T0325239

Advance Praise for *Drone Wars*

"A riveting account of one of the most significant developments in contemporary warfare—the evolution and proliferation of drones. Seth Frantzman provides a compelling description of this development and of the challenges facing the US and other countries as they grapple with the rapidly emerging threats posed by the new technology. He also conveys a sobering analysis about how this technology is transforming warfare and a convincing case for better defenses against drones in the hands of terrorists, non-state actors, and near-peer adversaries. This is a very important book."

—General David Petraeus, US Army (Ret.), former Commander of the Surge in Iraq, US Central Command, and Coalition and US Forces in Afghanistan, and former Director of the CIA

"A fast-paced account of the pioneers behind today's military drones, in *Drone Wars,* author Seth J. Frantzman sheds light on the shadowy world of military drones and how these new technologies are changing the modern battlefield. The global proliferation of drones and their incorporation by militaries and terror groups creates an urgency for developing and fielding defenses against drones and keeping up with countries and groups that may pose an increasing threat."

—Richard Kemp, former Commander of British forces in Afghanistan and led the international terrorism team at Britain's Joint Intelligence Committee

DRONE WARS

PIONEERS,
KILLING MACHINES,
ARTIFICIAL INTELLIGENCE,
AND THE BATTLE
FOR THE FUTURE

SETH J. FRANTZMAN

BOMBARDIER
BOOKS

A BOMBARDIER BOOKS BOOK
An Imprint of Post Hill Press
ISBN: 978-1-64293-675-9
ISBN (eBook): 978-1-64293-676-6

Drone Wars:
Pioneers, Killing Machines, Artificial Intelligence, and the Battle for the Future
© 2021 by Seth J. Frantzman
All Rights Reserved

Cover Design by Cody Corcoran

Post Hill Press
New York • Nashville
posthillpress.com

Published in the United States of America
1 2 3 4 5 6 7 8 9 10

For Daniel and Amit

CONTENTS

PROLOGUE

The concrete staircase felt claustrophobic. At the bottom was the sound of gunfire. Above, beyond a small door that led to the roof of this three-story building in Mosul, was an imperceptible buzzing. And somewhere in the distance, hiding behind a mattress or secreted in a similar stairway, an ISIS sniper was watching us. That's what the Iraqi major said as he motioned to three of his soldiers to move quickly up the stairs to avoid a gap in the wall that overlooked an alleyway. It was Iraq, 2017.

We were being hunted. Hours ago we'd entered the city as the hunters, the ones with the US Air Force at our backs and an endless supply of ammunition and Humvees and a mass of soldiers. But the enemy was here, waiting. Their inexpensive weapons, including quadcopter drones armed with grenades and mortars they made in underground factories, were deadly. So were their booby-traps in homes and vehicles laden with bombs. But it's the buzzing of an ISIS drone that I still can hear, years later. It is endless and unnerving, like the distant reverberations of explosions and other sounds of war. It also represents a new generation of warriors. The drone warriors.

Prior to the battle, the drone threat had seemed surreal and distant. We were at a makeshift Iraqi base—someone's one-story house on a hillock, transformed into a soldier's squat. One Iraqi soldier laced up his boots, sitting on a black plastic chair in a concrete-wall enclosed courtyard. The boots were khaki-colored, with spots of dirt around the bottom.

He pulled them tight, looping the laces around the clasps at the top to hold them more tightly to his ankle. He was a member of the Emergency Response Division (ERD), an Iraqi army unit that was supposed to be used in a crisis. Today, and for the last several weeks, the ERD had been slogging its way into the city of Mosul's western edges. The offensive to retake the city from the horrors of ISIS was in its fifth month.

I'd come to Mosul because of a vow. It was here that ISIS proclaimed its "caliphate" in 2014, when it took over parts of Syria and Iraq and began a genocide of minority groups. On the road to Mosul, the deserted towns that had been home to Christians in the plains of Nineveh spoke to the depredations of ISIS. In Qaraqosh, the churches had been burned or used as bomb factories, their crosses torn down. In some villages, ISIS had turned each house into a small fortress, with tunnels underneath and walls blown open so their fighters could move from room to room without being seen from above by American drones.

Now the Iraqi army was squeezing ISIS in Mosul. It had surrounded them in the city, some 60,000 Iraqi soldiers against 5,000 jihadists. In the fall of 2016, the Iraqi special forces of the Counter-Terrorist Service had fought street by street to push the enemy back. Now in the spring of 2017, I was a journalist embedded with the Iraqi units tasked to clear western Mosul. The Mosul battle had been so horrid that whole units had lost columns of US-supplied Humvees. We were next into the meat grinder that March. I'd vowed to go into the city with the Iraqis to be there when it was liberated. In a naïve way, I thought it would be like going into Berlin in 1945, to see justice done.

The man with the boots, his thick black hair closely cropped, slung his Croatian VHS-D2 rifle over his shoulder. The rifle had a bull-pup nose with a magazine behind the trigger. It looked a bit futuristic, and it fit the battle we were heading to. Since January 2017, ISIS had increasingly been using drones to attack the Iraqi army. These drones were spotted almost every day. ISIS had built factories to convert civilian-use quadcopter drones, basically the kind you buy at a tech store, which have four little helicopter blades, into death from above. ISIS put grenades and mortars on them and also used them to film attacks and conduct surveillance.

There was no way to fight the drone threat. Soldiers had tried to spray gunfire into the air, but it's hard to shoot a drone the size of your forearm from a hundred yards away when it is moving. Some Iraqi and US-led coalition forces tried jamming the drones. Bizarre-looking jammer guns, that look more like big toy squirt guns with an antenna on them, were offered to the troops. The jamming was spotty, and soldiers, like the man with the boots, hadn't been trained to use them.

Driving into Mosul that day in late March, we felt naked to the drone threat. It was always there, more than the snipers or mortars, because it was from above and otherworldly. To get to Mosul we drove from the town of Hamam al-Alil, where ISIS had left behind a path of destruction and mass graves, through fields and pastures to Mosul's ruined airport. The factories lining the airport's western edge had been turned into a post-apocalyptic landscape, deserted, with all their windows broken and concrete hanging in chunks from a web of steel girders. We were in an SUV following an Iraqi Humvee and a camouflaged van full of ERD troops. This area of the city had been liberated a week before. The soldiers played music, religious ballads, that wafted through the air. Between the music and the hum of the engine we felt secure. When we stopped, however, we could hear the "pop-pop" of gunfire. An officer of the ERD, taller than the man with the boots, and with the first appearance of jowls on his cheeks, tilted his head. "Drone?"

There was a distant buzzing. We were at an intersection of what had been a major thoroughfare, divided in the center, and a road running into a neighborhood, lined by two-story duplexes. The buzzing came and went. We looked up. It was there, somewhere. A drone. Ours or theirs? No one knew. "Stay by the side of the street when we walk," one of the Iraqi soldiers said. So we walked along the street, passing shops that sold appliances and gardening equipment, all deserted. We eventually came, after several blocks, to a smaller alley. Here the soldiers had set up curtains at each alley-crossing. Constant machine-gun fire reverberated down the alleys. ISIS held one side of the block and the Iraqis the other. We were supposed to sprint across each alley, avoiding snipers, and ascend a small wooden ladder into the second floor of a house. Then, through a hole that had been blown in the house, we would ascend to the second floor and then to the roof. I sprinted, climbed, crawled, and made my way through the warren of rooms of the house to a central staircase. At the top of the staircase an Iraqi officer pointed up and to the right. Snipers there. I guessed the upward motion was supposed to indicate drones too.

On that day we emerged unscathed from the claustrophobic staircase. One of the ERD soldiers fired an RPG from the roof of the building and then we retreated back into the warren of alleyways with the decorative blankets strung across the street to obscure us from snipers. The drones would keep up their deadly work for several more months as ISIS was pushed back and the city was liberated. Iraq and the US-led coalition would use their own drones to hunt down ISIS and even to destroy ISIS drone-making factories. The drone wars had begun.

As I sat in a small apartment in Erbil in the Kurdish region of Iraq over the following days, I felt relieved and stressed at the same time. What were these machines that seemed to come from the future to remake warfare? Drones appear in movies, such as the remake of *Blade Runner* or *Terminator 2*. They're sinister, or sometimes they are an ally. Today's drone wars, between states and terrorist groups, are rapidly expanding. From Syria to Libya, Afghanistan, Iran and Kashmir, the drone is ubiquitous and used by all sides of major conflicts.

How did we get here? What will be the future of this technology? Will we still need multi-million-dollar warplanes if we can replace what they do with drones? Will the next *Top Gun* be sitting in a box in Nevada while he shoots down enemy drones 8,000 miles away?

A soldier on a rooftop in Mosul in March 2017. After the drone threats from ISIS had passed, the Iraqi soldiers were able to place heavier weapons on roofs in the battle for the old city of Mosul. But they constantly kept an eye skyward. (Seth J. Frantzman)

The more I looked at the world emerging from the war on ISIS, the more it became clear that the next phase of warfare will be dominated by drones and unmanned technologies, full of gadgets and what are called "autonomous weapons systems." When I was a kid I was fascinated by the world depicted in the film *Aliens*. There are scenes in the film that depict where we are heading: soldiers networked to a computer screen that shows where each fighter is located, and remote piloting of aircraft and guns that fire automatically at targets without a person in the loop deciding which target to shoot at.

The drone wars that we are already witnessing in Libya, Syria, between the US and Iran, and between Iran and Israel are rapidly changing the environment we live in. The US and China are rushing to build more and more drones with more technology and more weapons on them. This is like the revolution that saw airpower go from a man chucking a bomb out of a bi-plane to strategic bombing in World War

II and the sinking of the *Bismarck*. Drones are a "disruptor" in how they provide commanders and governments a new swath of possibilities. Today they are only being used in one or two roles, whether surveillance or targeted airstrikes. But they won't stay in those niche roles for long. Militaries face this fork in the road: to decide how many drones they will have for all their forces, from special forces with little tactical drones, to giant drones the size of an F-16. The drone is expendable, more so than human life in a kind of warfare where the public demands low casualties. This enables us to fight forever wars across borders in places like Somalia or Afghanistan without boots on the ground.

The questions that I set out to answer after Mosul were whether those wars, the drone wars, are a new kind of warfare and how effective they are. The new technologies must be harnessed to become a gamechanger, and they will be matched by enemies who have the same technology. The drone wars coincide with changes in American national security strategy and the rise of other countries such as China into this military competition.

INTRODUCTION: CITY OF FEAR

D rones are everywhere. In January 2020, mysterious drone forma-
tions appeared in Colorado, terrorizing farmers and leaving people
fearful about what might come next. They might be lingering near
nuclear power plants, posing a threat to millions. In the Middle East, the
US used a drone to kill Qasem Soleimani, a key Iranian commander in
2020. Drones are transforming the battlefield from Syria to Azerbaijan,
Libya, and Yemen.

For militaries and security agencies, the main users of drones, the
UAV market is expanding as well. There were more than 20,000 military
drones in use by 2020. Once the province of only a few hi-tech militaries
like the US and Israel, drones are now being built in Turkey, China, and
Russia, and smaller countries like Taiwan may be joining the military
drone market. It's big business too. $96 billion will be spent on military
drones between 2019 and 2029. Militaries may soon be spending more
on drones than tanks, much as navies transitioned away from giant vulnerable battleships to more agile ships. Terrorists are using them too,
buying civilian drones and putting grenades and bombs on them. This is
a turning point in military history, like the jet-propulsion revolution or
the development of the rifle.

Drones are inherently a sexy topic, but also one that is not well
understood. They are seen as otherworldly and their use possibly uneth-
ical because they conjure up images of faceless evil machines dealing out
death from above while unseen humans monitor the lives of others. Yet

drone operators see themselves as pilots, even if they aren't exactly Tom Cruise from *Top Gun*.

In the fast-moving narrative of *Drone Wars,* we will explore the history, the present, and the pioneers and terrorists of drone warfare. Moving from the Israeli soldiers carrying their light-weight drones over hills to launch them over Lebanon, to the rooms where American "strike cell" operators follow top terrorists, the book will provide an account of the people and the machines, blending personal experience and interviews with operators, generals, and insiders, from different countries, technologies, and eras of the ever-expanding empire of drones we now live under. This is not an exhaustive history of all drones, but a look at key technological vectors and riveting applications of drones. Each chapter examines how these unmanned aerial vehicles are being used in a new way. Themes include targeted assassinations, surveillance, terrorism, and future uses. Interviews with players from industries, activists, innovators, or those running various parts of the drone wars combine for a sweeping narrative covering a large canvas.

Through the course of researching *Drone Wars,* I spoke and corresponded with former US general and former CIA director David Petraeus; George W. Bush administration official Douglas Feith, who monitored the hunt for Bin Laden; UK forces commander Richard Kemp, who served in Afghanistan; a retired Irish special forces officer; Pentagon and US Air Force officers; Libyan drone operators; ISIS detainees; Kurdish fighters; and experts at Lockheed Martin in the US and Israel's defense companies, including the engineer behind Israel's first drones: From Blackhawk pilots to US National Guardsmen who first used tactical drones, to those fighting against proliferation and experts on Iran's secretive drone program, to researchers looking at artificial intelligence transforming warfare.

The biggest focus initially is more on Israel and the US—the main pioneers of drones—but also reflects my own experiences encountering drones across the Middle East. The book looks at both the military objectives of drones (surveillance and killing) and the challenges linked to drones, such as making them smaller, faster, or more capable; and it spotlights the theorists who have posited that drones could replace warplanes and can be used in swarms. It is based on interviews with Iraqi Kurds trying to avoid Turkish drone strikes in the mountains, as well as air defense officials planning to fight off Iranian drone swarms.

The future for drones is largely already at our fingertips. The technology to make drones fly for several days aloft, or to give them long-range missiles, has arrived. There are mini-drones that soldiers can use in the jungle to police other drones that can drop tear gas. The problem that countries face today is largely twofold. First, you have the existing "platforms" for drones that are successful. Militaries tend to be slow at designing new platforms, so once you have an F-16 or an M-16 rifle, a main battle tank or a destroyer, you stick with it for decades. Once you have a Predator model drone, all you do is make more of them and make them slightly larger and faster, or pack them with more munitions, radars, and cameras. This is called adding more "sensors" to the platform. The first problem, therefore, is that militaries came to a bottleneck before the next drone revolution. What we will see in this story is how that happened. Why aren't there more stealth-like drones? Why does it take the European countries a decade to design a drone that will monitor civilian and foreign airspace? Why did the US not export drones and allow itself to be slowly overtaken by China? That all is rooted in lack of platform change and conservative unwillingness to see the future.

Second, the problem is militaries not coming to terms with the power in their hands. While futurists have predicted skies full of drones, just like flying cars, the actual commanders have eschewed these flying machines. One counter-terror police commander I spoke to said his unit only had several drones for a huge area he was tasked with securing. Why? Budgets and lack of vision. This means that there is no drone military visionary, a kind of drone Patton or drone Rommel, someone who sees in drones the revolution that tank commanders saw in the 1930s.

Unlike when warships were fashioned into dreadnoughts prior to the First World War, there is no prophet of drone power. There is no country that has decided to build thousands of these machines and outfit entire divisions with them, flooding the battlefield with the machines. Instead, militaries want precision strikes, and when they do acquire these products, they want them so full of technology that the price tag is upped to the millions and billions. Case in point: NATO took years to acquire US Global Hawk surveillance drones and then only bought five at a price tag of some $1.5 billion.

As we shall see, these twin problems are the hurdles that the drone revolution must get over. We are beginning to see points of light break through. Drone swarms used by Iran have forced Western countries to rethink air defense. Libya's war, where Turkish inexpensive drones ripped apart Russian air defense systems, shows that drones can be a kind of instant air force to transform the battlefield.

Over the years, the prophets of drone warfare have come and gone. There have been false hopes and dead-ends and false prophets. On the horizon is the idea of armies that go to war with drones, and whoever has the best drones and air defense will win. But to get to drone vs. drone wars we have a long way to go. The number of large drones being used in war and shot down has multiplied, from several a year in the 1980s, to hundreds a year by 2020. However, we are still in the era of the biplane and early tanks, and drones have not realized their potential. This book will explore how that happened and how the turning point is approaching.

Today's commanders are rooted in the past. They didn't grow up with tablets and drones. They were trained for a war fought in the 1990s. As younger men become generals, the desire to have every platoon with a drone operator and tablet to fly them, layers of drones, and access to air defense to fight off the swarms of enemy drones, will materialize. To get there, we need to see how drones came to exist in the beginning.

To understand the emerging drone wars, I began with my own experience with drones. Going back to the 1990s, I read about advances in unmanned aerial systems and technology and how they would transform the future of war. Later, during Israel's wars in Gaza between 2009 and 2014, I saw how drones became more common on the battlefield. I saw drones used in Iraq and Ukraine and, as a journalist, covered the threats and air defense systems being developed.

In Israel, I met with drone pilots, soldiers, and police commanders and went to the leading manufacturers of drones to tour their assembly lines and speak with their experts, many of whom are former pilots. I spoke with the pioneers of Israel's drone program and then interviewed key American officials and soldiers who led the drone wars in the 1990s and 2000s. These included pilots and generals as well as executives at key US defense companies and former staffers who had worked in Congress. To understand how other militaries were using drones, I sat down with commanders from the United Kingdom and Ireland and spoke to experts from the Persian Gulf to Turkey as well as those who cover Iranian drone technology. This book is based on years of working in the field under the threat of ISIS drones, and seeing how militaries are using drones, as well as a year of interviews with the most knowledgeable individuals across the spectrum, from critics of armed drones to prophets of how they will change the world as we know it.

The development of drones was a slow process, but their use has expanded exponentially. In just the last few years, the use of drones by both sides of conflicts and the development of air defense to shoot them down has been rapid. Lasers are being rolled out, and the types of drones are expanding, even as militaries continue to struggle to find a place for the new platform. The drone has not reached its potential, and those who continue to imagine that there will be an era without air force pilots will be surprised to see how slow progress is being made in Western countries. But the revolution is shifting to China, Turkey, and other countries, and it is happening quickly. In that sense, the story of the drone wars is not just about machines. It is about the change in the balance of power between the US, which was a global superpower after 1990, and rising states like China and India. The rise of drones was intimately linked to America's global war on terror. Now, as that conflict shifts to US-China and US-Iran competition, the drone wars shift as well, and around the world, drones are coming into their own.

CHAPTER 1

DAWN OF THE DRONE: PIONEERS

I n 1983, US Secretary of Defense Casper Weinberger received a surprising briefing. He had returned from a trip to Lebanon and was
shown video of him, taken during his visit by an Israeli unmanned
aerial vehicle. Weinberger was considered one of the coldest members
of the Reagan administration in dealings with Israel.[1] Throughout all
the rocky relations, however, the drones intrigued him. In June of 1983,
the US wanted Israel to revive a memorandum about confronting Soviet
influence in the Middle East.[2]

This was at the height of the Cold War when US President Ronald
Reagan wanted to confront the "evil empire" in Moscow. The race for
new defense technology was intense. In the Middle East, the Israelis,
often operating western military technology, faced off against the Soviet-
supplied Syrians. If the Israelis could develop a new weapon, everyone
would want a piece of the action.

The US was wrestling to fill a void in its own defense technology.
The Americans had experimented with what were then called Remote

Piloted Vehicles in the 1970s, using them against radar-emitting targets at the Utah Test and Training Range. But it was thousands of miles away in Israel that a revolution was about to take place that would change war as we know it.

In 1974, Yair Dubester was a young Israeli engineer. Israel was reeling from losses in the 1973 war. More than 2,500 Israelis had been killed, 1,000 tanks lost, and more than one hundred aircraft destroyed. For a small country that had been drunk on the success of the 1967 war, when multiple Arab armies had been crushed in six days, the experience was sobering.

Dubester was studying at Israel's elite Technion university and working at Israel Aerospace Industries, where the first unmanned aerial vehicle was being built. "We weren't the first to think of it, but the first to develop the first operational system," he says. I called Dubester in early March 2020, before the coronavirus crisis broke and engulfed the world. He was cheerful, discussing decades of his life working with drones. Looking back to the late 1970s, he recalled that the main problem Israel had was getting real-time intelligence of the enemy. That means not just sending planes up to take photos, but having them send back video simultaneously.

Prior to 1973, Israel signed a contract with Teledyne Ryan in the US for a drone.[3] The first twelve, called Firebees, got to Israel in 1971. They were big beasts, weighing more than 2,000 lbs., and had a turbo-jet engine, flying up to 60,000 feet at 485 miles an hour.[4] They were basically rockets with little wings. Their origins were actually as flying targets. The origin of the Israeli drone program was thus an American flying decoy. Israel thought they could be used to deceive enemy radar and missiles. The Egyptians had a massive army with Soviet-supplied anti-aircraft missiles. Any unmanned aircraft that could reduce losses for irreplaceable pilots was badly needed.

A special UAV unit was inaugurated at Palmachim Air Base in Israel, a base ensconced in the dunes near a popular beach. The Firebees were used as decoys against Soviet-supplied surface-to-air missiles that Egypt. Flying from Refidim Airbase beginning in September 1971, they proved effective. Israel sponged up other drones, including the American-made Chukar. It was to be used as a decoy, and the twenty-seven acquired were called *Telem*. The Chukar was less a real drone than it was a suicide drone, designed to be destroyed. Twenty-three were used in the 1973 war, and five were destroyed. The Firebees were also eviscerated in the war. Only two survived.

The Israelis decided they needed more options that could give them what the air force called "intelligence at the moment of truth."[5] A delegation was asked to go abroad and find out what else could be acquired. Israel looked at drones built by Philco-Ford and RT. The Americans had plenty of these vehicles sitting around. Think of these drones in the tree of evolution as a missing link between piloted aircraft and UAVs, one of those kinds of dead-ends of evolution. Some of them looked like large model airplanes or missiles, and their designers had ideas to stick laser designators on them or other gadgets that would later become commonplace on drones. Drone versions had been used in Vietnam to decoy and gather info on surface-to-air missiles.[6] More than 980 had been built in the 1960s and 1970s, and 441 were lost in Vietnam.[7] Like many innovative American projects of the space age, they had been abandoned and left to gather dust, with only a few dozen still around by the early 1980s. In short, it was like inventing gunpowder but not figuring out how to use it on the battlefield. To that problem, the Israelis brought a solution.

In the wake of these experiences, an Israeli company named Tadiran built the Mastiff drone, which had live high-resolution video and could fly for seven hours.[8] At the time it was called a "remote piloted vehicle." It looked like a big model airplane, thought *New York Times* writers who saw it in 1981.[9] It had propellers and a two-cylinder engine. It weighed around 150 lbs. and could fly to 10,000 feet at seventy miles per hour.

An IAI Scout, an early drone. IAI's pioneering drone technology
began in the late 1970s and early 1980s. (Courtesy IAI)

The Israelis innovated further with the IAI Scout, which had a live
broadcast link and stabilized camera. It was also called *Zahavan*, or
Oriole. Think of these early Israeli drones as the origin of species for
everything that comes next. The Scout had a twin-boom or dual tail, a
short angular body that ended in a kind of snout. Small wheels sprouted
from the fuselage. Twenty were rolled out by June 1979 at Hatzor Air
Base in central Israel, hidden behind the fields of pretty villages in the
area. The Scout was short-winged and took off with the help of a rocket.
That would soon change as the wings grew by two meters, to a total of
five meters, and a pilot with a joystick could do takeoffs. Operational
in June 1981, a squadron of Scout drones flew into Lebanon to capture
video of Syrian air defenses.

Dull, Dirty, and Dangerous

Dubester speaks with a young man's curiosity despite his age. He loves to talk about drones and technology and the pluck and accidental discoveries that led to Israeli breakthroughs. He remembers the difficulties Israel faced after 1973. "We found out the Egyptians and Syrians bought from Russia the anti-aircraft missiles, the SA-3 that were mobile, not stationary." When the anti-aircraft systems move around, it doesn't help to just photograph them, you need to be able to find them in real time using a system that can hover in the air without a pilot so if it is shot down you don't lose people, he says.

UAVs are good for dull, dangerous, and dirty missions, Dubester says. It's kind of "D-cubed." They were dangerous indeed, he remembers. The Teledyne Ryan's UAVs crashed too often. That is why Israeli engineers designed the Scout, which helped locate surface-to-air missiles. It was this ability, to fly slowly and bring back video, that led to greater investment. "Before that," he says, "no one cared about it." Dubester and his colleagues designed the Scout to be lightweight and fly for several hours. In fact, it was based on a French Nord Noratlas, which was sold to the Israelis in 1956. Israel and France once had a close military relationship, and the design was arrived at by accident because Israel was familiar with the Noratlas twin-boom model. In the end, the engineers realized the design was phenomenally stable and worked well for slow-moving UAVs. Dozens of designs would grow out of this choice made in the 1970s.

When the Scout was first demonstrated to the Israeli army, the ground forces shrugged off its abilities. A large exercise was underway in Sinai. Ehud Barak, then an officer serving in Sinai, didn't seem interested at first. "Let *them* fly it," Dubester recalls the officers saying at first, dismissing the UAVs as a kind of toy. The drill was supposed to practice crossing the Suez Canal, but the officers quickly realized that the UAVs, giving real-time video, aided the troops in the exercise. A bridge that was supposed to be mistakenly left unassembled to confuse the troops could be seen easily, giving away the point of the exercise.

"We had only four hours' endurance [flight time] at the time, and when we needed to land, the troops said no, it's not acceptable," recalls Dubester. Suddenly the toy that was dismissed had become essential. "I will never forget that. It was a game changer." Dubester would go on to write a book with two colleagues who pioneered the Scout: David Harari, head of the UAV division at IAI, and production manager Michael Shefer. "We were there from day one until our retirement," he says. Invention is sometimes the mother of necessity, and within a short time, the drone would prove its necessity.

"Tomorrow's War": Operation Peace for Galilee

Twenty-four hours was all it took for Israel's UAVs to wreak havoc on Syrian air defense in the 1982 war in Lebanon. The Israeli operation, called Peace for Galilee, was launched to stop Palestinian rocket attacks on northern Israel. Former IAI engineer Shlomo Tsach recalls how in just one day, a "drone revolution" occurred.[10] Real-time video of SAMs and their radar was sent back by Israeli Mastiff and Scout drones, and the IAF went to work destroying the Syrian air defense. It was in those twenty-four hours that Israel's multi-billion-dollar drone industry was truly born and formed the progenitor of the American love for drones.

Lebanon is a small country, and though its border with Israel appears short, only sixty-five kilometers as the crow flies, it is actually a warren of winding roads and hills. Palestinian terrorists were launching missiles at Israel, and to defeat them Israel would have to deal with the Syrian army in Lebanon as well. The Syrians should have been a formidable obstacle, with 25,000 men dug in along the Bekaa Valley in central Lebanon. They had seventy-nine missile launchers and hundreds of radar-directed guns and SA-6 batteries. But they weren't quick enough to move against the Israeli threat, as drones helped guide Israeli jets to their targets.[11] The new drones could be used for laser designation of targets and helping guide artillery rockets.[12] This was "tomorrow's war," a British defense analyst concluded when comparing Israel's crushing of the Syrians with the Falklands conflict that pitted the UK against Argentina the same year.[13]

Israel combined its drones with the use of an E-2C Hawkeye, a kind of flying radar dome, and a Boeing 707 to conduct surveillance and electronic warfare, with jets firing Shrike missiles to destroy the SAM radars.[14] Dubester says the drones gave Israel the ability to do a battle-damage assessment rapidly and to gain air supremacy in a "single afternoon."[15] Israel used a combination of an air-launched decoy to trigger the radars and then identified the SAM sites with the Mastiff drones, which relayed communications back through the Scouts to crews operating the missiles. Seventeen deadly SAM batteries were destroyed.[16]

The Americans took notice, and the US Navy came calling. A partnership between IAI and a company called Textron in the US led to the Pioneer drone. Each cost around $500,000 and had a $400,000 camera inside, transmitting back detailed images taken up to 2,000 feet in the air, up to one hundred miles away.[17]

Pioneer was a direct descendant of the Scout, adapted to be launched from a ship with a rocket and land in a net on return. It was used in the 1991 Gulf War to help with targeting for the one-ton shells fired by battleships. Beginning in 1985, the US used the Pioneers, and they would help with naval targeting during the Gulf War. Iraqis even surrendered to one of them in the desert, bewildered by this new pilotless form buzzing around them. The incident happened on Faylakah Island, and the men waved undershirts to signal their concession.

Dubester flew out to the American high desert at Mojave to demonstrate the drones to the US. The desert is a mix of reddish rocks and tan dunes, with Joshua Tree cacti dotting the landscape. The test range is desolate. "We had to integrate the system on the USS *Iowa* and *Wisconsin* [naval ships]." The problem is the Americans wanted something bigger that would fly longer and higher.[18] It needed to fly in all-weather conditions and around the clock. It would help do signals intelligence (SIGINT), including electronic surveillance (ELINT) and communications intelligence (COMINT) missions. Dubester and his team went to work on what became the Hunter, Searcher, and Ranger UAVs.[19]

As the Israeli drones grew, the prophets of drone warfare envisioned several "families" of drones such as Tactical UAVs (TUAV) and mini-UAVs. What began as just one platform expanded rapidly to "multi-mission UAVs" with numerous sensors, gadgets, and antennas. Jargon came with the new field. Terms like ISR were created to describe intelligence, surveillance, and reconnaissance missions that would be perfect for drones. By 2002, Israeli drones had logged 120,000 flight hours and were being exported to twenty countries. The little country was a drone superpower.

Back to the Drawing Board

In the US, the road to drone warfare passed through the US Air Force's mountain of target drones. At Holloman Air Force Base in New Mexico and Tyndall Base in Florida, the US used drones for target practice. Drones were linked to a number of innovative American projects. At Skunk Works, Lockheed Martin's super-secret advanced development program, drones were used for target practice.[20] The company also developed the GTD-21 drone in the 1960s that could be dropped from B-52s for experimental supersonic reconnaissance missions over China.[21]

Target drones were an evolutionary dead end.[22] But drones in general could help solve military problems and fill necessity niches. This meant, for example, helping armies find mobile air defense or conduct battle damage assessments. Since the dawn of war, the goal has always been to stay one step ahead of the enemy, to neutralize threats and to leverage new capabilities. Balloons once helped militaries see further, for instance. Drones may have first helped spot Soviet air defenses in the Middle East and save pilots' lives, but soon they would develop into their own world.

In 1983, terrorists in Lebanon bombed the US Marine barracks in Beirut. The USS *New Jersey*, an 880-foot World War II-era battleship, was sent to retaliate with its sixteen-inch guns pounding the shore. This was old-style war, when what was needed was more precision to take out terrorists who ran around streets with AK-47s. Enter John Lehman, secretary of the navy. He wasn't much of an orator, even when speaking about "exciting" programs for his ships, but what he lacked in rousing speeches, he made up for in practicality. With his interest in new technology, and Weinberger's, the Americans tapped the Israeli company IAI and the Tadiran Mastiff. Mastiffs were brought to the Marine's Camp Lejeune RPV platoon in North Carolina. Marines who had excelled at model airplane competitions were invited to pilot the drones.[23] The stocky, square-jawed General Al Gray of the Fleet Marine Force Atlantic, who had first served in the Marines in Korea and Vietnam, would drop in to see the drones' progress in both North Carolina and Arizona.

The Israelis and Americans worked with AAI, a company in Hunt Valley, Maryland, to tweak the drone for naval needs. They put it on the USS *Tarawa*, a lean, new amphibious assault ship that has a long deck, and flew it in freezing conditions in Adak, Alaska. It was also flown in Australia and the Philippines.

Soon the US was looking at both the Scout and Mastiff, and their descendants the Hunter and Pioneer. We've already met the Pioneer, which had a five-hour flight time and a range of one hundred miles. By 1990, it had flown 2,550 missions for 5,200 flight hours. By today's standards, it doesn't look sexy or pretty. It's a workhorse, with rough edges and straight lines, boxy and boring: single wing on top and a twin tail.

The US ejection of Saddam Hussein's massive Iraqi army from Kuwait during the first Gulf War showed how useful new drones could be to the world's most powerful army. One Pioneer UAV mission had found three Iraqi artillery batteries, several missile launch sites, and an anti-tank battalion. The drones were always in the air during the six-week war. When it was over, every field commander wanted them. The

Department of Defense said the Pioneer had proved excellent at immediate, responsive intelligence collection.[24] By the mid-1990s, there were
nine Pioneer systems deployed, with five drones per system. The US put
them on four ships, including the USS *Cleveland*, an amphibious war-
ship.[25] Army researchers argued they needed to give them to units down
to the battalion level.

The Marines used Pioneers in Bosnia in 1994 and Kosovo in 1999,
flying them from the *Ponce De Leon*. Meanwhile, the Hunter, built by
IAI and TRW, was submitted to the US Army to meet its needs for a
short range UAV for reconnaissance missions for corps commanders.
The Hunter had a twin tail and a long, sausage-like fuselage.[26] A larger
order for fifty, costing $200 million, came in 1993.[27] The prophesied
multi-billion dollar program was eventually canceled, although Hunters
were used by the army, navy, and air force. The Hunters, named RQ-5A,
were used in Kosovo as part of Operation Allied Force and eventually
flew 30,000 flight hours by 2004.[28] Overall the Hunter shows how
drones have long-term reliability but also how armies were not ready to
fully incorporate them.

"For 25 years I delivered to US Army, Marines, and Navy, and the
main reason was that for many years the US failed to develop a decent
UAV system," recalls Dubester. "I was asked by colleagues in the US: How
did it happen, the US got to the moon but didn't built a UAV? Why?"

Indeed, why couldn't the US make what appears to be a simple
remote-controlled plane? Washington had experimented with a program
called Aquila, back in the RPV era.[29] Weighing 146 pounds with an
almost eleven-foot wingspan, the Aquila drone was supposed to be trans-
ported to lift-off with a truck and return to a net. It would fly at speeds
of up to one hundred miles an hour for several hours, for multiple sorties a day up to twelve miles from the launch site. The flying wing was
envisioned as loitering, not necessarily being manually piloted. Using
lasers, video, and infrared sensors, it would find targets and transmit
information back.

The US Defense Advanced Research Projects Agency (DARPA) wanted to develop Aquila for surveillance and targeting. A 1974 report noted that "technological advances quickly rendered light aircraft obsolete and forced the forward observer to evolve different techniques. The net result was a reduction in the range at which artillery targets could be effectively and accurately located."[30] The idea of Aquila was to find targets. But unstabilized cameras could only find targets at around 3,000 meters on a road at the time. They wanted it to be able to find tank-sized targets at 1,000 meters with a "fifty percent probability." The needs the US was trying to meet in the 1970s are little changed today, when a central question posed by militaries before acquiring a drone is how good it is at finding enemy targets.

Aquila was given the name MQM-105. It soon became evident that the requirements of the contract to jam so many avionics and payloads conflicted with the vehicle's size. It failed to meet its goals on ninety-eight of 105 test flights. It was supposed to be stealthy and impossible to jam, which also degraded its communications link. The program was a total failure.[31] It shows what happens when you have "mission creep." The Israelis, by contrast, built a simple drone for a simple mission. The US had built a Frankenstein drone.

The technological innovations in the 1970s would resurface many years later. Brig. Gen. Hillman Dickinson said that the RPV could locate targets, conduct "post-strike analysis" and be used for radar, jamming, or even be "flown into a target loaded with an explosive."[32] He was forward thinking, arguing they could reduce or eliminate the loss of human life; they were cheap and were not limited by "human frailties" such as fatigue. He cautioned that it was right for the spendthrifts in Washington to be wary of new programs and ordering large numbers of potential products.[33] The US should not try to run before it could walk. The Aquila decade of development was finally ended in 1987 after more than a billion dollars.[34] Washington's quest for a drone that could fly further, faster, and longer than planes had produced nothing so far.

Other American Frankendrones followed. In 1989, the US Army and Navy wanted a short-range UAV (UAV-SR) for surveillance and target acquisition. The IAI and TRW Hunter was put forward, along with the McDonnell Douglas Sky Owl. The Sky Owl was sort of a flying box with a twin tail. The Hunter prevailed, designated BQM-155A. The Sky Owl was launched from a catapult, and some versions foresaw it delivering an unguided rocket.[35]

When America did finally build its own successful drones, it was due to an Israeli named Abraham Karem. Born in Baghdad, Iraq, he built a drone in his garage in the 1980s, eventually becoming the godfather (or "dronefather") of the Predator.[36] Karem had also looked at the Aquila with puzzlement. He had come to the US in 1977 from Israel. The Aquila needed thirty people to launch it. Cumbersome and expensive, it was a product of the US system of slow defense procurement. It was made like a sausage, with different things all mangled together. "I was not the guy who put missiles on the Predator," he said in 2012. "I just wanted UAVs to perform to the same standards of safety, reliability and performance as manned aircraft."[37]

As Karem, a former IAI employee, entered the picture, Israel's drone revolution was already on the way. *The Diffusion of Military Technology and Ideas* noted that "UAVs have now evolved into more sophisticated unmanned aerial vehicles, and their new capabilities suggest the potential for significant changes in the organization and force structure of future air forces." World War II general Henry "Hap" Arnold had once said the next war would be fought by planes with no men in them. Analysts were already forecasting that UAVs could replace manned aircraft. This was also a far cry from being clunky decoys and targets.[38]

The initial drone revolution of the 1980s showcased a new technology. These drones could do surveillance or act as decoys and targets. They could conduct electronic intercepts or electronic war, but there were only a handful of them. They were built on a legacy of similar unmanned vehicles that had been used for spying and other missions.

But these decoys, targets, and surveillance assets had never transformed war. They were tools, and it was by accident that the tools had helped Israel revolutionize the battlefield against the Syrians. The Americans saw this potential and, through some luck and daring, decided to build more of them. This would set the US and Israel on a course to change history and build the kind of technology that had previously only been imagined in futuristic movies.

Historic weapons on display at a house in Washington, D.C. As warfare has changed over time the drone could revolutionize combat, the way armor and swords once did in the past. (Seth J. Frantzman)

In its essence, this revolution was about protecting soldiers. Just as knights had put on heavier and heavier armor, and trench lines of World

War I got deeper and deeper until they became the Maginot Line in World War II, so drones were supposed to keep soldiers from harm's way. They were not otherworldly and futuristic at first. They were just a practical, clunky way to solve a problem. That's also how naval ships first got clad in iron and tanks first arose. Now we must see how drones broke through and took over war.

CHAPTER 2

SPIES IN THE SKIES: SURVEILLANCE

The Air and Space Museum in Washington sits on the National Mall. It was being renovated in January 2020. Nevertheless, after a short walk through security and a left after the coat-check, the American history of space flight towers over visitors. There are giant missiles and rockets. The German World War II-era V-1 and V-2 are both on display. One was the first cruise missile, the other the first ballistic missile.

Drones, missiles, and airplanes all have something in common. They all have an ancestor. Like animals, they are part of a tree of technological development. Every drone has an origin story, sometimes stretching back, like the Teledyne Ryan company, to the time of Lindbergh. When we think of drones, we tend to think of some that resembled flying bombs or decoys, dropped from planes or catapulted and landing in nets. Then there are true flying machines, initially more like model airplanes. Today that has all progressed, and there are families of drones of different types at different altitudes and performing different functions. I thought of that in Washington in 2020, driving from the Air and

Space Museum to its counterpart out by Dulles Airport, the Steven F. Udvar-Hazy Center. It is there that a Predator drone hangs over the hall. It's not the most beautiful or the biggest drone. It might go unnoticed if one isn't looking at the brochure to find it. Many revolutions go unnoticed at the beginning.

Origin of Species

Surveillance was the first job of the drones. Their limitations are immediately obvious. In 2012, when US Ambassador Chris Stevens was in Benghazi, a mob of armed terrorists attacked his compound, murdering him and several other Americans. Stevens was a true believer, a brave and dedicated American diplomat. There were drones that might have helped save him, but none of those in range were armed. Despite the overwhelming impression of America as a drone hegemon astride the world, the same lack of armed drones was a problem in Niger in 2017, when US special forces were ambushed while on patrol with the Niger army. After a brief skirmish in the bush country near the border with Mali, four Americans were killed by a mass of armed jihadists. Even though the US and France had a secretive drone base nearby, drones couldn't do anything but record the tragedy.[39]

We've come to expect a lot from UAVs now. They are supposed to do more than just watch. They are supposed to bring us takeout or even help stop pandemics. It's important to take a step back to the 1990s and consider just how revolutionary the surveillance aspect was. The idea of having not only real-time video and the ability to use laser designators for targets, but also to monitor and loiter for days over a target, is important.

US President Lyndon Johnson had proposed in the 1960s that American success against the Soviets was because the US had been able to dominate the air the way the British had once dominated the sea and the Romans had once dominated land using roads. Twenty years later, drones would provide a new way to dominate the air. Israel's experience was important, but it was also limited. Once the Americans got in the game, they could change the face of war because of the size of the US military and American influence over the world.

At this time in the 1980s, the ability to experiment with drones came about because there was a window, with the decline of the Soviet Union and the advent of smaller complex wars such as in Lebanon, that would require more intelligence and fewer large munitions. As war transitioned from the era of the tank and the era of mass destruction, such as strategic bombing, to precision, the UAV would fill the gap between all these large machines like tanks, naval guns, and large bombers. The full picture, using UAVs to support vastly expanded special forces on the ground to fight terrorists, was coming into view, with prophecies that the drones might replace manned flight.

The key change in thinking was like planting a new tree, as it were, in the air. Instead of building on remote-controlled decoys, something new was needed. The 1980s were a revolution in technology in general. Computer companies such as Apple, Microsoft, and Oracle were founded in the late 1970s, while video and image processing, satellites, and all the technology needed for drones were improving. Computing power was expanding exponentially. Improvements would include making all these cameras and payloads more lightweight. To get to the disruption that drones were about to cause required standing on the shoulders of technology that was available. And, suddenly, it was available.

Building a Model

In 2010, the US Department of Defense task force on drones summed up its drone inventory. There were 8,000 of the vehicles, and they made up 41 percent of all military aircraft. Less than 1 percent were armed. They were mostly doing intelligence, surveillance, and reconnaissance missions.[40] Fifteen years before that report, Air Force Col. James Clark was in Hungary and his men were experimenting with a descendant of the Gnat, a drone called Predator. "We had three or four over there," he recalled in 2013. Developed in San Diego by General Atomics, the Gnat had a video camera and was flown in twelve-hour shifts.[41] They wanted something that could build on the Israeli success with the Pioneer. The Pioneer had a wingspan of seventeen feet and a range of 100 miles. It could stay in the air five hours and was catapulted at lift-off. Flown with a joystick, it was more like a model plane and cost $500,000 a pop. Images could be transmitted up to 100 miles away.[42] The navy invested a further $50 million to develop the nine it acquired to "minimum essential capabilities."[43]

The Gulf War had shown what these machines could do. They needed to be in the air at all times. The US had flown 522 sorties with the Pioneer, one hundred by the navy, ninety-four by the Marines, and eighty-four by the army in the 1991 war.[44] They helped naval gunners, aided the Marines at the Kuwaiti border to find troops using infrared sensors, and also helped map the ground for Tomahawk cruise missiles.

There was a problem though. An intelligence officer from the Marines said that the units desired three times as many as existed. The army also wanted more. Everyone agreed. We need more, officers told the US House of Representatives Oversight on Investigations Subcommittee that was looking at intelligence successes and failures.[45] Success has many fathers, the saying goes, but failure is an orphan. US military history is littered with many failures costing billions of dollars, evolutionary and experimental dead ends that sponged up resources. The Predator was a success, and it has many fathers.[46]

It fell to Director of Central Intelligence James Woolsey to navigate the hallways that led to the Predator. "We live now in a jungle filled with a bewildering variety of poisonous snakes," he said in the early 1990s, describing the changes the US faced after the fall of the Soviet Union. It's hard to keep track of all the snakes.

After the Gulf War, fighting in Bosnia led to calls for US intervention to stop ethnic cleansing. The Clinton administration wanted information on Serbian artillery firing on Bosnians. Frank Strickland, a senior officer at the CIA's Directorate of Science and Technology, was working closely with Woolsey at the time.[47] "US satellite reconnaissance capabilities were limited to coverage of only a few minutes each day," Strickland recalls. The US needed something that could linger over an area the size of West Virginia. CIA's director of espionage, Thomas Twetten, had already reviewed the agency's past work with drones, including a clandestine program called "Eagle" that used model airplanes and cameras in Lebanon in the 1980s.[48] Inspired by the Kennedy-era, he gave up academics for the CIA. Twetten spoke in a short, deliberate manner, with a slightly nasal voice.[49] He brought the review to Woolsey.

Woolsey had a background in the Johnson administration as an intelligence systems analyst and had analyzed overhead reconnaissance needs under CIA Director Robert Gates. What was needed was a long-endurance UAV. DARPA had already been in contact with Karem about a drone called Amber, which could fly for thirty hours. Two Ambers were brought to the Dugway Proving grounds in Utah for tests.[50]

Amber was unique in that it didn't use motorcycle engines like some previous drones, but had its own unique engine and had already stayed aloft for forty hours at a time by 1988. It could be launched from a canister with a rocket. DARPA thought the 800-pound light-weight drone was marvelous, but Karem's Leading Systems, Inc., saw its fantasy crushed by politics and sloth-like procurement. Congress pushed for a joint service short-range UAV developed as part of the TRW and McDonell Douglass rivalry. Leading Systems developed the larger Gnat with a Rotax engine and offered it to Turkey and other countries. But LSI went bankrupt, and General Atomics snarfed it up via a purchase of Hughes Aircraft Company, which owned its intellectual property.[51]

The product the Americans needed for the problems in Bosnia had already been built in a garage by Karem. Enter Jane, a CIA pilot. "Jane and her team discovered the Amber vehicles during their market survey. After some investigation with General Atomics, the team defined a more mature concept featuring Amber," recalls Strickland. Jane and CIA Deputy Director of Operations Ted Price brought the Gnat to Woolsey. "That is Abe's design," Woolsey said when he saw the Gnat. Woolsey knew Karem from a different missile project.

Woolsey's path to the drones had also come from knowledge of Israel's successes. Woolsey had suggested drones as a solution to a variety of problems in 1989. His ideas were dismissed at the time. So when he finally took up the helm at the CIA, he immediately asked for a meeting about the US's UAVs. Langley needed to be able to see what the drone was seeing in Bosnia. It had now come full circle for the director, and he pressed ahead, discussing the project with the Department of Defense, which had a joint UAV program. The price tag for the program was a $100 million, he was told.[52] He phoned General Atomics co-founder Linden Blue, and Karem came on as an expert advisor on the initiative to deploy the Gnats to Bosnia as soon as possible. They had to quiet the engine, which sounded as loud as a flying lawnmower, but otherwise the operators liked the new aircraft. Soon Woolsey was watching a video link of the Gnat, and the drones were sent to Bosnia in a C-130.[53] In one flyover, he looked at a bridge and asked the drone to zoom in on a man in a big, funny hat, to prove its abilities. The Gnats had proved their worth.[54]

First based in Italy, the communications relayed through a Schweitzer-manned aircraft to a ground base. Its data link initially interfered with Italian TV, and a new base had to be found.[55] At the time, it was to fly out of Gjadër, Albania, more than 140 miles to its target. Luckily it had a 500-mile range and twenty hours of flying time to do its mission.[56]

Rick Francona, a retired US Air Force intelligence officer who had first seen early US drones in Vietnam, was in Bosnia aiding the hunt for persons indicted for war crimes. He looks back at the changes he saw. "We had access to drones to conduct surveillance, but we didn't control them," he recalls. "It was often hard to get them for what the command structure regarded as low priority." While he ended up relying on helicopters more than drones, he says the experience was eye-opening.[57]

What was needed now was mass production. Woolsey and the Department of Defense worked closely until an Advanced Concept Technology Demonstration (ACTD) could be done with General Atomics. The team put a satellite link into the UAV and extended its size, giving it more range and payload. The Predator was born. Woolsey would later joke that his role was as a matchmaker or *shadchan*.[58]

Why does the Predator look the way it does, with a sleek body and a big head, as if someone took the cockpit out and filled it with clay? This design has become iconic, symbolizing how drones are supposed to look. The Predator and the less sexy Scout are the two basic models for most of the world's drones. So why the bulbous nose on the Predator? The drone needed an antenna to relay signals. The antenna was put in the nose. It was given a better engine, and General Atomics President Thomas Cassidy gave it the Predator moniker.[59]

General Atomics' first contract was for $31.7 million for three Predators in January 1994. The Predator faced immediate political and interagency challenges back home. Air force officers wanted to fly it, so CIA teams joined them at Nellis Air Base in Nevada. Nellis is on a flat plain, framed by mountains on one side and the bright blue skies that hang over Nevada. The Predators have enjoyed their home there for decades, that hot sun beating down on them.

The Predators were used first in 1995. They were slow, around seventeen miles per hour, and hard to fly. In rainy Albania, the operators sat in a van, one holding the joystick and others monitoring images. When the drone was beyond line-of-sight, control would pass via relay and a manned flying plane. It was a slow process, and the video was muddled until a satellite link could be developed.[60] One of those images came from a Sony camera that could swivel around. It had radar and electronic intercepts.[61]

The Predators were used for surveillance in Bosnia. They were not invulnerable. One was shot down by Serbs as it flew below cloud cover to conduct its surveillance mission.[62] By then only thirteen were still usable.[63] During the Kosovo campaign in 1998–1999, the navy pushed to have Predators help with targeting for submarine-based cruise missiles while the air force put laser designators on them to help guide bombs. Kosovo proved to be a UAV watershed. The British brought their Phoenix drones from the Thirty-Second Regiment of the Royal Artillery for twenty sorties, while French and German CL-289s Pivers (*Progammation et Interpretation des Vols d'Engins de Reconnaissance*) flew 180 missions, and the French Crecerelle drones also crowded the skies. Around twenty-one UAVs were lost in total.[64]

When Kosovo was over, the Predator's next mission emerged immediately. National Coordinator for Counter-Terrorism Richard Clarke, his infectious broad smile often illuminating the room, joined National Security Advisor Sandy Berger and others from the Clinton administration who agreed to send them to monitor Afghanistan.[65] The CIA was hunting Osama bin Laden after the attacks on US embassies in Africa. Could the cameras see well enough to find bin Laden and justify a cruise missile strike from submarines operating near the Persian Gulf? In the summer of 2000, the Predators packed up their vans, satellite dishes, and other equipment and went to Uzbekistan. Uzbek President Islam Karimov had agreed to their deployment but kept it a secret from most of his staff. By September, the drones had images of the sheds at a place called Tarnak Farm near Kandahar in Afghanistan, where bin Laden was thought to be.

Satellites had searched in vain for months. Now he appeared on drone video, with his flowing robes and white beard. CIA Director George Tenet handed the video to Clinton and Berger. More flights were made. The process of tracking down bin Laden involved a lot of interservice red tape.[66]

Big Safari

When the US finally got Predators, the question was who would control them. Air Force General Ronald Fogleman, who dominated the service in the 1990s, wrangled control of them in 1996. Fogleman had a long history in the air force, dating back to the 1950s. The grandson of a railroad worker, he was a mild-mannered and modest man, but with an intense drive for his service branch. He appeared to have bad memories of the Aquila program and congressional meddling. Defense Secretary William Perry agreed and signed a memo in 1996 designating the air force as the lead service to operate Predators.[67]

US servicemen were getting their first glimpse of the new drones that would come to play a greater role in US airpower. Brad Bowman, a US helicopter pilot who had graduated West Point in 1995 and was flying a Blackhawk at Fort Huachuca in the late 1990s, recalled the first time he saw a drone. "I was doing training and qualification for EH-60, the electronic warfare version of the Blackhawk, and we were there doing flight training and doing a flight pattern, and I looked out my window and saw a drone behind us in the traffic pattern, it was probably a Predator, an early version of it, and it was a deeply unsettling feeling, the technology was so new," he recalled in March 2020.[68] "I was marveling at this unmanned aerial vehicle and it was remarkable and I hoped the junior enlisted person sitting in some room or van [controlling it] was well-trained and taking his job seriously…I wasn't sure we were supposed to combine manned and unmanned aircraft in the same flight pattern." As drones entered US airspace, a whole new way of life was beginning.

James Clark, then a Colonel in the US Air Force and assistant to the vice-chief of staff for modeling and simulation, went to Bosnia in 1997 to see the 11th Reconnaissance Squadron.[69] The biggest problem for the Predator was that everyone wanted drones. The army was jealous it had lost the program and wanted more money for the Hunters. The navy wanted control. A joint navy and air force attempt to build a medium-range UAV had failed in the early 1990s, and the air force canceled the contract in June 1993.[70]

Undersecretary of Defense John Deutsch, who would later lead the CIA, argued that the US needed a UAV to fly to a range of 500 miles for twenty-four hours, up to 25,000 feet, and to carry up to 500 lbs. It needed to carry radar and high-resolution video, have satellite link-up and operate in all weather conditions.[71]

Meanwhile, the first operational Predators were stuck in Taszár, Hungary, with operators living in tents. Usually based in Indian Springs, Nevada, the squadron was now in a very different landscape. Three Predators and fifty personnel had come to operate them. Another group of operators were taking a ten-week course and would arrive in June 1996.[72] Airmen complained of bad weather and wanted to be in Italy. Albania was tried, but it was politically unstable. Bad weather also crippled the system. The quality of life provided by the army was also intolerable. Airmen resented the "harsh" tents. The Predators had to take off from a wood taxi-way.[73]

"The USAF has no direct control over its own destiny with Predator as long as the Navy is in charge," Clark groused. General Atomics was also too small, he claimed, asserting it could only make up to seven of the planes a year. But Cassidy had support from Congressmen Jerry Lewis and others.[74] Fogleman would persist through 1997 in getting Congress in the Defense Authorization Act to move authority from the navy to the air force and designate the 645th Aeronautical Systems Group, known as "Big Safari," for the Predator. Congressman Lewis was impressed with Big Safari, and Undersecretary of Defense Jacques Gansler signed off on the move.[75]

That is why it was under the air force that the Predators were brought to Uzbekistan to hunt bin Laden. With the 32nd Air Intelligence Squadron in control, through links from Ramstein Air Base in Germany, USAF intelligence director Col. Edward Boyle and Maj. Mark Cooter put the unit on the trail of bin Laden.[76] They caught him on video twice.

Dark Star

Meanwhile, back in the US, General Atomics had swept the defense industry off its feet with the Predator. Pentagon bureaucracy was also looking to fill more gaps in the UAV sector. It wanted what it called tier I, tier II, and tier III planes: a tactical drone, a medium-altitude long-endurance aircraft (MALE), and a high-altitude long-endurance aircraft (HALE).

Congress, which had backed a joint-service UAV program since 1988, established a Defense Airborne Reconnaissance Office (DARO) to push the program through Advanced Concept Technology Demonstrations (ACTD). AeroVironment had already tinkered with a bizarre high altitude solar (HALSOL) UAV that was funded from the 1980s to 1995, when it was cancelled. Another Boeing project called Condor also failed to materialize. It would have filled the HALE category needed. Lockheed Martin's Skunk Works was also working on an idea called Quartz.

The US Air Force still needed a drone that could fly high, for a long time, and deep into an enemy airspace defended by surface-to-air missiles. General Joseph Ralston was mildly optimistic in the mid-1990s about these new UAV programs.[77] The then commander of air combat command at Langley Air Force Base, Ralston said the US was moving into UAVs in a "big way." But the systems would take a long time to develop. "Air Force technology does not change quickly, as is commonly thought," noted Ralston.[78]

Ralston was skeptical that the combatant commanders, formerly known as "commanders-in-chief" (CINCs) of various regions, would have drones available in the near future.[79] By the time funding was put into UAVs, a decade might have vanished. Enormous potential and enormous challenges lay ahead, he said.[80] Col. Ronald Wilson called the programs "Eyes in the Sky" in 1996 when he reviewed the successes so far.[81] A "family" of UAVs would be built that would be planned for "multi-service" use and "intended to be as interoperable as practical and connected to service command, control, communications, computers and intelligence structures."[82]

The challenges were already being examined in two programs. When the US envisioned its drone needs it had imagined it as a tiered system, with the Hunter as tier I, the Predator as tier II, and something else for tier III. What the air force got was two ideas, a "Tier III minus" called Dark Star, and a "Tier II plus" called Global Hawk.

Tier I had been a rocky road. It's worth summarizing this disaster to show why the US failed to develop a successful small drone in the 1990s. Wilson argued that tactical UAVs should have electronic warfare abilities and a moving target indicator. They were intended for first use by the Fourth Infantry Mechanized Division in Fort Hood. Envisioned as a two-year development, flights were scheduled for 1997. They would have electro-optic (EO) and infrared (IR) capabilities as standard. They would also fill the need for reconnaissance, intelligence, surveillance, and target acquisition (RISTA).

Wilson appeared nonplussed that the Predator, having been used for two deployments in the Balkans, would be used by the air force with army military-intelligence units waiting for information to pass to their commanders. Army Major-General Charles Thomas agreed that the system was needed at "all levels from brigade through theater…our plan is to access it for army use through forward control elements (FCEs) that will be in place at division and corps."[83] He was worried about the time it was taking. "What needs to happen first is the fielding of a well-tested and trust-worthy system that is capable, durable and proven."[84]

The Hunter drone had the ability to fly up to 300 kilometers for eight hours. Cancelled in 1995, the remaining few were at Fort Hood and Fort Huachuca. Only seven were delivered from a program that envisioned fifty-two at a cost of $2.1 billion.[85] Another, called the Outrider tactical UAV (TUAV) was supposed to have a range of 200 kilometers and fly "on station" for three hours.[86] Called RQ-6A, it was a bizarre dual-wing drone, and it was cancelled in 1999.[87] Initial high hopes for the plane, which was supposed to replace the Hunter, faded after only six were made for a cost of $57 million.[88]

Some Hunters were used in the 2003 invasion of Iraq and were armed with anti-armor munitions called "Viper Strike." An airfield was later constructed for them by the V Corps near Najaf so they could help hunt for targets for Apache helicopters.[89] By 2004, the Hunters had flown 30,000 combat hours. An MQ-5B Hunter was developed in 2005.

For high-altitude drones, the US turned to its legacy defense companies. Lockheed and Boeing were rumored at the time to be building a "secret, stealthy" UAV.[90] Those ideas would eventually lead to the X-45 and X-47 swept-wing concepts of the early 2000s. Unfortunately, an innovative drone they built didn't pan out. Dark Star was a stealth-like drone, long and flat like a flying ruler with a disk in the middle. It vaguely resembled part of the Enterprise from *Star Trek*. It could operate over hostile countries at 45,000 feet for up to eight hours. Its cameras could keep an eye on 18,500 square miles and could fly 575 miles from its base.

Built by Boeing and Lockheed, Dark Star was tested at Edwards Air Force Base. It had a sixty-nine-foot wingspan and was only fifteen feet long. It weighed 8,600 lbs. and could carry another 1,000.[91] "Testing will continue this summer," the air force said in the spring of 1997. Maj. General Kenneth Israel, director of the Airborne Reconnaissance Office, was hopeful it would have the "ability to supply responsible and sustained data from anywhere within enemy territory."[92]

To compliment the Dark Star, Teledyne Ryan built the Global Hawk, a high-altitude, long endurance UAV which was about to be flown for the first time. Capable of a 2,000-pound payload, it would "permit ground commanders to switch among radar, infrared (IR) and visible wavelengths." It was supposed to fly for forty hours at 400 miles per hour up to 65,000 feet. It had a range of 3,450 miles and was designed to "loiter" over targets for twenty-four hours. A prototype was ready on February 20, 1997.[93]

Military bureaucracy and chain of command created a web of headaches for developers. When Wilson previewed the Global Hawk program, he noted that if it or Dark Star ever got off the ground and was used by a joint task force, the video it took would then be allocated to different processors, either the Army's Enhanced Tactical Radar Correlator and Modernized Imagery Exploitation System or the Air Force Contingency Airborne Reconnaissance System (CARS) or the Navy and Marines' Joint Service Imagery Processing System (JSIPS).

Dark Star was supposed to compliment the Global Hawk, being able to penetrate areas defended by air defense with a low-observable signature to radar. But the sleek black aircraft crashed on its second takeoff in 1996. Called RQ-3A, more test flights followed in 1998, but it was cancelled in 1999. It would have given the US the ability to go into enemy airspace. Instead, the US fell back on several classified programs in the 1990s, and the Dark Star became one of the examples given to Congress on why UAV procurement had become a lackluster sinkhole of costs.[94] Lockheed continued to tinker with the idea of a flying wing UAV, based on some experience from Aquila. In 2001, it built a flying-wing drone with a thirty-foot wingspan called X-44A. It was only shown to the public at the Los Angeles County Airshow in 2018.[95]

Another drone called Polecat was unveiled in 2005 by Lockheed's Skunk Works, with a ninety-foot wingspan and weighing 9,000 lbs. Vaguely resembling the B-2 bomber, it was tinkered with for basing in the Gulf. It could carry 1,000 lbs. of payload and fly up to 60,000 feet.[96] Called P-175, Lockheed developed it without government support and flew it publicly at the Farnborough Airshow in 2006. The flying wing design was racecar-like and simple, but it suffered an "irreversible unintentional failure" near the Nellis testing grounds in December 2006, and Lockheed operators pushed a self-destruct button.[97] That failure led to the development of yet another stealthy drone, the Sentinel RQ-170, which we will hear more of later.

The Great Debate

The US had once put a man on the moon within a decade, but it had been unable to put more than a few drones into the hands of warfighters, US Representative Duncan Hunter of California raged to his fellow representatives on a procurement subcommittee in 1997. Born in 1948, Hunter had served in Vietnam as an Army Ranger. First elected in 1981, he was a skilled politician. He was also deeply interested in UAVs. On April 9, 1997, he brought together the leading American military personnel involved in developing and fielding them. A hearing like this had never been conducted before.

The hearing examined challenges that America's military faced. While Eglin Air Force Base had just established a UAV battle lab, the rest of the services were struggling to get what they wanted. Louis Rodrigues, director of defense acquisition issues for the US General Accounting Office, provided sobering testimony. Billions had been wasted, and out of eight programs only one had succeeded fully: the Predator.

The committee reviewed how UAVs had performed in Desert Storm. They had been mostly unchallenged. New technology would enable new platforms to fly longer, penetrating enemy air space while satellites looked down from above. Less maneuverable than manned aircraft, their video could be linked to local commanders. The Congressmen heard how the US Navy had pushed for UAVs under Secretary of the Navy John Lehman and had bought Israeli Mastiffs and Pioneers. Lehman was credited for this "single-minded focus."[98] But then the focus shifted. "It became a major challenge to ensure that tactical command levels had the necessary skills and understanding to deploy tactical collection systems," Rodrigues said.[99]

"The more you ask the UAV to do, the harder it becomes to build," he said. The military pointed out that programs had tried to put too much into the UAVs and not considered if the technology was mature.

These drones were only the most visible part of a larger system, with computers, data links, and ground control being part of them.

General Paul K. Van Riper, bespectacled and lean, of the Marine Corps Combat Development Command, said that the Corps wanted more drones. "In contrast to early success, the history of UAV development over the past ten years has not been a happy one for our operating forces." He said his testers at Quantico wanted a new system, but all they had were the Pioneers. Next up to bat was Maj. General Kenneth Israel, director of Defense Airborne Reconnaissance of the US Air Force. With a wry smile and tuft of close-cropped hair, he said that UAVs saved lives and that they were worth the investment. "I would like to find the father or mother who do not think their son or daughter is worth $10 million." He said that, in drills, UAVs had shown they could hunt down opposing forces. "They aren't looking up in the sky at the Hale Bopp comet, they were looking for UAVs because it basically exposed where they were." Hunter grilled Kenneth Israel on how many UAVs the US currently had and expressed displeasure at the paltry amount: some thirteen Predators, forty-five Pioneers, and fifty-six Hunters.

The men then moved into discussing what was necessary in the future. The Marines said they wanted vertical take-off and landing drones that could operate easily from ships. At the time, the military was sharing its Joint Vision 2010, looking thirteen years into the future. One concept was a drone called Cypher, a flying donut developed by Sikorsky. There was also a small flying V called Exdrone built by BAI Aerosystems. Both were tactical drone flops. "The technology and the information and data distribution is within our grasp today," said Israel. "It is just seeing it through."[100]

Hunter agreed, but he noted that the US was downsizing after the Cold War. UAVs represented a kind of synergy of new technology as the US Navy reduced its size from 546 ships to 346 and the army sent home eight divisions' worth of men. "We like UAVs...we wonder why we are not doing more right now and why the programs have not moved more quickly." The air force agreed, said Lt. Gen. Brett Dula, vice-commander of air combat command. But the air force wanted the Predators to do more, such as being ready for "precision engagement," which would pave the way for arming them.[101] In concluding remarks, after hours of testimony that ran to hundreds of pages, Richard Best of the National Defense Congressional Research Service noted that the services wanted a family of UAVs for different ranges and groups, but it was a struggle to get there.

In addition to the problems raised, all the existing UAVs had problems. Predators couldn't fly in the hot temperatures, which reached 113 degrees in Kuwait. They also need 5,000 feet of runway. Rain ruined the propellers of Pioneers. Fog and crosswinds kept them on the tarmac. Drones were seventeen times more likely to crash, and by 1998, fully twenty-three of sixty-five Predators had been lost.[102] These were fragile little creatures. Infighting, bureaucracy, waste, and "requirements creep," where platforms were jammed with add-ons, was strangling the colossus in the cradle.

In the Footsteps of Lindbergh

It had all begun with a sketch by Alfredo Ramirez on a pad in 1994.[103] His concept was selected by DARPA in 1995. It had to be cheap as well, for a "flyway price" of only $10 million. Teledyne Ryan planned its first Global Hawk flight. They waited and waited to fly them for a year. Finally, they got a go-ahead on December 16, 1996, and prepared for the first flight in February 1997.[104]

With a 116-foot wingspan, the drone resembled a flying Beluga whale. Unlike the stealthy Dark Star, this was a lumbering beast and was specifically not designed to evade enemy radar.[105] But it also had whale-like endurance, flying for forty hours and 13,000 miles. Finally, after more delays, it flew in 1998. The behemoth was designed to navigate in any weather.

It was a pristine day on February 28, 1998, when it taxied and took off at Edwards Airbase in California.[106] The DARPA-supported prototype was all white. Mike Munski, of Teledyne, flew it from a console. It was dubbed AV-1, and it flew for just under an hour and reached 32,000 feet.[107] It had been brought from Teledyne Ryan's Lindbergh field. "Today's flight was an exceptional accomplishment for the Global Hawk team. This is a key milestone towards giving warfighters a powerful new capability," said Col. Doug Carlson of DARPA.[108]

"It has shaped aviation history," said Northrop Grumman Vice President Lauren Stevens years later. Northrop Grumman acquired Teledyne Ryan in 1999 for $140 million, and the project shifted a bit. They worked twelve-hour shifts to bring the two test aircraft up to standards. Engineers remembered working on Thanksgiving.[109] Not everything went perfectly. In March 1999, AV-2, the second plane, crashed after takeoff.[110] As it fell 41,000 feet, a chase plane monitoring it kept shouting "pull up" to the unmanned vehicle.

The brass were impressed with the Global Hawk. A $71 million contract was given to the company to build more in February 2000.[111] One flight to Eglin Airbase and then over the Atlantic became its first trans-oceanic flight. Operators at Fort Bragg watched the images beamed back. Another Global Hawk, AV-5, flew 7,500 miles, from Edwards to Edinburgh, Australia, in twenty-two hours. It was the first crossing of the Pacific by a UAV. It set records as well, flying for thirty-one hours at 65,000 feet. It got an award in May 2001: the Collier Trophy from the National Aeronautic Association. Rolls Royce and Raytheon shared the award with Northrop Grumman.

The terror attacks of September 11, 2001, prodded the company into an even faster pace. Global Hawks were rapidly deployed over Afghanistan. Here they could finally showcase their abilities, flying for hours and providing real-time intelligence on the Taliban and Al Qaeda. For Operation Enduring Freedom they beamed back 17,000 real-time images and flew sixty combat missions. Lt. Col Thomas Buckner, Twelfth

Expeditionary Reconnaissance director of operations, was impressed. "They are in huge demand," he said.[112]

A year later, the drones were sent over the skies of Iraq for Operation Iraqi Freedom. They flew only fifteen missions and sent back 4,800 images. This was "time-critical" data for the operation, and it found thirteen surface-to-air missile batteries, fifty SAM launchers, and 300 tanks. It also did a battle-damage assessment on airstrikes on Saddam Hussein's palaces.

These drones accelerated Iraq's crushing defeat, the Joint Forces air component commander concluded. Global Hawks would eventually have a slightly larger wingspan of 132 feet for the RQ-4B model. "The group that went out there—air force and contractor—were among the most committed I've ever seen," developer Anderson recalled. Both Anderson and Ramirez went on to work to develop further models, eventually resulting in what is known as Triton.[113] By 2018, Global Hawks had flown 250,000 hours in operations since being presented to the air force in 2001.[114]

The Global Hawk was fantastically successful. Built of graphite composite, the V-tail helped provide reduced radar and infrared signature. Its engine was an AE turbofan supplied by Rolls-Royce of North America. Eventually, payloads were increased to 3,000 lbs. in "block 10" of the plane's modification.[115] The way the drone works is that it may have a separate launch and recovery station than the mission control, and it communicates with them via satellites. The launch-and-recovery element (LRE) has an acronym, as does the mission-control element (MCE).[116] While it is in the air, it can track moving targets using its radar and put a target designator on them. During a twenty-four-hour on-station survey, it can cover an area the size of Illinois (40,000 square miles).

The whales were built in batches or "blocks," with the first seven drones forming part of the prototype block, with subsequent editions in 2006. The first two were provided to the navy that year. Six more were built in 2009, with fifteen planned for 2011, and twenty-six for 2012.[117]

The Global Hawk was better than the U-2, which the US had used in the past for broad-area surveillance. It also had new technology and sensors such as the electro-optic infrared imaging (EO/IR) and synthetic aperture radar (SAR). SAR basically meant it could provide a finer scan of the landscape, while better cameras provided more detailed images. It could stay on station for twenty-four hours, while the U-2s could only stay for ten hours. Because of the limited number of Global Hawks that were built, they were highly valued, and their histories are well known.[118] AV-3, for instance, logged 4,800 flight hours in 167 missions in three deployments as part of the global war on terror.[119] Building on that success, the fourth Global Hawk began flying in 2004 and flew 422 missions; it was eventually disassembled at its home at Beale Air Force Base and sent to the Museum of Aviation in September 2011.[120]

The Global Hawks became astronomically too expensive. In the 1990s, they were supposed to cost $10 million apiece. When one was damaged in December 2001, just repairing it cost $40 million. Was this cost-saving program now "gold plated"?[121] Northrup Grumman received a $299 million contract in 2002. It was building the RQ-4B by this time, increasing endurance to twenty-eight hours and 3,000-pound payloads. It could fly 10,000 miles. The program also got an air worthiness certification in 2006 after three years of tests and 77,000 hours of flight. It was still restricted from flying over populated areas to the "extent possible."[122]

Counting the Cost

The Permanent Select Committee on Intelligence threw a fit. How did this $10 million plane balloon to $48 million and then $473 million? "The continual addition of new features and capabilities was making the program unaffordable. There is now an effort to flood the Global Hawk program with money, there are ad hoc plans for rapid, major upgrades before requirements have been established, and no sign of serious examination of where and how Global Hawk fits into an overall collection architecture."[123] Whoops. It was now a billion-dollar program. But at least it worked, unlike the Aquila.

The eighth Global Hawk was delivered in 2003, and a base was built in Al Dhafra in the UAE for some of them. From there, they provided 15,000 images for operations in Iraq and Afghanistan.[124] The Pentagon wanted to add a SIGINT package to them and multi-platform radar technology to the block forty edition, planning to have forty-five of them in service by 2010 and seventy-eight by 2020.[125] They were also doing more things. NASA and the National Oceanic and Atmospheric Administration began using them for science.[126] It could even monitor hurricanes.

As the U-2s were being retired, the Global Hawk would replace them. The problems with America's fleet of various spy planes were already apparent. The need for more Global Hawks was made clear in April 2001, when a Chinese People's Liberation Army J-8 jet collided with a US EP-3 navy plane, forcing it to land on a Chinese island. Its crew members were held in China. They were released ten days later.

Considering how much could have been done in the 1990s, it is surprising that only the Global Hawk and Predator came out of the era as success stories. Both played a major role in the war on terror that would dominate the world for the first two decades of the twenty-first century. But it is extraordinary how many failures there had been. From 1979 to 2000, the US had wasted more than $2 billion on eight UAV programs.[127] Congress heard that the efforts were "disappointing."

This left huge holes in the concept of a multi-tiered UAV system. There were no tactical UAVs for the army, the navy didn't have a replacement for Hunter, there was nothing that could penetrate radar at high altitude or fly quickly like a medium-range concept.[128]

The Global Hawk program eventually transitioned to the "Triton" UAV for use with the navy in 2012. It cost more than $1.16 billion. Five were converted from existing RQ-4s. The US Navy said it wanted 68 MQ-4C aircraft to complement the manned P-8. It was to be put through trials for the Broad Area Maritime Surveillance Block 10 (BAMS-D).[129] It is called RQ-4N.[130] This monster was to fly to altitudes of 50,000 feet for thirty hours over a target with a range of 2,300 miles at 360 miles per hour. Global Hawks in all forms helped the US monitor North Korea from bases in Japan, as well as operations in Africa against Boko Haram and also against ISIS.[131]

One of the RQ-4Ns was sent to patrol waters off the coast of Iran in June 2019.[132] It was at the height of US-Iran tensions after Iran had carried out attacks in the Gulf of Oman. There had also been rocket attacks from Yemen on Saudi Arabia. The navy had only four of the Global Hawk variants at the time. In the first hours of June 20, the drone was struck by an Iranian missile and fell in the Strait of Hormuz.[133]

The shootdown was carried out by an Iranian 3rd Khordad air defense system. How did one of the most expensive US planes, more exorbitant and precious than an F-35, get shot down by an Iranian missile? As with the incident back in 1960, when a CIA U-2 piloted by Francis Gary Powers was shot down over the Soviet Union, there were many concerns, but at least there were no people lost or captured. *Defense One* said the US had nickel-and-dimed its way to being shot down by a mediocre radar and missile.[134] That question would plague the US, as it wondered whether twenty years of drone development had become complacent after years of fighting enemies that didn't have the ability to shoot them down. To understand how the US became so complacent, it is necessary to understand how drones got the ability to be armed in the first place. That story began in the 1990s with bin Laden, and reached is crescendo at Baghdad International Airport on a balmy morning in January 2020. Let's start at the end.

CHAPTER 3

HELLFIRE FROM ABOVE: DRONES WITH MISSILES

Two men at Baghdad International Airport kept a close watch on the Cham Wings flight from Damascus on January 3, 2020. It was two hours late and finally touched down just after midnight. Several heavy-set men exited the plane first, via a staircase, crossing the tarmac at the sprawling airport and bypassing customs. They were met outside the terminal, beyond security, by a Toyota Avalon and a Hyundai minibus.[135] Abu Mahdi al-Muhandis, an Iraqi militia leader, wore the same style untucked button-up shirt and a similar cropped white beard as Qasem Soleimani, the legendary commander of the Iranian Revolutionary Guards Corps' Quds Force, whom he was now receiving in the van. Muhandis had arranged the special greeting, asking his contact at the airport Mohammed Redha to get his motorcade as close to possible to receive Soleimani. Meanwhile the airport security men watching had done their job, confirming to US officials that the plane had arrived and that a man matching the description of Soleimani had disembarked.[136]

Twenty-five minutes after the plane had landed, at 12:55 a.m. Baghdad time, the first of the two vehicles was making its way along a road leading from the airport to central Baghdad. The vehicle was eviscerated by two missiles fired from a US drone. A third missile destroyed the Toyota. All that remained to identify Soleimani, Iran's premier general, was a bloody finger with his ring attached. Locals reported the mysterious explosions and assumed they were errant rocket fire aimed at a nearby US base. No one suspected the US had decided to kill Iran's most well-known and feared general.

Sixty-two-hundred miles away in the US, President Donald Trump was briefed on the successful operation. Narrating as the missile followed the vehicle live, a soldier told Trump what was happening. "They have one minute to live sir, thirty seconds, eight seconds, they're gone sir."[137] At the same time, Iran's general in charge of aerospace operations and intelligence, General Amir Ali Hajizadeh, who has a passing resemblance to George Clooney, was flustered. His agents in Kuwait were monitoring a US drone base at Ali al-Salem Air Base. There had been increased activity.

US MQ-9 Reaper drones were in the air. Helicopters operating in Baghdad's skies were also reported. Soleimani had not informed Hajizadeh of his whereabouts. "We always monitor the US activities, but we didn't know Hajj Qasem's schedule," he said, using the honorific title for Soleimani. Soon it would dawn on Hajizadeh and others that the mysterious explosions at Baghdad Airport signified the end of their famed commander.

It was a 4,900-pound drone with a wingspan of sixty-six feet that launched the missiles that killed Soleimani. In operation since 2007, the Reaper is one of many unmanned aerial vehicles in the US arsenal. Days after the Soleimani strike, for instance, when Iran targeted Ayn al-Assad base with ballistic missiles, US drone operators flying MQ-1C Gray Eagles were caught in the crossfire. They stayed in their containers and worked for hours to make sure their UAVs landed successfully.[138]

To understand how drones got to play such a pivotal role in history, killing Soleimani and Muhandis, it's important to remember whom they didn't kill: Osama bin Laden.

Can We Arm It?

One of the first interagency meetings Douglas J. Feith attended after taking his job as under-secretary of defense for policy in 2001 dealt with drones. It was August. Washington was humid. "What we talked about was there were some satellite imagery of a guy who was tall and had white robes and they thought it might be Osama bin Laden in Afghanistan,"[139] he recalls. It was before 9/11, but Bin Laden already had a lot of blood on his hands from attacks on the US in Africa and the Middle East. "There was a debate about what we could do, and we had just put Hellfire missiles onto drones, and it was a brand new technology, never used. Drones were thought of at the time as intelligence, surveillance and reconnaissance (ISR) assets, they were not thought of as having lethal capabilities. We were just told in August 2001 we had been able to put a Hellfire missile on a drone, and there was discussion of should we use this new Hellfire missile capability to kill bin Laden."

Debates followed. "If we do it, what about collateral damage?" asked concerned policymakers. Who should operate it? Could the CIA do it? Who would physically pull the trigger? The military shied away from responsibility at first. A general said, "The military doesn't do manhunts," Feith recalls. They had bad memories of the hunt for Panamanian strongman Manuel Noriega in the 1990s. Targeted killings just weren't what the military did, they said. "After 9/11 the military had to go through a cultural readjustment, to make the operations against terrorist leadership a military mission. We stopped hearing about not doing manhunts, instead we had lists of Al Qaeda leaders being captured or killed. So this was tied in with the drone debates of August 2001. Is it a military mission? Military people said no [at the time], let intel do it. If the UAV is a military asset, do we transfer them to CIA, and who pulls the trigger?" Feith remembers.

Then came 9/11.

The possibility of killing bin Laden would haunt some after the terror attacks. The administration had not seen it as a priority, and the small price tag related to the operation was apparently batted back and forth between CIA and the air force.[140] The Air Force Combat Command General John Jumper had been seeking to arm the Predator since May 2000.[141] The Predators were about to be sent to do Afghan missions by George Tenet. The State Department was non-plussed, arguing that arming them might violate the 1987 Nuclear Forces Treaty because it would be a "ground launched cruise missile."[142] The air force pushed ahead with backing from Undersecretary of Defense Jacques Gansler, who wanted the Predator armed, and who also insisted that a DARPA project called X-45A to build an armed UAV go forward.[143]

The Hellfire idea was watched from the highest levels. Deputy National Security Advisor Stephen Hadley, CIA Deputy Director John McLaughlin, Deputy Defense Secretary Paul Wolfowitz, and Air Force General Richard Myers looked at sending armed Predators on Afghan missions. Richard Clarke at the NSC helped get permission by illustrating it didn't violate the 1987 treaty. The Big Safari program, which was developing the armed version, swung into action. First, a $2 million demonstration had to be done. Air Force General Stephen Plummer acquired ten Hellfire II missiles and three M299 launchers. Clarke called the idea of sending the Predators to find bin Laden again in March 2001, "see it/shoot it."[144] Bush agreed to send the armed Predators on September 4.[145]

The wheels moved too slowly, and it wasn't until September 18, after the attacks on Washington and New York, that a team was assembled at CIA headquarters in Langley to form Detachment 1, Air Combat Command Expeditionary Air Intelligence Squadron.[146] It would carry out operations from under some trees in trailers at Langley. It was later replaced with the Seventeenth Reconnaissance Squadron, called the "Predator unit" and sent to Indian Springs Air Force Auxiliary Field, Nevada, now called Creech Air Force Base.[147] The CIA now had permission to find and kill "high-value targets."[148]

At General Atomics, Predator orders poured in, recalls Thomas Cassidy. He had been a bit concerned days earlier, pitching the Predator for scientists and firefighters.[149] In Afghanistan, the Predator found its footing, designating 525 targets in just two months after 9/11. Tommy Franks, the US commander, said the "Predator is my most capable sensor in hunting down and killing Al Qaeda and Taliban leadership."[150]

The Hellfires were arriving too. They had already been tested at China Lake in February 2001.[151] Big Safari helped put in place the communications system to enable the drones to be flown from within the US.[152] The first Predator to fire a Hellfire flew 261 sorties before being retired and given to the Air and Space Museum.[153] There were only ten Predators available, but more were rushed into production, until there were 180 available by 2007.[154] Continuous live-feeds were now being watched in Washington and at US air bases as the drones hunted for targets.

David Glade of the Center for Strategy and Technology at the Air War College believed in 2000 that the "development of uninhabited aerial vehicles (UAVs) could potentially revolutionize how military force is used in the future."[155] He was right. On November 4, 2002, the Predators expanded their operations to target a black Toyota Land Cruiser traveling near a farm in Al-Naqaa, Yemen. Hellfire missiles ripped the vehicle apart, killing six people. It was a "revolution" in robotic warfare, according to the *Times* of London.[156] The operation had been made possible by an undercover agent on the ground, using bribes to local tribesmen and a cell phone, who was able to get information to other operatives and drone operators. When it was all over, the vehicle was a smoking hulk, and Al Qaeda commander Abu Ali al-Harethi, was dead.

The US had hunted down the man responsible for the Cole bombing of October 2000.[157]

The Predators over Yemen were flying from Djibouti, armed with AGM-114C Hellfires. They'd been waiting for this day for months, and US President George W. Bush had spoken to Yemen's long-time leader Ali Abdallah Saleh. The killing of al-Harethi helped spawn a debate about the legality of these targeted killings.[158] It also led to controversy in Yemen, as politicians feigned no knowledge of the US "freelancing" operation and slammed US Ambassador Edmund Hull.[159] It was a clean strike, US officials said after.[160]

The CIA was pleased with the strike. Its origins went back almost thirty years, ever since Vice-President George H.W. Bush had pushed for a task force on counter-terrorism and the creation of the Counterterrorism Center, consecrated under Duane Clarridge in 1986. Focusing on rescuing hostages and punishing Iranian-backed terrorists in Lebanon, the Americans had funneled money into a super-secret "Eagle Program" for a flying machine. It would have an infrared camera and a wooden prop.[161] Its descendant was the CIA's use of Predators after 2001.

Now, preparing for invasion of Iraq in 2003, the US and its allies could finally go to war with UAVs in support, as opposed to just having a handful at hand. They were also taking losses. On December 23, 2002, a MiG-25 shot down a Predator that was over the southern no-fly zone. Several other Predators were lost in the invasion. The shootdowns showed that drones were not ready for air-to-air combat and that more stealthy versions were needed. At the time, the US was already working on, and perhaps using, a stealth drone similar to the Sentinel that would appear years later.[162]

Eventually, the drones were stationed at Balad Air Base in Iraq as part of the Forty-sixth Expeditionary Recon Squadron. Commanded by a major, the team had only around twenty-five UAVs. They helped in the battle of Fallujah in November 2004 and killed Iraqi snipers. The Marines were also using Pioneers to help guide their 155 mm. mortars.[163] The US was also finally integrating drones into the air force structure. A squadron consisted of around five flights of four aircraft each. Each flight has around fifty-five officers and crew. By 2006, the Eleventh, Fifteenth, and Seventeenth Reconnaissance Squadrons had 1,000 officers and crew.[164] From June 2005 to June 2006, Predators carried out 2,073 missions and flew for 33,000 hours, following 18,490 targets and conducting 242 attacks.[165] By 2011, they would reach 1 million combat hours.[166]

The Predators were supposed to be in the air for twenty-four hours over targets as they and their operators rotated in and out. But there were hurdles. There weren't enough satellites for all of them, and in 2001–2002 only two Predators and one Global Hawk could be in the air at the same time. Nevertheless, the air force wanted one hundred of them by 2004. It managed to lose a third of them along the way.

Other issues arose as the Predators expanded. The air force demanded a monopoly on flying them, using pilots who were officers. This was despite the fact that most people who want to be pilots don't envision themselves sitting in a trailer. The navy, army, and marines didn't mind using enlisted personnel to fly drones.

As the UAVs' role grew, so did demand. By 2007, there were around 180 Predators deployed and various units were demanding some 300 hours of information from them a day. They didn't have the capacity to provide it all. They were operated from the US, but they frequently took off from near the war zones, such as at Balad Air Base in Iraq. In the early 2000s, they were usually piloted and controlled from Creech or Nellis AFB. One airman told P.W. Singer in *Wired for War* that his role was to make sure "our own guys aren't walking into danger." The pilots were able to speak to commanders, other flight coordinators, and intelligence assets.

While the Predators were armed and conducting surveillance, they could also use laser designators or an infrared "beam" to pinpoint a target for ground troops.[167] It was a revolution from what had been available to soldiers before. When soldiers of the V Corps were preparing to go into Iraq in 2003, they had only a handful of Hunter UAVs. It appears that US drones in this era also began to be used in other ways, both for border patrol in 2008 and also as a kamikaze weapon. This happened by mistake when a Raven drone operator flew a drone into a terrorist.[168]

By 2006, there were thirty-two countries developing drones, and there were more than 250 models. Forty-one countries were already flying eighty operational types as well. The US had 1,000 UAVs.[169] This included a micro-UAV called the Wasp that weighed 250 grams.[170] The US was operating 250 large UAVs and expected to spend $13 billion on development, with a target of employing 1,400 by 2015.

Beyond Line of Sight

On June 6, 1967, Israeli soldier Yaki Hetz fought in one of Israel's toughest battles. He was one of the men in Israel's Fifty-fifth Paratrooper brigade assaulting Ammunition Hill in Jerusalem against Jordanian forces during the battle for Jerusalem in the Six Day War. The hill was festooned with trenches. From the top of the hill, one can see the Old City of Jerusalem in the distance and the Ottoman-era walls of the city. "It all happened so quickly," he later recalled. His platoon commander was hit by the Jordanians, and he helped take command of the assault at just after 2:30 a.m. Hetz won the Medal of Courage.[171]

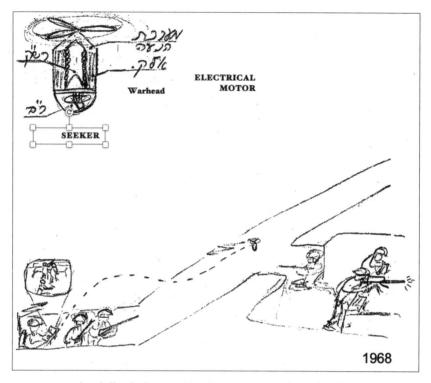

Jacob Hetz's drawing based on experience from the 1967
war inspired Rafael's Spike Firefly decades later. (Courtesy
Rafael Advanced Defense Systems and Jacob Hetz)

The battle for Ammunition Hill led Hetz to the conclusion that
what was needed was something infantry could use to see around a
trench or over a hill while fighting in close combat. He made a sketch
of a weapon that could hover, see, and then kill the enemy.[172] He had
moved on from the trauma of 1967 to study engineering and then work
at Israel's Authority for the Development of Armaments, later called
Rafael Advanced Defense Systems. Hetz would work at Rafael for forty
years, and his dream of a loitering munition would eventually take shape
in the early 2000s. Eventually called Firefly, it would be a three-kilogram

missile with two rotors that could be put in a backpack, launch easily, and fly around a building to attack concealed or dug-in enemies.

Israel's Ministry of Defense and Rafael developed Firefly, which was eventually procured by the IDF in May 2020. The system is designed with a small warhead and can slam into an enemy at seventy kilometers per hour. It uses the same electro-optics that Israeli anti-tank missiles use, with infrared night and day sensors. Operated by a tablet, any soldier could learn to use it. Where platoons once had a mortar expert, radioman, medic, or squad automatic weapon carrier, now there would be the drone operator. While Hetz and Rafael were only imagining this weapon eventually rolling off the assembly line, others were getting in the game of building killer drones, much higher up in the sky, like the US Predator.

"My first exposure to drones was in 2002 or 2003," recalls Col. Richard Kemp, a British army officer who rose to commander during the war in Afghanistan. The tough, imposing colonel recalls being in the cabinet office in London on the Joint Intel committee when the US killed a terrorist in Yemen. "To me that was a revolutionary act of warfare." His activities had been monitored, his communications tracked, and then he was gone. "I was aware of the development of drones. It was the first time I'd experienced their use. It brought home to me the immense power of these things. It was in the hands of the CIA, not the military, and after that the US conducted more strikes in Pakistani tribal areas," he recalls.

But the commander did not use them himself in those years in Afghanistan. He worked closely with the Americans in Afghanistan and observed the capabilities that the drones brought. As he discussed the role of drones in Afghanistan over drinks in Washington, Kemp looked back at the arc of recent conflicts. He was involved in Northern Ireland in the 1990s, trying to improve surveillance for British forces. He called it "Project Convertible," the development of an airship, often called an aerostat today, that could hover above areas to provide information on IRA terrorist activities. "We were keen to enhance capabilities."

Like early drones, the concept was to give intelligence to headquarters, not lower-level troops. "That was a tiny fraction of what a drone can do, and that would change situation capability, and a drone or series of them would have revolutionized the conflict in Northern Ireland. We constructed observation posts that were manned, and each had twenty to thirty soldiers. And they were constantly attacked. They didn't need troops in them, they weren't there to react but to observe. Drones could have made a big difference."

The radical changes necessary to incorporate drones and make troops comfortable with them was clear to Kemp. "In 1977, the technology we had when I joined the army, with the exception of night surveillance thermal imaging, it was no different than in World War I, the radios and all that was similar." Now technology means coming to grips with the power of drones. "To my mind, the major difference is that it doesn't give you a fundamental capability that wasn't there before, we have had aircraft that can monitor and attack for many years. It's not fundamentally different, but the options it gives you on the battlefield, it enables you to maintain surveillance and adjust it over a longer period of time. Except for satellites, we didn't have that. For politicians it also gives the capability of applying military force in a way they haven't had it before, without risk and deniability that was never available and without infrastructure in the area. I would say that if anything, the revolution is at that level more than at the tactical level."[173]

In the end, the drone was the next logical development for the battlefield. It reduced the threat to soldiers in the field, sending in armed drones instead of special forces. Now drones would hunt the enemy down. Predator was mostly hunting down enemies in "permissive" or "non-contested" airspace, where shoot-down risk was low. This was a result of US global hegemony and funneling investment into a weapon that was tailored to the war on terror. It was a product of the 1990s, evolving for the post-9/11 wars.

For Kevin McDonald, a former senior officer in the Irish Defense Forces, the appearance of drone technology fundamentally changed the way wars are fought. The affable Irish soldier, a mountaineer who laces his serious discussions with humor, is enthusiastic about technology and war. "Even though it's just the latest technological development, it gives the army using it greater 'reach' than its opponents." This is what is called "standoff" ability so that one can strike from further away and not endanger one's own soldiers. This is true from the largest drones to the smallest tactical ones being used by platoon commanders. He compares it to the first tanks being introduced in 1916. The tank helped the soldiers leave their trenches to take on a dug-in enemy, and the drones would do the same.[174]

Hunter-Killer

"The new Predator pilot, with their air-to-ground expertise, worked with engineers to develop the procedures, displays and checklists necessary for the successful employment of weapons from the aircraft," a 2006 report said.[175] The Predator was so successful, other ideas were pushed aside.[176] But there was a need to figure out how to transition pilots trained to fly aircraft to sit in trailers thousands of miles away and hunt down terrorists. Initially, the Predators used laser designators to guide others to do the killing. Once the Hellfires had been affixed, the pilots developed tactics, techniques, and procedures (TTPs) to improve their work.

By 2010, the US had some 7,500 drones.[177] The experience of flying these drones took a toll on operators. A former drone operator who asked that his name not be used described some of the process. Let's call him Captain Black. A former pilot who worked with special forces and had flown for decades, he trained to become a drone operator during the early years of the presidency of Barack Obama, as the US armed drone program got into high gear. Trained at Holloman Air Force Base near Alamogordo in New Mexico and then at Randolph in San Antonio, he went to Creech to fly the drones. Training involved qualification on a simulator and a more academic course to qualify for the fundamentals of remotely piloted aircraft.[178] Once the real flying began, it was the "most stressful" mission he had flown, he said.[179] It was also the most demanding.

What made it difficult, in part, was the contrast between normal civilian life in Las Vegas and then driving almost an hour to Creech to do missions. Unlike F-16 pilots sent to the Persian Gulf or aviators in Vietnam and the Second World War, this kind of war was different. "You get up at six in the morning," he said. "You drive to the base, have a briefing and then sit down in front of the screen to start flying the drone. A sensor operator sits to your right. One flies the mission and the other operates cameras. You work until four in the afternoon and then do a debrief. It's a 12-hour day. You work five days and are off three, or sometimes six days on and then off for two."[180]

Capt. Miles, 489th Attack Squadron pilot, and Airman 1st Class Darriette, 489th ATKS sensor operator, prepare for a sortie via simulator at Creech Air Force Base, Nevada, Nov. 24, 2020. The 489th ATKS provides expert launch and recovery aircrew that enable world-wide combat MQ-9 operations. (U.S. Air Force photo by Airman 1st Class William Rio Rosado)

There was a constant shortage of drone crews compared to the demand. With never enough personnel, it was difficult, and pilots rarely had days off. "They want to fly more missions, and tensions are high and morale is difficult because they want to fly the existing crews into ground because they have more missions than crew," said Captain Black. He went on to fly for almost three years.

Brett Velicovich, author of *Drone Warrior*, recalled his experience in 2009 as he sat in the "box," the trailers where operators worked south of Mosul in Iraq. They had eight flat-screen TVs, and they watched live feeds from the drone, which showed the speed, missile laser designators, and maps. He worked in a team of six, including military intelligence and other soldiers.

He described one mission hunting a suspect using a drone.[181] Next to him in the hot seat was an air force tactical controller. They could speak to specialists in other US spy agencies and with helicopters and ground forces. The enemy was using a bongo truck, a white truck typical in Iraq. Using electro-optical and infrared, the operators stalked their prey. The mission that time would involve using the drone to follow the enemy and calling on air support from Black Hawks. The raid was a success. The bongo was bumping along the road when the choppers fired near it and dropped soldiers to detain the suspects. This was the drone war: round-the-clock monitoring, the ability to kill as well as the ability to coordinate with ground forces. One servicemember in the US who was awarded for his service spent seventy-four days chasing one target. In the end, he identified it, and a warplane took out the target.[182]

For those on the ground in Iraq, the early years were a bit cumbersome. One US National Guard commander I spoke to described going on raids among the reeds and wadis that make up rural Iraq north of Baghdad, where Sunni jihadists were hiding. Despite having access to drones, the need to call back to command and then speak to the drone operators made operations cumbersome. Drones might spot the enemy, but by the time soldiers arrived, the jihadists had melted away. How to coordinate the drones with the men on the ground would take years to sort out.

The air force was transitioning from rotating pilots into unmanned work for several years to the training of an actual force of unmanned aerial warfare pilots. This would be its own career path. Some of those careers would end up piloting the Predator B, later known as the Reaper. Developed and flown as early as 2001, it had a Honeywell turboprop engine and longer wings than the Predator, at sixty-four feet. It could carry 3,000 pounds of weapons up to 55,000 feet for twenty-five to thirty-six hours. General Atomics paid for the initial development, and in October 2001, after the 9/11 attacks, the air force took interest.

An MQ-9 Reaper aircrew flies a training mission over the Nevada Test and Training Range, Jan. 14, 2020. MQ-9 aircrew provide dominant, persistent attack and reconnaissance for combatant commanders and coalition partners around the world. (U.S. Air Force photo by Airman 1st Class William Rio Rosado)

The Reaper or MQ-9 was specifically designed as a hunter-killer as opposed to a surveillance aircraft that missiles were added to. They would still be cheap, around $5 million each. By 2006, the Reapers were ready for action. With six pylons on the wings, they could carry more than a dozen missiles. The drone would have versatility in its weapons, like an F-15 had in the 1980s and 1990s. It could carry Hellfires, Stingers, or Viper and GPS-guided Joint Direct Attack Munitions (JDAM). It looked like more bang for the buck.[183]

The Reaper's Westinghouse radar and Raytheon laser designator were state-of-the-art.[184] It was also intended to have better optics, with up to nine cameras, showing an image within a diameter of 2.4 miles of terrain. While the Reaper was giving US operators awesome killing power, it was also deceptively inviting for policymakers. As the Bush administration wrapped up its time in office, the incoming Obama team saw drones as way to hunt down terrorists without having to lose troops.[185] They wanted to end the quagmire of Iraq and Afghanistan, wars that had cost trillions of dollars and where many lives had been lost. The global war on terror could be won from the air.

This idea of winning from the air had also been a deceptive dream for American warriors in the 1990s, when the Clinton administration had carried out air-driven wars in the Balkans, Kosovo, and even against Al Qaeda. These interventions, born of US global hegemony, were based on a kind of new world order of humanitarian intervention. September 11th burst that illusion, showing the US was vulnerable. Now the US was vulnerable again, to the doubt that came with not winning in Iraq.

If there would be no "mission accomplished," at least there could be a mission.[186] The Obama administration would use Reapers to deadly effect. In Pakistan, for instance, the Bush administration had carried out only forty-eight strikes. The first occurred on June 19, 2004. The Obama administration would order at least 353 known attacks.[187] Up to 2,683 terrorists would be killed by the Obama team, but concerns were raised that up to 162 civilians were also killed. The Obama team would concentrate on killing Taliban members.[188]

Creech Air Force Base was the heart and soul of this operation. The pilots praised the Obama administration for never wavering in authorizing strikes on high-value targets. Crews rapidly expanded from seven or eight people in a squadron in 2010, to 250 or more, with one squadron having up to 500 members. "These are big organizations and they expanded quickly and there were growing pains. It was a small community and they were trying to train as many as they could," recalled Captain Black.[189] "When I first went to Creech it looked different, they have demolished the buildings we used to fly in, they moved the buildings inland from the highway." As the drone program expanded, the controversy about the operators expanded, and there were fears terrorists might target the base. "We flew a lot of important missions and I am proud of what we did and knocking out bad guys and I take a lot of pride in those missions."

High-value strikes gave way to "signature" strikes, striking groups of fighters or alleged terrorists who followed a pattern. Days were spent with eyes on target, from above and from other sources, sometimes on the ground. After the strike, the pilots, sensor operators, and intelligence experts would watch those fleeing and kill the "squirters" who fled. They would debrief, go home and then work the same area the next day, following the funerals and waiting for another opportunity.

It was grueling work, and graphic: sitting at their screens, the pilot in the left seat and the sensor operator on the right, watching the enemy in the crosshairs, waiting for the order to pull the trigger. "Then the sensor operator guides the weapon…we have the option of the five-hundred-pound laser guided bomb and the three types of Hellfires," says Captain Black. Reports hint at other clandestine weapons, never revealed to the public, that were used.

Most of the Obama administration's strikes were carried out by 2012. "CIA attacks have struck Pakistan's tribal areas on average once every five days," a report noted.[190] For instance, Taliban commander Baitullah Mehsud was eviscerated in August 2009. The next year, another Al Qaeda operative, Ilyas Kashmiri, met with a Hellfire missile as well.

Obama liked the precision of the strikes. He emphasized that this made civilian deaths less likely.[191] The peak was 2010, with 128 strikes in Pakistan. John Brennan, National Security Advisor, said that the US was the first country to regularly conduct strikes using remotely piloted aircraft conflict. But in 2012, he noted that the US must "use them responsibly" if America expected other countries to do so.[192] The US became so concerned about implications it was running a "kill chain" that was out of control that it made sure to incorporate human controls into every aspect of drone warfare. Even though the intention was to show there were checks and balances, the emphasis created a perception that the US was doing something wrong.[193] While Washington put the brakes on, other American enemies would continue to develop drone killing technology.

The battlefields of the drone wars rapidly expanded.[194] UAVs were sent to Africa as part of operations in Libya and also to Niger and Camp Lemonnier in Djibouti. In 2014 they even flew over Chad.[195]

There were 104 Reapers by 2010, and the air force wanted up to 346 of them by 2019.[196] In 2011, these drones flew 2,227 missions for Enduring Freedom in Iraq, and then flew 1,889 in 2012, including operations in support of "Copper Dune" in Yemen against Al Qaeda. The older Predators, by contrast, flew 7,797 sorties in 2012 in Iraq, of which 238 were to support Turkey's anti-PKK operations (dubbed Nomad Shadow), and 1,119 to hunt down terrorists in Libya.[197]

Turkey was so impressed, it kept pressing the US to buy them.[198] Instead, the US provided Turkey intelligence from drones on the whereabouts of the PKK. In 2019, Washington stopped sharing the information after tensions rose with Ankara. Turkey responded by increasing its own drone arsenal, now made at home.[199]

Congress and Joint Chiefs head Mike Mullen loved the "game changing technology" so much that funding was increased by 75 percent in 2011.[200] But the operations were taking a toll. Michael Hayden was concerned that the CIA was focusing too much on fighting terrorists, leaving the US handicapped to respond to the Arab Spring, the ISIS threat in 2014, and Russia's annexation of Crimea.[201] Brennan agreed, and the administration shifted to ending the CIA's commitment to Afghanistan and Pakistan. The Trump administration, coming to power in 2017 with an idea of ending the Afghan war, reduced drone strikes in Pakistan dramatically, until they appeared to end entirely in 2018.

The drone war saved American lives. By 2014, a total of 2,356 US servicemen had been killed in Afghanistan and 3,485 members of the Coalition. "The high number of militants killed helped reverse the Taliban's momentum."[202] Drones helped keep the US public from complaining about the endless war. The drone had become the "weapon of choice" for the war on terror, a US task force on drone policy concluded in 2015.[203]

As the number of Reapers and Predators expanded to 303 aircraft in service, the number of missions they were doing rapidly increased. It had taken a decade and a half to get to the million-flight-hours mark in 2011, but it would take just two more years to get to two million.[204] The 432nd Air Expeditionary Wing at Creech flew 12,000 sorties in 2017, for 216,000 flight hours. The air force credits the machines with helping liberate vast areas from ISIS, enabling millions of Iraqis and Syrians to return home.[205] The drones had come of age, from precision strikes and being a novelty, to a war-winning system. Historically the US was getting more out of these sorties than mass bombing missions of past wars.[206]

The number of US drone units was expanding also. In addition to the 432nd, there were other units recruited for the drone wars: The 732nd Operations Group, the Seventeenth, Twenty-second, and 867th attack squadrons with their Reapers, the Forty-fourth Reconnaissance Squadron and the Thirtieth Reconnaissance Squadron, which operates the Sentinel.[207] There was even talk of a special medal for drone warriors.[208]

Col. Stephen Jones, 432nd Wing/432nd Air Expeditionary Wing commander, stands in front an MQ-9 Reaper Remotely Piloted Aircraft (RPA) in a hangar at Creech Air Force Base, Nevada, Aug. 8, 2020. As commander, Jones leads more than 5,000 people across five groups and twenty squadrons, in addition to serving as the Installation Command Authority for Creech Air Force Base. (U.S. Air Force photo by Airman 1st Class William Rosado)

The commander of the 432nd Wing in the US Air Force in 2020, Stephen Jones, was a member of the initial team that weaponized the Predator. "I can tell you this entire enterprise was born of innovation," he said in an interview.[209] At Creech Air Force Base he led 5,000 people in five groups and twenty-one squadrons.[210] A graduate of the University of California, Berkeley, he was a B-1 pilot in the past and served at bases from Alabama to Ramstein. With more than 700 combat hours in Iraq and Afghanistan, he is one of the America's most knowledgeable drone commanders.

"The RPAs we have fielded today are remarkably resilient: our fleet is airborne three-hundred-sixty-five days a year, with each platform airborne for sixteen to twenty hours at a time," Jones says. "The aircrew of the 432nd Wing regularly top 350,000 combat hours per year and prove the versatility of the weapon system daily; CSAR and strike, coordination, and reconnaissance (SCAR) tactics are examples of how the MQ-9 is being utilized in ways never before realized."[211]

Drones were proving also that they would save the lives of pilots too. By 2018, some 254 large drones had crashed worldwide, with 196 of those being US drones such as the Predator or Reaper. Predators had a particularly bad time, with sixty-nine destroyed completely in crashes between 2009 and 2018.[212] By contrast, known crashes show only a handful by Israel, India, Turkey, and Pakistan in the same period, illustrating the volume of use by the US.

The problem with discovering a new, relatively cheap, and expendable weapon, is that one can become addicted to it. As the US found itself hunting terrorists in up to eighty countries around the world, it became addicted to killing them the easiest way possible, through Hellfire missiles and drones. What comes next is the story of those who felt drones were trending toward becoming a Terminator-like killing machine.

CHAPTER 4

KILLING MACHINES: THE ETHICS OF DRONE WARFARE

On September 11, 2012, US Secretary of State Hillary Clinton called David Petraeus at the CIA. She wanted to make sure they were on the same page regarding an attack on a US diplomatic annex in Benghazi, Libya. US Defense Secretary Leon Panetta was also in the loop. The Pentagon was monitoring events. A US drone was pulled from surveillance near Darna to help see what was happening. The machine was already over the target by 5:11 p.m., Washington time. It was eleven in the evening in Benghazi. Buildings were burning.[213]

It was too late for the men on the ground. US Ambassador Chris Stevens was dead, along with three other Americans by the time the night was over. The Predator drone that provided surveillance was unarmed. Washington was also reticent to use drones to target the attackers. "The individuals related in the Benghazi attack, those that we believe were either participants or leadership of it, are not authorized use of military force," Army General Martin Dempsey, chairman of the Joint Chiefs, said in October 2014.[214] The US didn't have the capability to find and kill them, he said, because the army wasn't authorized to do so.[215]

His statement was an extraordinary reversal of what the US had been doing for years. Suddenly the armed drones had been muzzled, and surveillance missions took precedence. In 2009, a US Scan Eagle launched from the *Bainbridge* helped in the rescue of Captain Richard Phillips[216] of the *Maersk Alabama*.[217] The Scan Eagle, one of a new generation of small, catapult-launched drones used by the navy since 2005, had seen some 500,000 combat hours and 56,000 flights.

The White House was gun shy. Mistakes kept being made. In 2015, a counterterror operation killed two hostages held by Al Qaeda: Dr. Warren Weinstein and Giovanni Lo Porto.[218] Obama's use of drones became a major point of contention. Articles called his administration the "Reaper presidency," and numerous reports chronicled the drone strikes that killed civilians in Pakistan and elsewhere.[219] By one account, "Between 2004 and 2014, US UAV strikes in Pakistan are estimated to have killed approximately 2,000 to 4,000 people, while US strikes in Yemen are estimated to have killed several hundred people."[220]

The new dronephobia came after years of success. In Libya, the UAVs helped topple dictator Muammar Gaddafi. After months in which the tyrant had been suppressing protests and rebels, he was riding in a convoy leaving Sirte on October 20, 2011, when a Predator droned him.[221] He fled into a drainage ditch and was caught, sodomized, and killed by rebels. It was the end of four decades in power.

Similarly, the Obama administration ramped up operations in Africa. David Petraeus, then at CENTCOM, pushed for a Joint Unconventional Warfare Task Force executive order.[222] Camp Lemonnier in Djibouti became the hub of operations. Lemonnier is laid out like a long rectangle, abutting the water, with a runway parallel to the base's housing and buildings. It's a dry landscape, and there is a kind of trench separating the base from areas around it. The housing is a depressing series of containers laid out in a grid. A gym with StairMasters and weights gives people something to do.

Joint Special Operations Task Force 84-4 would manage operations in Somalia and Yemen, which are separated only by a small amount of water at the Bab al-Mandab straits.[223] More naval drones were involved as well, including the MQ-8 Scout, a helicopter, and the ScanEagle. The MQ-8, built by Northrop Grumman since 2000, was introduced in 2009 and was supposed to provide an easy way for ships to have a drone without using a runway. The Boeing ScanEagle, developed since 2002 was also used.[224] The ScanEagle was built by Insitu, a company in Washington State founded in 1994, and was initially designed to search for tuna at sea. Partnering with Boeing brought the machine to fruition. It looks like a large V with a bulb at the crest.

Some of the first strikes were carried out in Yemen, while dozens of strikes were carried out in Somalia. The African operations were never very large, and they were hampered by manned aircraft needing to operate over a huge expanse of land. There were only ten Predators and four Reapers in Djibouti in 2012. Reports on this largely clandestine operation say there were several drones in Ethiopia, a Predator in Niger, a Reaper in the Seychelles, and one Predator in Chad and Cameroon.[225] This appealed to Washington's desire to continue fighting terror, appear tough on Al Qaeda, and have a small footprint. While Osama bin Laden was killed in a Navy SEAL raid in 2011, his demise didn't end the need for these operations. Instead, the US increased them as Al Qaeda's various tentacles continued to function independently.

Public attention was concerned with controversies. On a relatively warm day in the hills of northwest Pakistan in October 2012, a sixty-eight-year old woman was killed in a drone strike. Her family wanted answers. Amnesty International tried to provide them, noting the poor people received no "justice or compensation" for the woman's death. Her name was Mamana Bibi, and she was one of the more high-profile civilians killed by US drones that led to questions about whether their use was becoming too widespread and indiscriminate.[226]

Amnesty looked at forty-five strikes between January 2012 and August 2013. The US was not providing even "basic information" on the strikes, which were ostensibly clandestine. But there were questions about what the "status" under international law is for civilians killed in strikes like these. "Based on its review of incidents over the last two years, Amnesty International is seriously concerned that these and other strikes have resulted in unlawful killings that may constitute extrajudicial executions or war crimes."[227]

A U.S. Air Force MQ-9 Reaper assigned to the 556th Test and Evaluation Squadron armed with an AIM-9X missile sits on the ramp on September 3, 2020 ahead of the ABMS Onramp #2. In the test, the MQ-9 successfully employed a live air-to-air AIM-9X Block 2 missile against a target BQM-167 drone simulating a cruise missile. (U.S. Air Force photo by SrA Haley Stevens)

War Crimes

The problem in Pakistan, as well as other places such as Yemen and Somalia, was that the US was fighting a shadow war. This was not under the jurisdiction of a state the US was either working with or occupying.

Blurred boundaries of countries were exploited by drones flying over ungoverned spaces, where insurgents or terrorists take root. This had been called the "non-integrated gap" by Thomas Barnett in his 2004 book *The Pentagon's New Map*. His map showed a world with parts of Africa, the Middle East, Central Asia, Pakistan, Indonesia, and several South American countries encircled as part of the "gap." These coincide with weak or failed states. Unsurprisingly, this was the area where the US drone war was racking up a body count. The drone army was operating there because no one had the ability to shoot them down and because the global war on terror seemed to give *carte blanche* to fighting terrorists wherever they are.

Amnesty International was concerned that the US was not providing information on the strikes and that Pakistan was failing to protect and enforce the rights of the victims. Amnesty accused Pakistani authorities of complicity in "in unlawful killings resulting from the US drones program...the failure to protect people in the Tribal Areas from unlawful drone strikes or to adequately assist victims of such strikes."[228] In addition, the researchers asserted that Germany, Australia, and others were giving the US intelligence for the strikes.

The reality was probably more complex. Because Pakistan had once supported the Taliban, it wanted to hedge its bets. If the US left Afghanistan, then Pakistan would want amicable relations with the Taliban if they returned to power. At the same time, it didn't want them destabilizing Pakistan. The Tehrik-i-Taliban in Pakistan murdered 148 students in a school massacre in 2014. Pakistan's leader Pervez Musharraf, who had come to power in a 1999 coup, resigned in 2008 soon after politician Benazir Bhutto was assassinated in 2007. It was a time of turmoil, with the siege of extremists in the Lal Masjid, the 2008 Mumbai terror attacks directed from Pakistan at India in 2008, and increasing terror targeting minority Shi'ites.

The drone war added to uncertainty in Pakistan. It generally killed terrorists, but one American pilot broke his silence and appeared in a

2014 documentary called *Drone*, speaking about his alleged role in a war that had killed 1,626 people.[229] Critics called on Pakistan to shoot down the American drones.

Mamana Bibi, a Pakistani grandmother, had become used to seeing them. "The drone planes were flying over our village all day and night, flying in pairs, sometimes three together," a resident of her village recalled. The family were out working the field when Mamana Bibi was "blown to pieces by at least two Hellfire missiles."[230] Why did the US target them? It may have been due to the presence of a Taliban fighter who used a satellite phone nearby. This looked like they were using deadly assumptions based on algorithmic evidence, the kind of faceless war that gave drones such a bad reputation. Was it worse than a bomber pilot flattening a city in the Second World War? Perhaps not. But today it is common to view US as a hi-tech moral democracy at a time when standards have changed, and it was waging a clandestine war led by the shadowy CIA.

In another 2012 incident, a group of workers were sitting in a tent when drones targeted them. Witnesses said they saw four drones flying in the area. The Zowi Sidqi village strike killed eighteen people. The Amnesty report raised the question of whether some of those in the group of workers were Taliban. It says that even if that were the case, and if "particular individuals could lawfully be targeted, could they have been attacked at a time and in a manner that did not put so many uninvolved civilians at risk?"[231]

Those who tried to take their cases to US courts were not successful. The American Civil Liberties Union and the Center for Constitutional Rights filed a 2012 lawsuit over the killings of Anwar al-Awlaki (Aulaqi), Samir Khan and Abdulrahman al-Awlaki in September and October 2011. In *Al-Aulaqi v. Panetta*, they said that the killing violated the Constitution's fundamental guarantee against the deprivation of life without due process.[232] Born in New Mexico to parents from Yemen, Awlaki became an imam in Falls Church, Virginia, and later moved to

Yemen in 2004, where he supported terrorists and inspired terror attacks in the US. He was killed after stopping for breakfast on the way to Marib, like the 2002 strike in Yemen. Obama called his killing a "major blow" to Al Qaeda. The case about his death was heard in July 2013 and dismissed in April 2014.

The ACLU was not only concerned about the killing of US citizens but also that they could be put on "kill lists" in the first place. They had filed a 2010 lawsuit also questioning whether Awlaki could be put on the kill list. The case was dismissed. The ACLU claimed the US was carrying out "signature" strikes as well, killing people based on patterns of behavior without even having intel on the identities of the victims. The US classified all "military-age males" as terrorists in such strikes, the ACLU claimed.[233]

In March 2019, a court in Germany also looked at the US drone program.[234] Unsurprisingly, the German defense department rejected claims it was responsible for US actions. By this time, estimates claimed that some 330 strikes had been carried out in Yemen, killing more than 1,000 people, of whom 200 might have been civilians. Some of the victims were children. It wasn't clear if US munitions, such as the GBU-12 Paveway II bombs now being put on the drones, were more accurate.

The UN began to take an interest in the drone strikes, and Christof Heyns, UN Special Rapporteur on extrajudicial, summary, and arbitrary executions, said in 2013 that drones were not "inherently illegal weapons." However, the UN warned that as more countries were using armed drones, it was important to understand a world where "multiple states use such weapons in secrecy."[235] The UN report argued that states should declassify their use of drones and make the aftermath of strikes more transparent. The demand was incumbent on the operator and states where drones were used. Already sixteen countries had called for the UN to look into the controversial use of drones. Pakistan topped the list, but other countries were in the spotlight as well.

In the debate on the use of drones, the role of Pakistan was heightened until such a point that the Pakistani government had indicated it did not consent to drones being used on its territory, and the UN agreed it was a violation of Pakistan's sovereignty. US State Department spokesperson Victoria Nuland said the US was in discussions with Pakistan on counterterrorism.[236] Former US Ambassador to Pakistan Cameron Munter said the problem was not that drones were bad at fighting terror, but that they needed to be used judiciously: "Do you want to win a few battles and lose the war?" CIA Director John Brennan, who would take the helm in March 2013, had just told confirmation hearings that the US only took action with drones as a last resort "to save lives when there is no other alternative."[237]

Israel's increased use of drones also came in for critique. The Hermes 450 and IAI Heron 'Shoval' had been used in the Gaza war, called Operation Cast Lead in 2008.[238] Israel was accused of relying on drones more for attacks in subsequent 2012 and 2014 conflicts in Gaza. I witnessed all those conflicts from the border, often coming under Palestinian Qassam and rocket fire. We would stand in the town of Sderot, or overlooking Gaza City from a field, and wait for the "red alert" sirens to blare. The haunting siren, in Hebrew, stays with me to this day. Those across the border in Gaza, under Israeli airstrikes, had no warning system. And they began to claim they were targeted by warplanes they couldn't see.

Israel doesn't admit that it uses armed drones, but human rights groups, foreign reports, and even US military studies have claimed in reports that Israel was using the Heron TP and Hermes 900 to conduct strikes.[239] Gazans claimed some 37 percent of their casualties were due to drone strikes.[240] But Israeli officers said the drones were improving their ability to make the right decision and distinguish terrorists from civilians, using better sensors and optics. While Israel was already acquiring its third- and fourth-generation unmanned aerial systems, other countries were on their first or second.

An Elbit Systems Hermes 900 equipped with maritime surveillance capabilities and life rafts. As drones are being used more they also receive new capabilities for different environments, not all of them military applications. (Courtesy Elbit Systems)

Since Israel doesn't admit it uses armed drones, it never weighed publicly the question of whether they should be used in war, relying increasingly on unmanned technology. There was little pressure on Israel to end drone strikes it didn't admit to. However, some evidence did emerge of Israeli drones and their weapons. One was spotted over Lebanon and posted to social media on May 19, 2020.[241] A missile dubbed "Mikholit" was even claimed to have been found in Sinai, Lebanon, and Gaza between 2014 and 2018.[242] Overall Israeli military operations increased rapidly in precision after 2014, so that by 2020, few civilians were dying in any kind of strikes.

Across the Atlantic, a turning point in the US use of drones came in 2013. The Obama administration was wary of its legacy being tarnished. They had come to office to end wars, and Obama had received a Nobel Peace Prize. Drones were supposed to cut down on casualties and enable the US to leave Iraq and Afghanistan. The US had reduced troop levels in both countries. But the war on terror continued, across Africa and into Libya and other places. The Arab Spring was fueling instability. Extremists were rising. Nevertheless, Washington wanted to quietly roll back the drone war.

The European Parliament joined the UN chorus in calling for restraint and more investigation of armed drones.[243] Expressing concerns over the use of armed drones outside the international legal framework, the EU parliament sought to "develop an appropriate policy response at both European and global level which upholds human rights and international humanitarian law." The resolution passed in 2014, calling on the high representative for foreign affairs and security policy to oppose extrajudicial and targeted killing. It sought to:

"Include armed drones in relevant European and international disarmament and arms control regimes; ban the development, production and use of fully autonomous weapons which enable strikes to be carried out without human intervention; commit to ensuring that, where there are reasonable grounds for believing that an individual or entity within their jurisdiction may be connected to an unlawful targeted killing abroad."

It also urged the EU to adopt a common position on the use of armed drones and called "on the EU to promote greater transparency and accountability on the part of third countries in the use of armed drones."[244]

The portrayal of drones as robotic killing machines operated by humorless bureaucrats or stressed-out soldiers became a cliché of Hollywood at the same time as the US government was reprising its role. *Eye in the Sky* came out in 2015, and drones appeared in *Homeland* and *Good Kill* in 2014. The 2015 film *Drone Strike* tells the story of an RAF drone operator who "fires Hellfire missiles 4,000 miles away," eventually destroying an Afghan family. These were followed by the 2017 thriller, also named *Drone*, where an operator is targeted by those who believe he killed their family. Almost all the films make drones appear to be somehow different than manned bombing missions, mostly because of the sterility of those sitting in an office watching the feed and making decisions. They then portray most of the victims, whether terrorists or not, as always being near their families when the operators have to make these split-second decisions. In fact, most drone strikes were not on family compounds, and most terrorists were not so ambiguous.

Former operators and pilots say the precision of the strikes didn't make them less traumatic. Captain Black recalled that there were many pilots with PTSD who suffered from the quixotic nature of the mission. The graphic nature of watching enemies die in high-resolution video was different than being an F-16 or B-52 pilot where you didn't see the casualties. In this sense, it's more like being a sniper on the ground. But snipers are in the field with their fellow soldiers. They are immersed in the war. The drone pilot goes home at night to a civilian life, and it is jarring. There is no way to get around it. The nature of the business is that cameras keep getting better, and therefore what the operator sees when the trigger is pulled is more graphic. Even without civilians being killed by mistake, the horror of war is right in front of you. There's no question about whether you killed the enemy. You can watch them bleed out.

Drones, because they appear futuristic, conjure up ideas of *Terminator*, and *RoboCop*, and artificial intelligence deciding to kill people. Even though the strikes in places like Pakistan would not have been less deadly had F-16s carried them out, the use of drones became an easy avenue of critique directed at America. Columbia University Law School and numerous other online and academic centers became interested in drones and the drone war. This included the Bard Center for the Study of the Drone and articles at the Bureau of Investigative Journalism, New America, Long War Journal, and Air Wars, The Intercept, and other publications who did extensive studies. The studies were aided by new information from WikiLeaks and other sources that gave readers a peek behind the curtain.[245]

Putting the Brakes On

US President Barack Obama, his voice sincere and vulnerable, told the National Defense University in May 2013 that "the use of force must be seen as part of a larger discussion we need to have about a comprehensive counterterrorism strategy." At West Point in May 2014, he went further, arguing that "we must uphold standards that reflect our values. That means taking strikes only when we face a continuing, imminent threat, and only where…there is near certainty of no civilian casualties, for our actions should meet a simple test: we must not create more enemies than we take off the battlefield."

The Stimson Center in Washington agreed and put together a task force on US drone policy. John Abizaid, the former US general, and Rosa Brooks, the American law professor at Stimson noted that "UAV technologies are here to stay. Used foolishly, they can endanger our interests, diminish regional and global stability, and undermine our values. Used wisely, they can help advance our national security interests even as we foster a more robust international commitment to the rule of law."[246] Abizaid was the former CENTCOM commander, so he should know. The task force was impressive and included Philip Mudd, former deputy director of the Central Intelligence Agency (CIA) Counterterrorism Center, and Lt. Gen. David Barno, former head of Combined Forces Command-Afghanistan.

The task force report said there was concern that the strategic value of drones was being eroded amid a Whac-A-Mole approach. Impunity also meant that drones were being used in a massive covert campaign all over the world, sometimes for targeted killing. There was little strategy involved now, just killing. "The seemingly low-risk and low-cost missions enabled by UAV technologies may encourage the United States to fly such missions more often, pursuing targets with UAVs that would be deemed not worth pursuing if manned aircraft or special operation forces had to be put at risk," the report noted.[247] Terrorist groups and "non-state actors" had already eroded states. This meant a changing battlefield and changing notions of what a combatant is. "The United States currently appears to claim, in effect, the legal right to kill any person it determines is a member of al-Qaida or its associated forces, in any state on Earth, at any time, based on secret criteria and secret evidence, evaluated in a secret process by unknown and largely anonymous individuals, with no public disclosure of which organizations are considered," the Stimson report noted.[248]

The task force considered bureaucratic oversight. The US had authorized military force against terrorists in 2001. But the US military is prohibited from covert actions. The CIA requires a presidential finding and notification to congressional intelligence committees. The military, by contrast, reports to the House and Senate Armed Services Committees. The military also appeared less interested in just killing people. SOCOM head Joseph Votel argued that the US got more information when suspects were captured rather than killed.[249] Lt. Gen. Michael Flynn, then head of the Defense Intelligence Agency, acknowledged that the drone campaign was primarily "only about killing."[250]

The US was now sending 8,300 special operations forces to some ninety countries, but new drones and missiles would be coming online soon.[251] As drones took on more missions with more weapons and became more interoperable, autonomous or artificial intelligence would also increase. The Stimson report concluded that Washington should "transfer general responsibility for carrying out lethal UAV strikes from the CIA to the military."[252] This conclusion could be a shot across the bow of the use of the drones so widely in counterterrorism tactics. This ran up against the fact that the US had been searching for just this tool since the 1980s to deal with new terrorist threats.[253]

Proliferation

"If you carry out operations in secrecy, and if you kill the wrong person, it's hard for people to get justice, and there is resentment, and that's counterproductive," says Wim Zwijnenburg, humanitarian project leader for the Dutch peace organization Pax. I called Wim in the spring of 2020 to get a sense of what the international community was doing today regarding drones and targeted killing. He is passionate about this field and aware of the bureaucratic hurdles involved in regulating drones in a world in which more countries are making them.

Since the Obama administration began to roll back its drones, there has been a shift.[254] Recent years have seen an expansion of the number of countries using drones. This includes wars in Libya, Yemen, and Syria. The countries using drones may be Saudi Arabia, the UAE and their allies, as well as Turkey and others. The Houthi rebels in Yemen began using their own drones, developed with Iranian technology, against Saudi Arabia. Canada has also used stout, box-like Sperwer drones in Afghanistan, managing to lose six of them. The Germans have deployed Luna Recon UAVs, a drone that looks like a white Egret bird in flight. New platforms, like tiltrotor or VTOL aircraft, a cross between helicopters and winged aircraft, represent a new leap and new options for arming.[255]

The concern in the first decades of the twenty-first century was over export controls. The US and European countries were reticent to export drones and sought to adopt common regulatory positions on armed drones. There are ways to get around the rules, such as building drones that carry less than the 500 lbs. payload and fly less than 300 kilometers.

More countries were getting into armed drones and trying to skirt export controls. The UK has carried out several Reaper strikes, while the UAE and Ukraine are building their own drones or buying from others, such as China. Pakistan and Nigeria are now using armed drones. Iraq has drones, and Turkey has rapidly increased its drone arsenal. This makes platforms like the MQ-9 vulnerable. To compete, the US launched a program dubbed MQ-Next in 2020 to replace the Reaper, hoping to have a new system by 2031.[256]

Western countries are concerned about proliferation. While NATO countries desperately wanted US drones, sales didn't often materialize because of US reticence to sell its technology, hogging drones to itself. Global Hawk surveillance drones only began to be based in Sicily by NATO for training in the summer of 2020. The same hesitation occurred elsewhere. An unarmed Predator was sold to the UAE. But the Chinese were running into the market as the US procrastinated. The US defense industry was unhappy. A draft document in early 2020 sought to provide principles for exporting armed drones. There is a push-pull between the desire to reduce proliferation and to not let others like China dominate. That leads to watering down agreements. Countries want the ability to carry out strikes and to have plausible deniability. Because drones are cheap and can be used without risk to a pilot, they are more likely to be used than special forces or commandos. That means drones are prone to abuse.

To reduce claims of abuse, the US developed the RX9, the "ninja" missile that has no warhead but rather has swords that flip out as it drops. How would a flying spear with swords weighing 100 lbs. be better than an explosive device? For one thing, it doesn't cause as much damage. If you hit the wrong person, at worst you kill that person and maybe one bystander. The "ninja" was used several times in Syria in 2019 and 2020. Images circulated online, showing cars diced up like tomatoes, and remains of their occupants left scattered about. In these cases, the weapon can kill a passenger in a car and leave others nearby alive. No more collateral damage.[257]

The future will be filled with more algorithms based on signals intelligence (SIGINT) and sensors that lead to artificial intelligence recommending whom to kill. This militarization of algorithm-based weapons systems can help militaries become more precise. But what happens when a computer identifies a threat and gives a commander the ease of pushing a button to eliminate the threat? If the data being input is wrong, a commander might use these increasingly autonomous systems to gun down innocent people. Western countries want to approach an almost zero-casualties result; no friendly-forces soldiers killed and no civilians.

While Western countries, learning from the American and Israeli experience, were trending towards caution and extreme precision, other states were going in the opposite direction. Terrorist groups saw drones as an easy way to upend their disadvantage on the battlefield. These groups, which look more like terrorist armies eating their way through states by preying off ungoverned areas across the Sahel in Africa and desert areas in the Middle East, all the way to Afghanistan and the Philippines, could get their hands on drones. US Pentagon planners had seen this whole swath of territory, where terror groups had grown since the 1980s, as the "non-integrated gap" of the world.[258] Now the gap was about to surprise the Americans and their drone army.

CHAPTER 5

IN THE HANDS OF THE ENEMY: TERRORISTS GET DRONES OF THEIR OWN

n Iraq, I got my first taste of being on the other side of the drone war. Crouching inside a large house during the battle of Mosul, I sheltered with Iraqi Federal Police as they bent their ears to listen for ISIS drones. It was a nerve-wracking experience. Used to being the hunters of ISIS, we suddenly became the hunted. It illustrated how vulnerable armies are to technology when they don't have a defense against it. All we had were RPGs and AK-47s. Iraqis had fired in vain at the sky over months of the battle for Mosul. ISIS drones wreaked havoc on the US-trained Iraqi army.

How did ISIS get drones? Throughout most of the history of the drone, only hi-tech countries have had access to this expensive and complex technology. That terrorists would eventually be flying them seemed unimaginable. It shouldn't have been so surprising.

A drone is relatively simple at its most basic element. A.M. Low made an aerial target in 1917, and Radioplane made target drones in the 1940s.[259] Terrorist groups already have sophisticated engineering they use to build bombs. There was no reason they wouldn't eventually build drones.

Many terrorist groups or "non-state actors" have built or used UAVs. This includes Palestinian Islamic Jihad, Hezbollah, Boko Haram in Nigeria, Hayat Tahrir al-Sham in Syria, the Maute group in Philippines, Houthis in Yemen, and various cartels.[260] Drones have also turned up in the Donbass war in Ukraine and are being used by factions in Libya, as well as by Venezuelan military defectors.

Hezbollah, an Islamic Shi'ite terrorist group, sought to pioneer a drone program to use against Israel. The group emerged in southern Lebanon in the 1980s with Iranian backing. When Israel withdrew from Lebanon in 2000, Hezbollah gained more freedom to stockpile weapons and import new missiles and drones from Iran.

A drone found by Kurdish Peshmerga that had been used by ISIS in an office near Kirkuk in September 2017. (Seth J. Frantzman)

On March 26, 2020, a small model airplane flew into Israeli airspace from southern Lebanon. Israel downed the plane, and bits of it were shown online. It was the latest attempt of numerous Hezbollah operations designed to show off its drone capability. Hezbollah was familiar with Israel's vulnerability to these attacks because of the Palestinian attack on Israel in 1987 using hang gliders, in which six Israelis were murdered.

Hezbollah leader Hassan Nasrallah acquired several drones from Iran in the wake of Israel's withdrawal. Nasrallah is the face of Hezbollah, a bearded, ranting figure who has lived in a bunker for the last decades because of fears of Israeli airstrikes. He should be afraid. Other Hezbollah members have met a bloody end, such as his former colleague Imad Mughniyeh, who was blown apart by a car bomb in Damascus in 2008.

Hezbollah wanted to test Israel. On November 7, 2004, the group flew one of its drones over the Israeli city of Nahariya and then out to sea. Later Nasrallah boasted that it could be armed with forty pounds of explosives and reach anywhere in Israel.[261] The UAV was thought to be modeled on Iran's Mohajer drone. It had two tail booms and straight wings, not dramatically different than some of Israel's early drones, which Iran may have modeled theirs on in the 1980s. It was utilitarian. Like Israeli drones and other early models of the 1980s, the Mohajer was catapult-launched and could return with a parachute. It may have been a Mohajer-4 model, of which Iran build some forty between 1997 and 2006, that Hezbollah renamed Mirsad.

The first Mirsad flight was a failure for Hezbollah, and the UAV crashed at sea. A second flight on April 11, 2005, was more successful. The UAV returned to Lebanon. A source close to Hezbollah told the US Embassy in Beirut that Hezbollah only had three of the drones at the time.[262] Syrian intelligence may have advised Hezbollah on the flight, a local source told the Americans during a secret meeting. Although Israel did not shoot down the drones, it responded with its own drone flights in the following years.[263]

Lebanon was a powder keg at the time. In 2005, Hezbollah assassinated Lebanese Prime Minister Rafic Hariri. Mass protests caused Syria to withdraw from Lebanon. Worried that its position could be eroded by mass protests, Hezbollah launched an attack on Israel in July 2006, killing Israeli soldiers and stealing their bodies. A month-long war resulted. Drones played a role, and several Hezbollah drones were shot down.[264] This marked one of the first times F-16s had engaged a drone. The three Ababil-style Iranian drones, carrying forty kilograms of explosives, were easily dispatched.[265] Israel sent an F-16 with Python missiles to down the first on August 7 off the coast and then downed another on August 13. Wreckage looked like an Ababil-T, more like a cruise missile than a drone.[266] It appears Hezbollah saved the drones to use toward the end of the war, but they failed to carry out their mission.

In 2008, Hezbollah muscled aside opponents in street fights in Beirut. Since then it has largely held Lebanon hostage and played an increasing role in Lebanon's politics, while building up its weapons arsenal. Israeli UAVs have kept constant watch on Hezbollah. Seven Israeli drones were observed by UNIFIL in 2009. One Israeli drone was shot at over Tyre in 2007,[267] and another downed in Beirut in 2019.

By 2008, Hezbollah had replenished its Mirsad drones and was arming them with explosives.[268] US Congressional reports identified Ya Mahdi Industries Group/Qods Aeronautics Industries as a supplier of UAVs and gliders for the IRGC.[269] Israel was growing increasingly concerned. Nitzan Nuriel, head of the Counter-Terrorism Bureau warned at a conference in September 2010 that Hezbollah had drones that could fly 300 kilometers.[270] Israel was also aware that Hezbollah was trying to intercept Israeli drone communications, leading Israel to better encrypt its drone transmissions.[271] Israel knew that terrorist groups like Hezbollah were already achieving technological successes previously available only to countries.[272]

Iran also sent its drones to Iraq. The small Yasir, a copy of America's ScanEagle, was given to Harakat Hezbollah al-Nujaba, a local militia similar to Hezbollah. During the war on ISIS, Iranian Mohajer-4 and Ababil-3 drones ended up in Iraq. Iran had been flying drones in Iraq since 2009 to monitor US forces but later relocated control to Baghdad to help fight ISIS and to use as targeting for Iranian F-4 airstrikes.[273]

Remains of an Iranian Shahed-123 unmanned aerial vehicle are seen at the Iranian Materiel Display at Joint Base Anacostia-Bolling, Washington, D.C., Nov. 26, 2018. The Department of Defense established the Iranian Materiel Display in December 2017 to present evidence that Iran is arming dangerous groups with advanced weapons, spreading instability and conflict in the region. The IMD contains materiel associated with Iranian proliferation into Yemen, Afghanistan, and Bahrain. (DoD photo by Lisa Ferdinando) *The appearance of U.S. Department of Defense (DoD) visual information does not imply or constitute DoD endorsement.*

Hezbollah continued to improve its drone program, bringing in components from Iran to fly another drone deep into Israeli airspace in 2012. Israel scrambled an F-16 again with Python air-to-air missiles and brought the vehicle down.[274] Nasrallah bragged about the incident, claiming the "resistance in Lebanon sent a sophisticated reconnaissance aircraft from Lebanon."[275] Nasrallah said it showed Israel's Iron Dome air defense could be penetrated. The new drone, dubbed Ayoub, was said by Hezbollah to be a response to some 20,000 incursions by Israel into Lebanese airspace.[276] Hezbollah sent footage from the Ayoub flight to Iran. There was concern the drone had flown near the Israeli nuclear facility at Dimona. Another drone flight followed in April 2013.

The Hezbollah drone flights were conducted from specially constructed airstrips in the Bekaa Valley. It also used them to carry out strikes in Syria against Syrian rebels. The group sent drones up to the picturesque Arsal region of rolling hills and mountains, where Syrian rebel groups and ISIS were operating. It used drones to track their activities. Hezbollah also used drones to attack Al Qaeda's Nusra front in Syria in September 2014, killing dozens. This was the first armed attack using a drone by a terrorist group or "non-state actor."[277]

For Israel, the Hezbollah drone war on Syrian rebels was a mixed blessing. Hezbollah's increased role in Syria during the civil war meant it was focusing on fighting groups in the Qalamoun Mountains on the Syria-Lebanon border, as the group boasted it was shielding Lebanon from extremists. The new airstrips were used for Ababil-3 and Shahed-120 Iranian-made drones.[278] In some ways, Hezbollah's use of Iranian drones doesn't represent a terrorist group making its own drones, just the proliferation of drones to the group which makes it a proxy in Iran's war against Israel.[279] Hezbollah's drone activities continued unabated. It sent another Iranian drone into Israel via Syria in September 2017, prompting Israel to use a Patriot missile to shoot down the drone.[280]

The growing threat coincided with technological improvements in Israeli air defense and radar. In addition, it coincided with an explosion in new drone technology in Iran. This was now an arms race. The original Mirsad drone was quite small when it first penetrated Israeli airspace in 2004, about 9.5 feet long or 2.9 meters, and was slow. Claims that it could reach 120 miles per hour were likely exaggerated. It appeared to have evaded radar, and the Israeli Knesset demanded answers from then IDF Chief of Staff Lt.-Gen. Moshe Ya'alon.[281] Israel was worried about the expanding program and Iran's trafficking of precision-guided missiles and other ordnance to Lebanon.[282] However, Hezbollah, eventually possessing some 200 drones, has since been frustrated in its drone activity.[283] It sought to launch "killer drones" from Syria in August 2019. But these attempts also reveal the vulnerability of terrorist groups using drones. Israel monitored Hezbollah's movements in Syria, watched as one team tried to hike the drones up a hill, and used clandestine methods, perhaps electronic interference, to stop the men from using the drones.[284]

Hezbollah can continue to arm its drones, but they pose less of a threat than the group's missile arsenal.[285] Nevertheless, the group has not stopped trying to upgrade its drones. Two men were charged in the US with conspiring to violate US export laws in March 2020 by purchasing drone parts for Hezbollah.[286] The men had tried to buy digital compasses, a jet engine, piston engines, and other products to help drones navigate. They fled to South Africa in 2018 but were picked up and brought back to Minnesota.

Iran's Ababil drones didn't just make their way to Hezbollah. Iran also made the technology available to Hamas in Gaza. Hamas had been carrying out terror attacks against Israel for years, but its takeover of the Gaza Strip in 2006 in the wake of Israel's withdrawal meant it could now import and build more missiles and drones. In November 2012, a Hamas drone flew out of Khan Yunis in the north of the strip.[287] Hamas also tried to build several small drones in the West Bank the next year. Hamas claimed it had built the Ababil A1B-style drone itself, and that it also had a reconnaissance version. These were around nine feet long. The name Ababil means "swallow," but the Hamas version resembled an Iranian Sarir H-110, more modern and with the common twin-tail design.[288] It showed them off, armed, in a video in July 2014.

Hamas kept tinkering with its drones, showing one off during a twenty-seventh anniversary march in December 2014. Armed men, their faces covered with scarves, celebrated these drones as a gamechanger that could threaten Israel. If you make drones, you also want to use them, and in September 2016, an Israeli F-16 found a Hamas drone flying off the coast of Gaza and shot it down.[289] In February 2017, Israel noted another Hamas drone taking off from Gaza and sent jets to kill it as it flew out to sea. It was an "immediate threat," Israeli officials said.[290] Israel shot down more Hamas drones in July 2019 and February 2020. Egypt even got in the game, gunning down a Hamas drone flying over the Egyptian side of Rafah after it invaded Egyptian airspace for ten minutes.[291]

The Hamas attempt to acquire drone technology was largely a failure. It was borne of Hamas being frustrated by the other failures it embarked on. It tried to defeat Israel with rockets in the 2009, 2012, and 2014 wars, but Israel built the Iron Dome air defense to intercept them. Hamas tried tunnels, and Israel created technology to stop the tunnels. Its drone war never got off the ground because it couldn't arm the drones, and Israel easily detected them using radar and other means of surveillance that make Gaza one of the most monitored places on earth. Even civilian-style drones that Hamas tried to import, disguising them for other purposes, were stopped at the border.

Israel's fears regarding what a drone war could look like were materializing a thousand miles away in Yemen, where Iranian drone technology showed what a menace it could be in the hands of terrorists.

Long Arm

The dhow floating in the Arabian sea on November 25, 2019, would have looked like any other poor trading vessel making its way, plying the trade routes between India, Iran, and Oman. But the USS *Forrest Sherman* suspected it had something more on it. A boarding party found a bevy of weapons destined for Yemen from Iran. Another vessel would be seized in February 2020. There were components for missiles, thermal imaging scopes, and pieces of drones.[292]

What they show is the danger of groups like Iran exporting their drone technology to terror groups. The danger was most pronounced in Yemen. The US had used drones extensively in Yemen to fight Al Qaeda, but by 2015 a new group emerged that would rock the Middle East. The Houthi rebels were an Iranian-backed group of fighters from the mountains that took over swaths of the country and threatened to take Aden, the country's principal port, in 2015.

The Houthis appeared at first to be rugged, rural fighters taking on a Goliath of a Saudi-led alliance and corrupt Yemenite government officials. They claimed to be fighting the US, Israel, and other Iranian enemies, incorporating terms like "death to the US, curse the Jews" into their rhetoric. Quietly, in caves and bunkers, they developed a sophisticated arsenal of drones and missiles with Iranian expertise. The technology was brought by boat and smuggled up to the hills. In September 2019, the Houthis brought in video cameras and showcased a room full of drones. Most were relatively small, several meters long, and intended to be used in kamikaze attacks. Riyadh had deployed Patriot missiles against Houthi ballistic missiles, of which 226 had already been fired, but the drones were a new kind of threat.[293]

The Houthis were the real pioneers of Iranian-backed drone technology. They were the first to use drones in a complicated drone attack. The Shaybah natural gas liquefaction facility was nestled in red sunsoaked desert, unsuspecting that it might be targeted. On August 17, 2019, ten drones struck the Aramco facility in Saudi Arabia. It was in the Empty Quarter near the UAE border, some 1,000 kilometers from Houthi frontlines in Yemen. The Houthis planned a "big, deep attack" on it and succeeded in sending armed drones to strike it. "We promise the Saudi regime and great powers that wider operations will come," a Houthi rebel told the Houthi Almasirah TV station.[294]

The group had stockpiled and improved their drones over time. They were a convenient way for Iran to fight a proxy war against the Saudis. As US-Iran tensions rose in 2019, the Houthi attacks also increased.[295]

Like most terrorist groups, the Houthis began by simply buying drones off the shelf. They used a commercially bought DJI Phantom to conduct surveillance of their enemies in 2015 and tried to build models based on instructions they found online. Eventually, they got engines and models from Iran to construct what they called the Qasef-1, which was a copy of the Iranian Ababil.[296] The UAE intercepted a shipment of drones from Iran to the Houthis in November 2016. The US established the Iran Materials Display in Washington at Joint Base Anacosta-Bolling in 2017 under US Defense Secretary Jim Mattis. The gruff, direct Mattis, known when he was a younger commander as "Call Sign Chaos," wanted to showcase the Iranian threat. Eventually, seventy-five countries would come to see the remains of Iranian drones and missiles, proving Iran was supplying the Houthis.

The Houthis claimed development of four drone classes, one a flying wing, the second a kind of cruise missile, and two that looked like model airplanes.[297] Washington was apoplectic. UN Ambassador Nikki Haley showed off wreckage of a Qasef-1 at Joint Base Anacostia-Bolling in DC. It looked like the Iranian Ababil-T.[298] Other wreckage from Houthi drones, including a gyroscope, were analyzed by Conflict Armament Research and linked directly to Iran. A V10 gyroscope was found on Ababil-3 drones and on the Qasef-1. Similar gyroscopes, called V9, were also found in September 2019 after a larger swarm attack on the Abqaiq facility.

The US Navy raid on that dhow in the Arabian sea linked Iran to the Houthi drones. US officials, who call the Iranian materials display in DC the "petting zoo," could now match what they found with known Iranian weapons, such as a Shahed-123 recovered from Afghanistan in October 2016, matching the V9 to the other gyroscopes.[299] The Shahed-123, with a body that looks like a giant tube with a wing bolted on top, is a decidedly un-sexy drone, painted khaki by the Iranians. One ended up in Washington at the Iranian Materials Display. The drone looked like the Iranians copied it from a Hermes 450, perhaps a Hermes being used by the UK that had crashed in Afghanistan.[300] This is the essence of the drone wars: countries stealing each other's designs from remote crash sites, shadowy wars in the mountains of Iran and Afghanistan, and US intelligence sleuths trying to piece it together before the Iranians and their allies can build the next threat.

The evidence illustrates that the Houthis launched their drone wars by using DJI quadcopters and then graduated to receiving Iranian Ababil-Ts from Iran. They then started to make some of their own components.[301] The drones used wooden propellers and internal components, such as circuit boards, scrambled together from all over the world. For instance, the Sammad drone the Houthis began building used an engine exported from Germany to Greece. Most of the components directly linked the Houthis to Iran, such as a motor that was found in a Shahed-141 that Iran flew into Israeli airspace in February 2018, and components from a Houthi Qasef-1.[302]

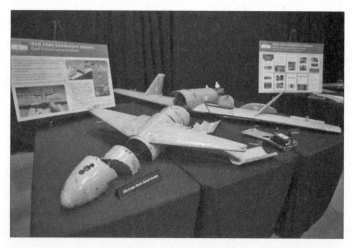

Remains of a Qasef-1 unmanned aerial vehicle are seen at the Iranian Materiel Display at Joint Base Anacostia-Bolling, Washington, D.C., Nov. 26, 2018. The Department of Defense established the Iranian Materiel Display in December 2017 to present evidence that Iran is arming dangerous groups with advanced weapons, spreading instability and conflict in the region. The IMD contains materiel associated with Iranian proliferation into Yemen, Afghanistan, and Bahrain. (DoD photo by Lisa Ferdinando) *The appearance of U.S. Department of Defense (DoD) visual information does not imply or constitute DoD endorsement.*

The Houthis became both drone master-operators and also a lab for Iranian exports. They used suicide drones against Patriot radar and air defenses. They successfully evaded Saudi air defenses to strike deep into the kingdom. They also attacked a military parade at Al-Anad, Yemen, in January 2019. The Houthis expanded their Qasef-1 design to the Qasef 2K, which they claimed to build locally. Then they built a group of the Sammad-class drones, modeled on the Hezbollah Mirsad or Iranian Muhajer.[303] The Sammad-3 was allegedly used to attack Abu Dhabi's airport in 2018, almost 1,500 kilometers away.[304] This drone acted more like a cruise missile, or what is called a "loitering munition," not intended to return to base.[305] The Houthis then began sending drones to attack airports in southern Saudi Arabia, striking Abha Airport in June and July 2019.[306] Images of the Sammad's alleged use continued to be published throughout 2020 as the group launched attacks in June and July with explosive-laden drones.[307]

The terror army also built a range of reconnaissance drones called Hudhud, Raqib, and Rased.[308] Most of these were similar to model airplanes and had a short range and endurance of around thirty kilometers and ninety minutes.[309] What the Houthis were showing was that they could create a hybrid drone force using Iranian technology, some gadgets sent from Iran, and indigenous designs. That meant they might need the gyroscopes or other technology from Iranian smuggling, but they could make wings or the fuselage at home. They could also figure out the GPS guidance and target sites far away. Characterized as "low tech, high reward," the reality is that they had built a significant threat to be used against some of the wealthiest governments which have access to hi-tech and Western air defense.[310] By the end of 2019, global powers were worried. The Houthis kept the attacks up through 2020 in a cat-and-mouse game with Saudi air defense. The US "petting zoo" displays and research backed by the EU and UAE all showed the Iranian link, and US Navy destroyers were prowling the seas to find more Iranian shipments. What the Americans and Israelis then knew was that Iran had exported its own kind of Predator, the Ababils, to terrorist groups around the Middle East.[311]

Black Flag

While Hezbollah, Hamas, and the Houthis were all piggy-backing on Iranian technology, another group had ideas of its own. Islamic State grew out of various jihadist groups that had been fighting the US in Iraq. It seemed to appear suddenly in Syria in late 2013 and early 2014, gobbling up areas along the Euphrates river. Its founder, Abu Bakr al-Baghdadi, was an Iraqi who had been imprisoned in the past for jihadist activities. He had a cadre of commanders in Iraq who had experience not only fighting Americans but who also had links to men who had served in Saddam Hussein's army. Some of these men had engineering skills.

Initially, ISIS faced little opposition. The Iraqi army retreated towards Baghdad, and ISIS found itself fighting Kurds in Iraq and Syria. ISIS faced a large and expanding global coalition in the spring of 2015. To fight the coalition, it absorbed 50,000 recruits from around the world, some of whom knew about drones. They might have been engineers or hobbyists or just knew that there were drones for sale that could be repackaged with small grenades and weapons.

The terror group bought small quadcopters that they smuggled into Syria and Iraq. Much of this came from smugglers in Turkey, until ISIS lost control of the border in 2016. The fanatics attached grenades and warheads to the drones they first began using in 2016. The US-backed Syrian Democratic Forces said that ISIS used drones frequently, every day on some frontlines. They used drones to monitor their own mortar fire and to make it more accurate and to help guide vehicles laden with explosives. Even as ISIS was beaten back in 2017 in Mosul and Raqqa, it continued to use drones daily. They were bombing people and the Iraqi army up to one hundred times a month.

The group also thought it would build its own drones. It contacted supporters abroad, including in the UK and Bangladesh, and sought to create front companies to acquire parts, such as cameras, antennas, and simulators. It was very interested in building fixed-wing model planes made from wood or other materials. After ISIS supporters were arrested abroad, the group transitioned to buying in bulk quadcopters and smuggled materials.

The US-led coalition was so concerned that it began to plow money into defeating the ISIS drones. Even though the drones didn't kill coalition personnel, US SOCOM Commander Raymond Thomas said that during one battle, ISIS put twelve drones in the air at a time in Mosul. They used seventy in one day.[312] This was the equivalent of a kind of drone "swarm" that worried military planners around the world. And these were not cheap drones: he estimated each cost up to $2,000. Do the math, and it's clear ISIS invested hundreds of thousands of dollars, if not millions, in its drone program. In response, at least $700 million was budgeted into a program for DARPA and other sources to create technology to stop the small drones.[313] Boeing, Raytheon, and other companies were mobilized to find solutions.

As ISIS lost ground, the coalition was also able to target drone workshops and other points that affected the ISIS drone war. Electronic warfare no-fly zones were put in place to try to disrupt the drone communications, and DJI even rolled out new software updates that should have made it harder for their drones to violate these "geofenced" areas. Unfortunately, the ISIS experiments with drones, which had turned them into a drone powerhouse between 2016 and 2017, also influenced other terrorist groups. Soon extremists of the Maute group in the Philippines were using drones around Marawi when they took over the city. A dozen drones were shot down by both sides in the battle. When it was over, US and Australian forces who had supported the Philippines concluded that small drones were absolutely necessary for infantry at the front. They also noted that disposable, cheap commercial drones can be helpful to identify enemies and draw fire. No need to equip a force with special military drones for everything.[314] ISIS supporters also began using them in Yemen and elsewhere. Cartels in Mexico may have looked at ISIS for inspiration, building a drone that could drop an explosive from the air.

Fighting off the ISIS drones had been difficult for the Iraqis. They had experimented with various devices, some of which looked like futuristic guns, that were supposed to bring down the unmanned vehicles through jamming. It also forced the Iraqis to move more slowly, as they were constantly looking up. The ISIS drones were not a strategic gamechanger, but they were harrowing.

When I entered Mosul in March of 2017, ISIS controlled part of the western side of the river. It was being slowly squeezed against the river by the might of the Iraqi army. At the front were units of the federal police. To get to Mosul, we drove from Erbil, the capital of the Kurdish region of Iraq, across fields and bridges that had been damaged in fighting. Burned cars and the remnants of ISIS "mad-max" suicide bomb-laden cars could be seen. The drive, about an hour and a half, snaked through abandoned Christian villages and then across Nineveh Plains to the Euphrates River.

When we got to the Federal Police compound on the outskirts of the city, we waited with the soldiers who were going in. There would be a convoy of several of their armored vehicles and our SUV. Eventually, after navigating broken roads and bombed-out fields and houses, we got to an area where we had to walk on foot through alleyways. In some ways, Mosul resembled any other city, with shops and stores, but as we entered the alleyways, the destruction was clear. Blankets were hung across the alleys to protect us from sniper fire. All the while, the men scanned the sky for drones. They were a constant threat. The threat wasn't worse than mortar fire or snipers, but something about being under a hidden enemy, buzzing about high in the sky, was disconcerting. The Taliban had felt the same apprehension facing Predators, according to accounts. There is something about drones that is different from fast-moving helicopters and warplanes. Because they are quiet and they loiter, looking, waiting, they are spookier. On those days I went into Mosul, whenever we heard a drone, we felt the fear of the unknown. There were no methods to shoot the thing down. All we could do was take cover.

It is not surprising that the US subsequently plowed money into various solutions to fight drones. Combat units got the Dedrone Drone Defender. The air force paid $23 million for the high-energy laser weapon (HELW) that can be put on vehicles. Raytheon also got a $16 million contract for the Phaser, which sounds like something from Star Trek but is actually a high-powered microwave weapon.[315]

These weapons were developed partly in response to the ISIS mini-drone threat. In war, militaries tend to train to fight the previous war. Just as Predators, Reapers, and Global Hawks were not meant to match up against modern air defenses, because the groups they were fighting didn't have air defense, so the US began to pour money into fighting a drone threat like the one ISIS produced. The next war, however, might not be against another ISIS.

Commercial drone manufacturers had a boom during the mid-2000s, but the security threats from the drones also ballooned. Regulations came with them. That will mean that ISIS existed at a unique niche in time when drones could be moved more easily across borders. However, in the years that ISIS grew and was then destroyed, many countries became more concerned about drone threats. Iran arrested a couple for flying a drone to take photos, accusing them of spying. Journalists and others have been detained at airports with drones.

Terrorist groups, too, have had to be more innovative. Hayat Tahrir al-Sham, a group that was once Syria's version of Al Qaeda but then morphed into a quasi-Syrian rebel group, used drones against the Syrian regime and Russian bases in Latakia. In one case, they even used a drone "swarm" against a Russian base in 2018. Russia sent expensive air defense to shoot down the Syrian drones. It launched offensives to root out the group in Idlib, forcing Turkey to intervene more in Idlib, where the drones were flown from. This played itself out in 2018 and 2019. The Russians blamed the US for the "drone swarms," showing off the technology and accusing the US of coordinating them with a navy P-8 surveillance plane.[316]

The rapidity with which terrorist groups, proxies, and "non-state actors" were acquiring drones was extraordinary. These were not just commercial quadcopters, but terror armies with drones that made them a real threat. It showed how quickly history had moved from an era when Israelis were pioneering surveillance drones, to the US hegemony in drone strikes, to the rise of everyone else. Not only were some eighty countries now acquiring drones, but the fears were being realized. In the 2014 *Drone* documentary, there is a quip about a drone one day threatening New York City, as if to suggest it won't just be the US carrying out secretive airstrikes. That day was now approaching. Whereas the prophecies of drones replacing aircraft were still myth, the threats were reality.

At the same time, the Russians learned something from the drone threat. The St. Petersburg-based Special Technology Center (STTS) built a rocket that could hone in on a drone. Samuel Bendett at the Center for Naval Analyses said the simple Russian weapon without explosives would reduce casualties on the ground.[317]

The HTS drones in Syria didn't look like commercial quadcopters but more like model airplanes with small armaments affixed to them. Russia said it could detect them easily from a distance and neutralize the drones with missiles.[318] The Russian experience showed that deploying air defense can work against modern drone threats. Many other countries were learning the hard way. How countries like Russia began to develop air defense is the other side of the drone equation. For each action, there is an equal and opposite reaction. Let's see how that reaction happened.

CHAPTER 6

FIGHTING BACK: NEW DEFENSES AGAINST DRONES

They called it the beast. First seen publicly in 2007 in Kandahar, the "beast" was a dark shape in the skies, a kind of flying wing. It was, in fact, a Lockheed Martin RQ-170, developed by Lockheed's Skunk Works. This was Sentinel, the latest US drone. At the time, observers wondered what the secretive drone was doing.[319] It was a testimony to how drones had become such a popular topic that the sighting of this new drone created a hunt for more photos and accounts. Its existence was acknowledged in 2009, and in January 2011 new photos emerged of the beast on the tarmac in Afghanistan. Rumors said it had also been seen in Korea.[320] Its development was still classified in 2020.

Almost a year after the 2011 photos were taken, Huma Abedin, the assistant to Secretary of State Hillary Clinton, shot an email to the secretary. Reports indicated that an RQ-170 had been downed in Iran. It was December 4, 2011. Iran's *Al-Alam* was reporting excitedly on the story of the "spy" plane that had been defeated.[321] US officials considered how to get the drone back, through a raid or airstrike, but opted against it to avoid increasing tensions with Iran.[322]

Reports over the next several days indicated the drone had been spying on Iran and may have been used in the May 2011 raid on bin Laden's compound in Pakistan.[323] The UAV was downed deep inside Iran, near Kashmar, almost 1,000 kilometers from Kandahar.[324] Over the next few days, Iran took the drone and put it on display. It looked mostly intact, and it was clear it had not been shot down, and no attempt to make it self-destruct had worked.[325] US President Barack Obama asked Tehran to return the vehicle. Tehran said it would crack its secrets. It now appeared Iran had tried to hack into its communications to bring it down. US media said "pilot error" may have been a factor. The CIA and air force were not commenting.[326]

This was a great propaganda victory and potential treasure trove for IRGC Aerospace Forces Brig. Gen. Amir Ali Hajizadeh. He told local TV that Iran had downed the drone after collecting intelligence about its flight path and using precise electronic monitoring. Now Iran could potentially let the Chinese and Russians reverse engineer any aspects that were new, such as its stealthy propulsion or unique eighty-foot wingspan that was three feet thick and fifteen feet long.[327]

Iran had been trying to down US drones for years. It had recently acquired Russia's Avotbaza Electronic Intelligence system. The capture of the RQ-170 was an embarrassment for the US and a coup for Iran in a high-stakes game of drone wars, in which the drone operator must be one step ahead of the adversary. In failed or weak states, like Iraq or Afghanistan, the US had used drones with impunity, and they didn't need stealth technology to hide them.

The Sixty-Second Expeditionary Reconnaissance Squadron of the US Air force had been based on Kandahar in Afghanistan in 2009, for instance. It helped make the area a center of the drone war as commanders in Kandahar pressed for more time for their pilots to fly the Predators.[328]

But reconnaissance missions over Iran, during the height of the concerns about Iran's nuclear program, were a different animal.[329] When more information was revealed about the RQ-170s, such as their being operated out of Shindand Air Base in Afghanistan, Panetta vowed they could continue.[330] Iran's UN ambassador Mohammed Khazaei was livid, calling for the "illegal acts" to cease. Iran also phoned Afghanistan's leaders and warned them that further US drone incursions would be seen as hostile acts.[331]

Breakthrough

The battle in the skies over Iran was about possessing the latest intelligence capability. Much like U-2 flights over the Soviet Union in the Cold War, the RQ-170 was supposed to be a gamechanger. It was supposed to be able to fly up to 50,000 feet and pack numerous sensors into its stealth body. It might be able to sniff for chemicals, a RAND Corporation analyst said.[332] Sentinels had full-motion video (FMV), the latest technology being affixed to drones. This video, eventually combined with high-definition (HD), when combined with a map that shows where the drone is, can help analysts see potential suspicious activity quickly and combine all the metadata with other sensors.[333] Moving from analog to digital and integrating it with forces on the ground so that everyone sees the same picture would change the way war is fought. Sentinel was a layer in that quiet revolution.[334]

Iran wanted to grab hold of that revolution like a man riding a bull and take advantage of US advances. Hajizadeh was leading those efforts from 2011 to 2020. He gained the personal blessing of Ayatollah Ali Khamenei, the supreme leader of Iran. Khamenei believed in the Iranian drone program and in efforts to counter America's drone army.

Having secured support from the leaders, Hajizadeh pushed Iran to down more US drones, eventually acquiring not only the Sentinel, but also the Predator, Reaper, ScanEagle,[335] and even an Israeli-made

Hermes. Tehran had grabbed up to eight foreign drones over Iraq, Syria, and Iran by monitoring and even "controlling" them.[336] In 2014, Iran showed off video it claimed it had taken from drones by hacking them. Iran showed off pieces of the Israeli Hermes on video. Iran boasted the Israelis were using the Hermes to spy on the Natanz uranium enrichment facility. That area is 1,000 miles from Israel. Experts told the *Jerusalem Post* that the wreckage Iran showed was not clearly a Hermes 180 or 450 and that such a mission to monitor Natanz was better suited to an Israeli Heron.[337]

Israel Aerospace Industries Heron TP, a multi-role, advanced, long-range medium altitude long endurance (MALE) unmanned aerial system. (Courtesy IAI)

The Iranians watched Israel's success closely. The Israeli Heron was one of the larger Israeli drones that had been its workhorse since the 1990s. It was one of the drones that had turned their defense companies into the leading drone sellers in the early 2000s.[338] The Heron family became a mainstay as its endurance increased to over forty hours and its range to more than 1,000 kilometers. Iran watched as Israel replaced its Searcher IIs with the IAI Herons in 2005 and began operating them from Palmachim Airbase. Amir Eshel received some of the first Herons for a squadron for the IAF in 2007.[339] Later he would play a key role in Israel's airstrikes on Iranian units in Syria.

In the drone wars, propaganda can be as important as actual advances. Everyone building drones seems to copy one another. For instance, Iran's Saegeh was a direct copy of the Sentinel. Iran's Shahed S-171 jet-powered Simorgh is also a copy of the Sentinel, first deployed in 2014. Hajizadeh pushed to arm the Saegeh with up to four missiles, claiming it could penetrate deep into enemy airspace.[340] It flew one from Syria's T-4 base in February 2018. Israel shot it down as it came into the country's airspace.[341]

The battle for the skies in the wake of Iran's downing of the Sentinel moved from a world that had one drone superpower to multiple drone makers. This fundamentally changed the equation and the threats that drones could pose. Iran's goal was to create an independent drone army, much as Israel had done in the 1980s, providing Tehran with the impunity Washington had previously enjoyed. Under Hajizadeh's guidance, Iran would bring down not only the stealth Sentinel but also the Global Hawk in 2019, and Iran would send drones to Yemen.[342] The world was entering a drone war revolution of rapid change in just several years.

To get to the point of confronting the Israelis and America, Iran had been down a long and bloody road. After the 1979 Islamic Revolution, it had a number of US target drones sitting around, remnants of the Shah's air force. These were basically large model airplanes with rockets on them. But Iran's new leaders had no time to learn how to use them. On September 22, 1980, Iraqi warplanes struck Iran, and the Iran-Iraq War began. Iraq was a technical giant, with Soviet weapons and poison gas. Iran's answer was religiously-motivated human wave attacks. But its new religious revolutionary guards were tinkering with drones. Soon they were carrying early models into battle. In 1986, Qasem Soleimani, the future IRGC leader, led his men across the canals that link Iran with Iraq's Basra, where fish breed amid the waterways. Accompanying him were new Iranian drone warriors. Nine-hundred-forty missions were flown, and 54,000 photos taken.[343]

Iran innovated. In the 1980s, it constructed the Quds Mohajer, first flown in 1985. Eventually, hundreds of the small planes, which could be carried by two men, would be built. The original HESA Ababil followed in 1986, with some 400 built. HESA, the company that built it, was actually founded in a former Textron factory that built Bell helicopters before the revolution. The Ababil was a loitering munition, more like a cruise missile, launched from a catapult on a truck.[344] The Ababil-2 followed in the 1990s, and the Ababil-T twin-tailed version in the 2000s. This one was exported to Lebanon and Yemen.

Iran's drone program borrowed heavily from 1980s designs, including Israel's IAI Scout and later the Israel-designed AAI RQ-2 Pioneer that the US used. For instance, these twin-tail designs look like an Ababil-3 that was developed in 2006 and has a range of 100 kilometers and a speed of 200 kilometers per hour for four hours. Several hundred were built by 2019.[345] Bizarrely, Israel's help to South Africa to build its Denel Dynamics Seeker UAV may have been leaked to Iran so that Iran could develop its Ababil 3.[346] In 2015, things came full circle when a UAE operated Seeker II was shot down in Yemen by the Iranian-backed Houthis.[347]

Iran may have also gained insight into Israeli drones through two Pioneers that were shot down in Iraq in the 1991 war, or a Hunter shot down during the Kosovo War in 1999.[348] In recent years, Iran may have gotten access to Predator wreckage in 2015 when one was lost over Syria, or to a ScanEagle and Reaper shot in Yemen in November and June 2019, respectively.[349] From outward appearances, Iran had no trouble relying on blueprints[350] or photos, but its real problem was trying to build up the endurance of its drones and their abilities to conduct surveillance, to relay communications back, or to target enemies. For instance, the kind of composite materials, guidance, and electro-optics that hi-tech industries in the US and Israel had were not widely available to Iran under sanctions. In design, drones such as Seeker in South Africa, Mohajer 4B, or the Pioneer in the US, and Aerostar by Aeronautics all look basically the same, with long wings and a twin-tail and a bubble for electro-optics at the front.[351] All Iran had to do was improve what was inside.

Iran was successful at turning its Ababils and Mohajers into advanced UAVs. In 2008, UN Peacekeepers inquired about drones they saw being used in Sudan. The government told them they were Zagils, an Iranian Ababil-3 that was renamed.[352] Two were shot down by rebel groups. Venezuela also bought Iran's Mohajer-2 in 2007 to use them for surveillance.[353]

An IAI Heron with a satellite and ELINT payloads. Drones have different systems depending on the mission. (Courtesy IAI)

Iran built several generations of each of these drones from the 1980s to 2010. Around 600 were produced in total. They were all limited in their range by line-of-sight, up to a little over one hundred kilometers. In addition, their small fuel tanks limited their range.[354] While the Ababil was used by the IRGC more extensively, the Mohajer was primarily used by the Iranian army, known as NEZAJA.[355] In April 2020, Iran unveiled a wide array of new Ababil-3s for the air force and army, claiming that they had new guided-bomb capabilities. It also showed off a new cruise-missile-like Karrar drone.[356] Tehran claimed they could fly 1,500 kilometers at speeds of 900 kilometers per hour and that its drones now reached heights of 45,000 feet. Iran copied an Israeli SPIKE missile that it then fastened to the Ababil-3 and dropped on a target, claiming it now had anti-tank weapons on its drones.[357]

Iran built a wide variety of drones after 2010, with names like *Yasir,* the *Hodhod, Roham, Ya Mahdi, Sarir, Raad 85, Haamaseh,* and *Hazem 1.* Much of this was designed to experiment and show off a large inventory.[358] Adam Rawnsley, an expert on Iran's drones, said that Iran created models that didn't go anywhere, boasting of just one or two prototypes. "What separates men from boys in drones is the network space and pushing imagery and data to people who need it."[359] Iran's Col. Akbar Karimloo noted in the spring of 2020 that the IRGC's UAV command was rapidly increasing its communications abilities. He told Tasnim News that his drones were advancing in using video imaging, GIS, and increasing ranges beyond one hundred kilometers. He pointed to the Ababil-3, Mohajer-6, and Shahed 149 as examples of his latest models.

Iran's goal after creating a drone force was to use them to harass its enemies. It had used them against Iraq in the 1980s. Now the great game would begin. Tehran sketched out an arc of countries where it wanted to project its influence. This would begin with the "near abroad" in Iraq and extend to Syria, Lebanon, Yemen, Sudan, Gaza, and Afghanistan. The Persian Gulf and Gulf of Oman would receive overflights of Iranian drones. Could Tehran go toe-to-toe with the Americans on drone power? The US was overstretched. It sought to establish permanent combat air patrols all over the world by having drones in the air twenty-four hours a day, called "CAPS," in some 240 locations.[360] In the end, America only could manage about sixty of these surveillance combat air patrols, which is a problem because there are more than sixty small locations full of terrorists and enemies that need to be monitored.[361]

The lobby of Israel drone manufacturer Aeronautics showing a model of the Aerostar Tactical UAS (TUAS), a cost-effective system that has flown more than 250,000 operational hours worldwide. (Seth J. Frantzman)

To break the Americans, Iran established a network of drone bases along and south of the Strait of Hormuz.[362] These would be located at a desert airstrip on Qeshm Island, near Bandar Abbas and the port of Bandar Jask, as well as at Minab and Konarak. At Konarak, Iran would base its new Shahed 129, modeled on the Predator. Ababil-3s would fly from Minab and Bandar Abbas beginning in 2010. A new airstrip would be built at Jakigur in 2015. By this time, Iran had a lot of experience moving its drones around. It had sent them to Syria and based them at a desert base called Tiyas, or T-4.

From here, it would launch a drone in February 2018 to test Israel's defenses. The drone flew near the Golan and infiltrated near Beit Shean in the Jordan Valley, likely violating Jordan's airspace. Israel scrambled an Apache helicopter and shot it down. In the course of retaliatory airstrikes, an Israeli F-16I crashed in northern Israel. I was awoken by news of the crash on the morning of February 10 while staying in Kiryat Yam, a suburban working-class beach community north of Haifa. I drove out near Shefa'amr, where the F-16I had crashed in a field near a row of giant chicken coops. Walking up a dirt road, in the still cold and wet morning, I could see the wreckage and one of the burned engines sticking from a field turned black from the crash. This is what Iran's drone war had wrought.

Iran had become increasingly brazen. On January 12, 2016, it sent a drone to fly over the USS *Harry Truman* and the French *Charles de Gaulle*. The message appeared to be that in the wake of the Iran Deal in 2015, Tehran felt it was winning in the Middle East. Kevin Stephens, a spokesman for the US Fifth Fleet, said the UAV was not armed and posed no risk. It was "abnormal and unprofessional."[363] Iran had sent its new Shahed 129 to conduct the overflight, which illustrated that while the US saw this as merely unprofessional, Iran was testing the drone's capabilities. Iran had conducted another overflight of the carrier in December 2015. The ayatollahs also sent drones to fly over Afghanistan in 2017. They were spotted in Herat province.[364] They then sent a *Sadegh* drone buzzing over the USS *Nimitz* in August 2017 in the Persian Gulf and said it flew over the USS *Eisenhower* in April 2019.

Iranian drone exercises followed, including a massive March 2019 drill at sea involving fifty drones that Iran dubbed the "way to Jerusalem" exercise.[365] Iran downed a US Global Hawk in June.[366] By July 2019, enemy drones were flying over the USS *Boxer* when the Americans began jamming them in the Strait of Hormuz.[367] The problem facing the US, Israel, and other countries was that there was no easy defense against Iran's drones. Washington had spent so long packing drones with technology to kill insurgents, they had ignored the importance of combatting states that have drones, or even how to deal with states that shoot back.[368]

Twenty Years of Ideas

The Pentagon had the privilege of total air superiority in the 1990s and 2000s. There was no near-peer rival. This meant the Americans weren't in a hurry. For instance, in 2005, the US considered pouring more money into the Hunter RQ-5A, re-named MQ-5B. The program had already sponged up millions in the 1990s and been canceled. Northrop Grumman sought to modernize the Hunters at Libby Airfield in Fort Huachuca. The Hunters had flown 14,000 hours in the Balkans and Iraq, but the new version would have a longer wingspan and be able to fly for fifteen hours.[369]

The result of the twenty years of the Global War on Terror was to stall the development of new UAVs. Because there was no necessity, various ideas came and went, and hundreds of millions of dollars were spent on prototypes that went nowhere.

Northrop Grumman was already building the Global Hawk and the Fire Scout UAV helicopter, which would be used by the navy. It was also taking part in the DARPA X-47 program to build a joint unmanned combat air system (J-UCAS). Boeing engineers who had worked on the manned Joint Strike Fighter X-32, which lost out to Lockheed's F-35 in 2001, went to work on the X-45. Northrop pioneered another design called X-47, and Lockheed made the X-44. The commonality of all these designs is that they were basically a flying "V" that looked like something out of science fiction, not really like previous aircraft. These designs were the future of a stealth infiltrator. Not very large, they borrowed heavily from the flying-wing design of the B-2 stealth bomber, which had been built in the 1980s. In that sense, the design hadn't changed much, but the technology on board had.

The whole program had challenges. These flying-wing concepts were supposed to be part of the Joint Unmanned Combat Air Systems, an idea that was canceled in 2006. The Boeing X-45, sleek and intended for the air force, ended up at the National Museum of the Air Force, although its autonomous take-off and landing software for carriers continued to be used by manned aircraft.[370] Some portions of the program lived on for the navy, first as N-UCAS and then in the Unmanned Carrier-Launched Airborne Surveillance and Strike (UCLASS) project, which itself survived as the Carrier-Based Aerial Refueling System (CBARS) and Boeing's MQ-25 Stingray. The slightly less stealthy X-47B continued to serve on the USS *Harry Truman*, USS *George Bush*, and USS *Theodore Roosevelt* with a series of test flights between 2013 and 2015. The X-47B eventually returned to Northrop Grumman in 2017. Elements of the Boeing X-45N, for the navy, and X-46 survived, along with another project called by Boeing the Phantom Ray that was also a flying wing.

The X-45 and its era were a product of the 1990s when DARPA had helped pioneer new ideas that worked. Mike Leahy, an air force officer, had pushed to provide funding to Northrop, Boeing, Raytheon, and Lockheed to build a killer drone.[371] They were supposed to destroy enemy air defenses, much as Israel had initially used drones against the Syrians and the Houthis had done with the Saudis. "It is a mission that doesn't directly threaten the white scarf crowd," Leahy said.[372] The term "white scarf" or "silk scarf" refers to traditional pilot-centric air-force circles. It turned out, in the end, that the F-35 and F-22 sponged up air force assets, and the Xs just didn't cut it. It would take years for new ideas, such as a stealthy XQ-58 Valkyrie, the super-secret RQ-180, and the General Atomics Avenger, or the Loyal Wingman concept to blossom.

The Russians were watching the US programs and decided to build their own futuristic flying-wing drone. They already had the Orlan-10, a small simple model that looks like a miniature plane, fielded in 2010, with around 1,000 made. Then they went bigger. Their UCAV was built by MiG and Sukhoi and resulted in the Sukhoi S-70 that eventually flew in August 2019. Russia calls this the "Hunter" or *Okhotnik* and describes it as a heavy attack drone. This was a vanity project for Russia, which was trying to show it could build planes that would rival the US F-35 and American drones. Deputy Prime Minister Yuri Borisov bragged about the flying wing at the MAKS-2019, claiming deliveries will be made of the aircraft in 2025.

The Russian large drone had flown for twenty to thirty minutes in 2019. It successfully landed. The "stealth" UAV is supposed to weigh around twenty tons and fly up to 1,000 kilometers per hour. It has the usual package of electro-optics and radar.[373] If this works, it will be important for Russia, which is trying to show it can browbeat the US in conflicts from Syria to Libya, and that it can sell its S-400 missile defense systems to NATO member Turkey. Having a real fifth-generation air force would improve Russia's image, especially since Russia has a paltry drone arm.

The overall picture of the drone wars after Iran's advances was that the US and its allies would be increasingly challenged in the air. US drones were segmented by service but relied on proven older vehicles. The MQ-1C Grey Eagle, for instance, is just another version of the Predator, made for the army between 2004 and 2009. The Army Aviation and Missile Command loved the Grey Eagle so much they initially bought eleven systems with twelve UAVs each.[374] Provided to the Eighty-Second Combat Aviation Brigade and then rolled out to more divisions, it was first used in Iraq's Diyala province.[375]

The AAI RQ-7 Shadow, also for the army, was supposed to replace the Pioneer with another small twin-tail design. All of these would use the same control system and have more fuel economy and potentially get better armaments.[376] The navy, meanwhile, was acquiring more tactical, smaller UAVs, such as the Boeing Insitu RQ-21 Blackjack. The twin-tailed grey plane was deployed to Afghanistan with mixed results. The navy eventually sought to get sixty more of them in 2019. It could fly up to 20,000 feet for one hundred miles with a seventeen-kilogram payload, and Boeing was looking to put better engines on it. But all of this still left the US and others vulnerable to enemy drones.

How do you stop a drone attack? From the beginning, drones have been downed as one would down an enemy aircraft. Iraq and Serbian forces had shot down US drones or caused them to crash. Israel shot down Iranian-made drones using F-16s or Apache helicopters and air-to-air missiles.[377]

Scrambling fighter jets isn't a solution to stop drones. First, radar may not pick up the drones, and there won't be time to send the jets. Second, depending on the kind of drone threat, using an expensive aircraft may be a waste to defend against a small threat. Third, there may be many more drone threats in the future and not enough jets to intercept them all. You could send up drones to fight other drones, but this technology was in its infancy. Only in September 2018 did the US use a Reaper for the first time to shoot down another drone.[378] Using F-16s was a stopgap measure against a new threat that suddenly emerged.

For Israel, the threat was relatively minimal at first, because Hezbollah and Hamas didn't have very many drones. When Iran brought drones to the windswept desert base called Tiyas, they could be seen by surveillance whenever they decided to make the several-hundred-kilometer approach. Israel took this threat seriously, targeting the Hezbollah killer drone team in a house near the Golan Heights in August 2019 before the men could try to fly their drones into Israel. Israel also reached deep into Syria, striking the Tiyas base itself.

When you can't prevent the threat, you need other technology. Israel already faced a widespread and growing missile threat from Gaza in the early 2000s. Israel faced a two-front rocket threat, including thousands of rockets fired by Hezbollah from Lebanon in 2006 and thousands more fired by Hamas from Gaza. To confront that, Brig. Gen. Daniel Gold, head of the defense research and development unit, pushed for the creation of what became Iron Dome, a missile defense system. First used in 2010 and supported by then Minister of Defense Amir Peretz, the idea was for a system that would confront current and future threats. Gold believed that Israel should not limit itself to classic methodologies but consider the future and use of technology to help it dominate that future.[379]

Iron Dome proved so successful that the US began to look at it for the multi-missile launcher aspect of its Indirect Fire Protection Capability Increment 2 (IFPC-2) in April 2016. The Iron Dome was brought to White Sands Missile Range and put through some paces. Its Tamir missile interceptor struck a drone.[380] The Iron Dome in the US, sold by Israel's Rafael and Raytheon, was called Skyhunter.[381] Israel also built other air defense systems with US support, including the David's Sling and Arrow-3, both of which were first used against threats from Syria in 2017 and 2018. Neither was designed to take out drones, although David's Sling could be used to defend against the UAV threat. In the last months of 2020, Israel conducted an unprecedented multi-layered integrated test with Iron Dome and David's Sling to test them against cruise missiles and drones. The systems worked. Meanwhile, the US was taking delivery of its first Iron Dome batteries from Israel to see if they would meet America's needs.

A David's Sling interceptor being fired at dusk in Israel.
It is one of Israel's multi-layered air defense systems.
(Courtesy Rafael Advanced Defense Systems)

While these systems would work against drones, they weren't the only air-defense systems that could shoot them down. The US was hesitant to invest a billion dollars in a program that they had questions about, including integration and cybersecurity issues.[382] The US Patriot missile system, first developed in 1990s, had been deployed to Israel. In 2014, Israel used Patriots to strike Hamas drones, with some pointing out the Patriot missiles cost $1 million each.[383] In June and July 2018, Patriots were fired at drones flying from Syria. The first missile flew at a drone, and the drone retreated into Syrian airspace. The second incident involved a drone that flew over Jordan from Syria and toward the Sea of Galilee before being downed.[384] In November 2017, Israel shot down a drone that flew into Israeli airspace from Syria.[385] Not everything was perfect: two Patriot missiles failed to hit a Hezbollah drone in July 2016.[386]

The 2016 incident, in which the Patriots failed and a jet also missed finding the drone, led to questions about how to stop the drone threat. Tal Inbar at the UAV Research Center at the Fisher Institute for Air and Space Strategic Studies told *Haaretz* that a complete defense was difficult because of the size, speed, and material drones are made of.[387]

There were also questions of overkill, to use Patriots to shoot down small drones. "We love Patriot missiles," US General David Perkins said in March 2017. He related a story of a Patriot shooting down a quad-copter. The $200 copter didn't stand a chance. "Now that worked, they got it," he said.[388] He told the story to the Associations of the US Army in Alabama. Using Patriot PAC-2 or PAC-3 missiles, with a range of thirteen miles, wasn't what the system was designed for.[389] The US army began sponging up new PAC-3 Missile Segment Enhancement missiles in 2018, buying 240 that year and another 240 the next. The new missiles, sixteen for a launcher, had ranges of forty kilometers and an altitude of twenty kilometers.[390]

The radar can track targets at one hundred miles out, but you'd need a plethora to defend a large country. There also aren't enough Patriots to defend against all the drone threats. Thomas Karako, director of the Center for Strategic and International Studies Missile Defense Project, said that the Patriot was in high demand in 2019 and early 2020. "They can't be everywhere at once."[391] Besides the batteries in Israel, there were also Patriots in Saudi Arabia and the UAE.

With its eight trailer-mounted launchers and AN/MPQ-65 multi-function phased array radar, the US has around eighteen Air Defense Artillery battalions with three to five batteries each. Some were in Japan, South Korea, Germany, and the US for training.[392] They were also in the process of upgrading their radars and moving from analog to digital. This would mean improving radar and also adding a lower layer of air defense or Lower Tier Air and Missile Defense Sensor (LTAMDS).[393] But unlike the Israeli Iron Dome, which was already part of an integrated multi-layered air-defense system, the Patriot was not yet integrated with either the High-Altitude US Air Defense (THAAD) or the lower level Short Range Air Defense (SHORAD) or the Integrated Air and Missile Defense Battle Command System (IBCS), the latter built by Northrop. All these acronyms would make the Patriot more versatile by 2031. But it would all take time, as batteries had to swap out technology or rotate back to the US.

The US Army began to wake up to the threat posed by drones in 2017, when it sought to retool its Raytheon-built Phalanx alongside the Northrop Counter Rocket Artillery Mortar (C-RAM) systems to deal with drones.[394] "We are looking at what we can apply as an interim solution," Col. John L. Ward, director of the Army Rapid Equipping Force, said in December 2017.[395] On the menu: electronic warfare, new sensors, and improved targeting tech, even making .50 caliber machine guns more accurate or "guided." The US Army and Northrop Grumman looked at the problem.[396] C-Ram had already been sent to Iraq and Afghanistan. It helped to defend against 2,500 rocket and mortar attacks. Equipped with a twenty-milimeter Gatling gun that can fire 4,500 rounds a minute on a thirty-five-ton trailer, it was imposing. But it needed more versatility against drones.[397] The US Army also acquired something called "Smart Shooter," which is an Israeli gunsight add-on that lets you lock on to a moving target and pull the trigger, and only release the bullet when the drone is back in front of the muzzle. On June 29, 2020, Israel's IAI also said it would partner with Iron Drone to use their drone interceptor technology, which uses drones to attack other drones.

Tracking drones is different than tracking a mortar because they don't follow a trajectory. They move around and loiter. The problem was moving faster than the US could keep up with, and tinkering with ideas like new sensors, missiles, and upgrades to existing systems wasn't solving the problem in time.[398] This left the US exposed in Iraq to possible Iranian drone threats in 2021 and also left US allies like Saudi Arabia exposed amid Iranian tensions in the fall of 2019.

As with drone wars in general, the technology to kill drones existed, but it hadn't been systematically put together. Because drone threats emerged rapidly, their abilities were not respected by Western countries that were resting on their laurels. This was a bit like the French in 1940. They had the same technology and access to tanks that the Germans had, but they didn't marshal it innovatively. The Israelis beat the Arab states in 1967 this way as well: using surprise and coordinating air power and armor better. Whoever was the first to dare to use drones as a threat against a sophisticated country would win the day. It was in Iran that this threat would emerge.

Somewhere in Tehran, deep within the headquarters of the Islamic Revolutionary Guard Corps, the planning for the ultimate mission to humiliate the Americans was beginning. Tehran's generals would strike at the soft underbelly of the US alliance system: the Saudi oil fields. They would use a new strategy called the "drone swarm."

CHAPTER 7

THE SWARM: OVERWHELMING THE DEFENSES

n May 2019, Iran's top brass gathered in Tehran. Tensions with the US were rising. It was time to strike a blow against the Americans. Major General Hossein Salami wanted to prove himself and the Islamic Revolutionary Guard Corps that he commanded. Iranians like Hajizadeh and Salami had waited for years for this opportunity. They would use drones against the Americans or a key American ally. In May and June, the IRGC struck at ships using mines. Then they shot down the Global Hawk and prodded allies in Yemen and Iraq to attack Saudi infrastructure.

On September 14, they went further. Supreme Leader Ali Khamenei blessed the plan. They all knew that killing Americans would provoke a response. They could read the US news reports that Trump had called off retaliation for the Global Hawk downing because no Americans were killed.[399] The Iranians planned a complex attack using twenty-five drones and cruise missiles. The drones would fly an arc through Iraq and then head south toward the Abqaiq oil facility, among Saudi Arabia's most important sites. The Center for Strategic and International Studies had warned in August that this massive oil facility, with its endless streets, a metal jungle of pipes and giant storage tanks, might be targeted. Riyadh put air defenses around it, including a Patriot battery, an Oerlikon GDF 35mm. cannon with Skyguard radar, and a French Crotale Shahine system. But the radar was pointing in the wrong direction, and the drones came in at a low angle. The huge facility got in the way of detecting the attack.

In the early hours of the morning of September 14, the eighteen drones began to impact. For seventeen minutes explosions continued, with two waves of drones hitting Abqaiq. Iran had sent cruise missiles as well, not all of which made it to their targets at Khurais, another nearby facility. Guided by GPS, the drones struck with precision at storage tanks and other areas on the site. No one was killed. The Iranians initially pretended the Houthis had carried out the attack. But the site was so far from Yemen, such an attack seemed too incredible to be true. In addition, Houthi drones would have been more likely to be detected because they would have flown through some 500 miles of Saudi Airspace. They would have had to fly around Riyadh or come near to Dhahran, Qatar, and Bahrain. These were sensitive areas, home to the US airbase at Al-Udeid and the Fifth Fleet in Bahrain as well as America's own drone base in Al Dhafra, UAE.

Iranian dissident groups said the drones were launched from near Ahwaz and flew around 650 kilometers. They came over Iraq and bits of Kuwait. Five percent of the world's oil supply was disrupted, and it took Saudi Arabia several weeks to restore production.[400] There was no major response to the Abqaiq attack. Other Gulf countries were concerned that something similar might be in store for other US allies.

In Israel, Brig. Gen. Pini Yungman, a former air defense commander with the Israeli Air Force, said that these drones, even in a swarm like at

Abqaiq, were not yet a major strategic threat because they didn't carry a large warhead. "They carry a very low weight of bomb or ammunition."[401] Uzi Rubin, former director of Israel's Missile Defense Organization who speaks quickly (like he is in a hurry to go through all the details of why missile defense is so important), in looking at the threat to Israel, said the country had an advantage over Saudi Arabia in being much smaller and able to monitor its airspace with radar.

The Abqaiq strike was a "Pearl Harbor" in its audacity. How does one detect so many low-lying threats? Yungman was confident that even if the threat included hundreds or thousands of drones, it could be defeated. Rubin says the major challenge is detecting them all. "When it comes to missiles, missile defense sensors will aim above the horizon because the missile is above it and you don't want clutter."

The Americans agreed with the Israeli assessment. CENTCOM commander Gen. Kenneth McKenzie, in olive-forest camo, speaking via Zoom due to the COVID-19 pandemic on June 11, 2020, said he feared that enemies using cheap drones could wreak havoc. His voice was soft, with a slight Southern accent, and he spoke for an hour about various challenges in the Middle East, coming to drones at the end. Large numbers of small UAVs were a threat, and he said the US needed to play catch-up to stop them.[402]

Drones can be interdicted by GPS-denied environments or jamming radio and other ways they are controlled. But if the drones are guided by their own optical system or artificial intelligence, the only way to stop them is a "hard-kill," meaning they have to be shot down. Yungman suggested in an interview that one way to deal with them is a five- to ten-kilowatt laser that has a range of around 2.5 kilometers. Karako agreed that after Abqaiq, a lot of new "solutions" to the drone problem would have to be put in play. "I think you'll see global demand signal for a variety of means to counter these threats."

The threat that Iran revealed in September 2019 was a watershed in several respects. It was sophisticated and took US allies completely by surprise. If the Saudis and others had been paying closer attention, they might have seen the August 2019 Shaybah attack on the natural gas liquification site by Houthi drones as a dry run for Abqaiq. Both revealed key defects in air defense and what the future might look like. Lack of radar coverage illustrated why defenders need 360 degrees of radar coverage. Then they need radar that can see beyond the horizon in every direction. The air defense system then needs optical ways to see the threat, to use lasers or various missile and gun interceptors, such as Israel's Stunner that is part of the David's Sling, or its Iron Dome Tamir missile. Lastly, jamming can be used as well as lasers or a C-RAM system with a machine gun. The best weapon against drone swarms is to use lasers because they don't require you to replenish their ammunition.

From *Star Trek* to *RoboCop*

Ben-Gurion University is based in the city of Beersheba in southern Israel. The city's origins are biblical: once upon a time, Abraham came to a well here. Later, the city was revived by the Ottomans in 1900 and became the scene of an epic charge by Australian Light Horse in 1917 during the First World War. In 2020, a new kind of war was being envisioned: using low frequency lasers to shoot down drones. Called Light Blade, the project was part of a small company named OptiDefense. A model was used with Elbit's detection system called SupervisIR to stop explosive-laden balloons on the border of the Gaza Strip. Prof. Amiel Ishaaya and two colleagues sought to develop a laser defense system that would make use of lower frequency lasers to defend against drones in urban areas.[403] Not far from their research project, another group was helping Rafael build a new generation of small surveillance drones.[404] All of Israel's most cutting-edge drone technology, and the technologies to counter them, are concentrated in this small country among people who usually worked together in the army or in university.

Rafael Advanced Defense Systems Drone Dome, showcasing
technology used to detect and counter increasing drone
threats. (Courtesy Rafael Advanced Defense Systems)

At Rafael, located near Haifa in northern Israel, lasers were also being
perfected to stop drones. Originally a part of Israel's Military Science
Corps national research and development defense laboratory for building advanced weapons, Rafael became a company in 2002 and had some
8,000 employees by 2019. It built anti-tank missiles, Iron Dome, and
the Trophy protection system for tanks. It was only logical that it would
also move into defending against drones, having created so many other
defensive systems.

In February 2020, Rafael testers took a handful of quadcopter drones,
the kind terrorists might buy on the commercial market, out to the desert to test their laser system as part of their Drone Dome technology. The
drones were sent to hover around while lasers mounted on a jeep burned
them and shot them down. They tried the lasers against three drones
acting as a kind of swarm. "Drone Dome is designed to address threats
posed by hostile drones both in military and civilian sites," Rafael said.[405]
Rafael said that its Drone Dome could be paired with other systems
such as its SPYDER air defense, which uses missiles on a truck to shoot
down threats, including drones.[406] Drone Dome was used at Gatwick
Airport in England in 2018 to stop commercial drones that shut down
the airport for several days, leading to 140,000 people being displaced

and 1,000 flights canceled. Other Israeli companies made anti-drone systems, including the IAI Elta's Drone Guard and Elbit's ReDrone.

In January 2019, I went out to a bucolic field in central Israel to see the Drone Guard demonstrated. Set up in a small collapsible tent with a plastic folding table and computer display, the system was easy to deploy and easy to use. A radar system deployed in front of the tent swung around on a metal pole, while a second small capsule provided optics so that the operators could detect and see the threat. As small quadcopter drones were launched overhead near a small knoll of trees, the system detected them. How does it know that it is detecting drones and not birds? These questions bedeviled designers over the years, but algorithms and the use of visual optics help the operator determine that they are seeing a drone. A jammer can then be used to stop the wavelength the drone is being guided from.[407] The drawback of the system is you would need large numbers of them to defend against any huge area, like Abqaiq, and if drones were not being guided but had a predetermined flight path, the jammer wouldn't stop them. They would need to be killed by weapons like lasers.

Lasers may work in a test, but they were largely unused in the field. The US, knowing it was having trouble downing new drone threats, was also considering lasers.[408] Israel was worried. The same month that Iran launched its Abqaiq "Pearl Harbor" attack, a Gaza drone dropped an explosive device on an IDF Hummer.[409] Jerusalem revealed it was the second such attack in 2019. Because of the threat, the Israeli Ministry of Defense Directorate for Defense Research and Development has pumped funds into several programs by its three major defense companies. The Iron Beam, a laser to defeat drones, was one of them. Israel said in January 2020 that there had been major breakthroughs.

"We are entering a new age of energy warfare in the air, land and sea," Brig. Gen. Yaniv Rotem said. The research was paying off. Israel was now a leader in drone defense technology, as it had once led in building drones. Israel's military wants a system that can do a number of tasks. It needs to be maneuverable so troops in the field can use it, also to complement the Iron Dome and potentially be able to be used in the air above cloud cover.[410] Three versions of the system would be built by Elbit and Rafael. Rafael's Iron Beam, for instance, can be used up to 4.5 miles. Lasers are also super-accurate, being able to hit a target the size of a penny. Iron Beam was developed over ten years beginning in 2009 and unveiled in 2014 in Singapore.[411] The problem with these systems is that they are still not operational as of 2020. The US Navy tried practicing with a solid-state laser developed by Northrup Grumman in May 2020. The awesome beam was fired from the USS *Portland* near Pearl Harbor. It shot down a drone, showing it did work.[412]

Like much in the world of future wars, there was a lot of talk about lasers, but they weren't actually in the field. The US Army had been talking about using them for many years, particularly since 2016.[413] The army had looked at a program called the Medium Experimental High Energy Laser, which did successfully down drones in 2017.

At Lockheed Martin, the best-of-the-best engineers built something called Athena, a laser system that successfully shot down numerous UAVs when it was used at Fort Sill. The US government lacked a road map for these defense systems, but the company believed in them.[414] They wanted to increase the power of the lasers to some one hundred to two hundred kilowatts. Upping the power would increase range from a few kilometers to ten, meaning the lasers could effectively defend bases or infrastructure without having to deploy dozens of systems in one place.

Doug Graham, Vice-President of Advanced Programs for Lockheed Martin said in an interview, "We have seen recent attacks, like the one on the Saudi oil fields, where directed energy systems could have made unique and important contributions, in part because of the situational awareness the weapon systems provide, as well as low collateral damage engagements. Aside from negating targets, Laser Weapon Systems provide long range precision sensor capabilities that complement radar and other systems."[415] The turning point for directed energy technology has been the advancement of solid-state lasers, he says. This specifically relates to fiber lasers that are compact and lethal, which have enabled laser weapon systems to be operationally viable and ready to affordably address real threats that exist today. "Now that laser weapon systems in the tens of kilowatts are ready to be fielded, and will be in the next year or two, we can build development roadmaps that show how lasers can scale to address more stressing targets like cruise missiles and eventually ballistic missiles," says Graham.

The technology was unlimited because lasers could be put on aircraft for offensive operations, and they don't run out of ammunition. There was no doubt that they would soon be deployed. When they were finally operational, it would be at sea.

Drone wars lend themselves to futuristic analogies. This is partly because unmanned vehicles have appeared in movies for years, from *Terminator* to *RoboCop*. They conjure up *Star Wars* and *Star Trek* and almost every movie that takes place in the future. *Angel Has Fallen* in 2019 featured a massive drone swarm, for example. While some of the futuristic aspects of these systems have come true, many of them have not. At the heart of the drone war are drones that still operate like planes or cruise missiles. However, at the heart of the defense against them, there are advances in detection and also other means of stopping them. All of these advances have come about because they had to meet a need. When Iran claimed to have hacked the Sentinel in 2011, the US worked to further encrypt its drones better.[416] Now the world was moving toward drone swarms. That would mean more autonomy for the drones so that they would have pre-programmed flight patterns and work together, maybe with a drone "mother ship."

The idea of swarming has been around for decades, but no one had ever really gotten it to work on the battlefield before the Iranian attacks on Saudi Arabia. The US had used large numbers of drones, sometimes in concert as part of the system of putting "CAPs" over targets and having others kill the targets.[417] When DARPA was looking at the X-45, its leader Michael Francis already saw a future drone swarm destroying air defenses before the enemy could stop them. At Edwards Air Force Base, the system was tested, showing for the first time multiple UAVs could be controlled at the same time.[418] Flown by operators in Seattle, the drones could work together and with other imaginary drones to conduct airstrikes or guide attacks on simulated air defenses. Unfortunately for Boeing and the various MQ-X ideas that were cancelled between 2005 and 2015, the original swarming technology seemed to be put on ice.

When it comes to drones, the technology is always a decade ahead of what the military brass actually wants to do with the system. China had perfected the use of hundreds of drones in concert for civilian purposes, using more than 1,300 for a light show to break a world record in May 2018 in Xi'an. Later, China put on extraordinary displays of drones flying in formation to look like medical staff, lighting up the skies of Zhuhai to commemorate healthcare workers during the coronavirus pandemic.[419] That civilians innovate while militaries ossify is due to the fact that many officers intended to command drone armies are veterans of wars of the past. That means that soldiers in the Gulf War remembered Vietnam-era technology and those who fought the war on terror had remembered the Gulf War and what was called the "Revolution in Military Affairs," a mixed bag of new technologies that didn't always work. Today's drone-war commander, however, has lived a whole life with drones.

A US Army poster depicts the future warrior fighting online.
In the drone wars the use of computers and technology
increasingly dominates military affairs. (Seth J. Frantzman)

When Kenneth Bray, acting associate deputy chief of staff of intelligence, surveillance, and reconnaissance at the air force looked to the future in 2017, he said the main goal would be to figure out what to do with all the data the drones were collecting. "We're starting to think from the data and decide, is it even collecting the right size data, or do I need to have different sensors on those platforms?" Bray said that the future of war is not against the low-tech terrorists with AK-47s being hunted in their cars or compounds, but rather against a complex enemy. That means densely defended areas that require a drone that relies on artificial intelligence, autonomy, and algorithms.[420] The US was looking at developing these future drones, dubbed MQ-X, that could survive in a "contested environment" and take a beating from weather and enemy weapons. General Atomics and its Predator C, the Avenger, hoped to meet this need.[421]

The Avenger, which General Atomics also made into an extended range variant to fly twenty hours and fly 400 miles per hour, was called YQ-11. The air force picked up at least one of these, but speculation was that they or another US government agency acquired more. It was tested in the Mojave desert and flown over Syria. This was not the weapon system that would be doing any swarming, though, at least for the foreseeable future.

Swarm Tech

P.W. Singer in *Wired for War* pointed out that drone swarms can cover wide areas, as the US needed to do during the "Great Scud Hunt" to find Saddam Hussein's Scud launchers. With some artificial intelligence, they can locate targets and show an operator which targets have not been neutralized. "The autonomous swarm would just figure it out all on its own."[422]

The US Air Force put out a "flight plan" for drones in 2009 that discussed swarms.[423] A group of partially autonomous drones would support manned and unmanned units on the battlefield using a wireless ad-hoc network. They would avoid collisions with each other and help select which drone would be best suited for each target. Seven years later, the US finally experimented with swarm technology at China Lake during what was called the Perdix Swarm Demonstration. Three F-18s dropped 103 drones over a target. Designed by students at MIT, the drones had twelve-inch wingspans and acted as a "collective organism."[424] On the computer screen they looked like little green dots moving from a long line where they had been dumped to circle a target. It was like a 1980s-era video game.

This was a far cry from anything that had been done before. The drones that were used by Syrian rebels against the Russians in Syria in 2018 included numerous drones, but not the hive mind "organism" of a swarm. They had no central control once launched. Unsurprisingly it was the US, with its vast resources and armies of computer geeks, that had cracked the code of swarm warfare.

DARPA liked the drone swarm idea enough that it pushed a concept called Gremlins, basically a swarm of loitering munitions.[425] The beasts, called X-61A, got to have a tryout at the Dugway Proving Ground aboard a C-130 Hercules that dumped them from the air. One crashed. They could be used against radar or for jamming, surveillance, and battle damage assessment.[426] The navy also fired off numerous drones into the air in a scheme called LOCUST or Low Cost UAV Swarm Technology. Lee Mastroianni at the Office of Naval Research said that UAVs are expendable and reconfigurable, and they could free manned aircraft and other weapon systems and "essentially multiply combat power at decreased risk to the warfighter."[427]

Raytheon also came up with the "Coyote" drone concept, a small drone that can fly and then attack at a distance of eighty kilometers for sixty minutes. The drones are shot out of a giant box either from land or on a ship. Raytheon said they could overwhelm adversaries or fly into dangerous areas. Officers could direct them using tablets or even using gestures.[428]

In the 2010s, Paul Scharre at the Center for a New American Security was quoted as a kind of prophet of the future of swarm drone war. In 2018, his book *Army of None* came out about autonomous machines and the future of war. "You imagine a football match, a coach isn't going to tell the players from the sidelines exactly where to run and what to do." Replace the players with drones and you get the idea. Between 2016 and 2020, the interest in drone swarms grew exponentially, with articles and research on it from Harvard to MIT.[429] There were some limiting factors involving communication and whether one drone would be used to communicate to the rest.[430]

What would the problem look like? DARPA tried to find out in the fading light of a March day at the Yuma proving ground with a "swarm" of six Navmar RQ-23 Tigersharks and its Collaborative Operations in Denied Environment (CODE) system. The Tigershark is a small twin-tailed grey UAV that had been used in Iraq and Afghanistan and was approved for experimental use in 2019.[431] It was meant to be a low-cost hunter that could seek out explosives or conduct CAP patrols.[432] The pioneers wanted to hand them over to the Naval Air Systems Command and paired the six real drones with fourteen imaginary ones flying using software from Raytheon and algorithms from Johns Hopkins University Applied Physics Laboratory's White Force Network.[433]

What if an enemy got a hold of this technology and used it against us? Marine Corps Commandant Robert Neller warned in April 2019 that drone swarms were heading our way. Neller was sure that the future was not defending against enemy bombers, but "I think the real future in enemy air attack is going to be swarming drones." The Marines put a compact radar and electronic warfare device that looks like a giant pastry on top of jeeps. Called the Light Marine Air Defense Integrated System (LMADIS), it can detect and kill drones. The Low Altitude Air Defense detachment of the Marine Medium Tiltrotor Squadron 166 of the Thirteenth Marine Expeditionary Unit got to try it out.[434] In July 2019, the Marines aboard the USS *Boxer* in the Persian Gulf used the system to kill an Iranian drone.[435]

The air force also built a satellite dish system called Tactical High Power Microwave Operational Responder (THOR) at Kirtland Air Base near Albuquerque that it tested in 2019.[436] The unexotic system moves around in a storage container and uses a microwave burst to kill drones, like a flashlight blasting insects.

The air force also wanted a medium-range anti-drone weapon and experimented with something called Counter-Electronic High-Power

Microwave Extended Range Air Base Air Defense (CHIMERA). The air force and army were also interested in yet another Lockheed Martin anti-drone microwave system called SHiELD or Self-Protect High Energy Laser Demonstrator. Apparently, concerns about the rapid need to confront drone threats came in the wake not only of what the Iranians and ISIS were doing but also an attack in Venezuela showing that a simple DJI Matrice commercial drone could be armed with C4 explosives.[437]

The technology to create drone swarms and confront them exists, but putting the anti-swarm technology at every base and location wasn't possible. Even if counter-drone technology was deployed after laborious testing, the chance that a country or terrorist group using a drone swarm would also run into a base defended by the latest anti-drone technology to see how both work in actual combat is not likely.

The development of swarm technology is interesting, but most targets, such as terrorist leaders, won't require drone swarm attacks. If the US ever had to go to war with a major power such as China, then it could get to see if the swarms work against other advanced technology, but that is also a big gamble to take with the technology for the first time. This means all the prophecies about drone swarms changing the face of war are exciting, but they haven't come to fruition.[438] Iran's attack on Saudi Arabia may have been a drone swarm Pearl Harbor, but just as another 1941 Pearl Harbor never happened again, it may be that another Abqaiq won't happen in the same way again. If it does happen, it will be faster, deadlier, and more destructive.

CHAPTER 8

BETTER, STRONGER, FASTER: A NEW WORLD ORDER

"UAVs are transforming current campaigns against extremists and enabling an entirely different way of pursuing combat operations, in which we enable host nation forces in a way that we never could in the past and help them defeat enemies like the Islamic State in their incarnation as an army, and then help host nation forces pursue the remaining ISIS elements operating as insurgents and terrorists," said former US General and former CIA Director David Petreaus in early 2020.[439] He says that drones, "unmanned ships, tanks, subs, robots, computers, and every additional conceivable system are also going to transform how we fight all campaigns. Over time, the man-in-the-loop may be in developing the algorithm, not the operation of the unmanned system itself."

A Tello drone, the kind of small quadcopters that can be purchased in stores worldwide. These types of drones became common after 2013 as companies like DJI rolled out massive numbers of small drones. (Seth J. Frantzman)

Petraeus had seen the advantages of UAVs in the early days of the war on terror. In March 2003, he was commander of the 101st Airborne during the V Corps offensive to take Baghdad. The whole corps had only one unarmed Predator drone, and the video quality it produced was not high resolution. By 2008, drones were available for the battle for Sadr City. One brigade was given vastly superior ISR than anyone had been supplied previously, he says, "including towers with optics ringing the neighborhood of some 2 million people, blimps with optics floating higher, low-level drones, and attack helicopters with optics, Predators, manned aircraft, all the way up to U-2s making passes overhead."[440] Petraeus was commanding the US and coalition forces in Iraq at the time. The multi-layered surveillance paid off, and seventy-five rocket and mortar teams who had been targeting the Green Zone were destroyed. In 2008, US Senator Barack Obama, a champion of drones, came to Iraq to meet Petraeus for a tour over Sadr City.

The search for better drones came about the way it did in large part because they were successful in Iraq and Afghanistan. However, that led to lethargy and complacency in the world's first drone superpower. There was no rapid need to develop new systems. Instead, there were experiments, and billions were spent on ideas. There was pushback from commanders who wanted traditional manned airplanes, like the F-35.

On the drone front, advances in technology were making drones more capable for everyone except the people with guns. Militaries were lagging behind in developing capabilities. Civilian drones led the way. Shenzhen-based DJI had begun operations in 2006 and introduced their Phantom I in 2013. Phantom 2 Vision followed, with twenty minutes' flying time and 300 meters of range. The Mavic was introduced in 2016 as a compact, portable drone. By then, DJI was on the way to gobbling up 72 percent of the global market for commercial drones, and by 2017 it had become a billion-dollar business.[441] It sold $2.8 billion in drones in 2017, an 80-percent increase from 2016.[442]

DJI drones were the most widely used drones that were not a "program of record" within the armed forces. US soldiers acquired these commercial drones and began using them for operations. There was a concern that China might be listening and learning. DJI drones were used throughout the US armed forces, along with some other smaller drones, such as Pumas and Switchblades, which were made by the US-based Aerovironment. But the army was becoming more cyber-savvy.[443] Lt. Gen. Joseph Anderson, deputy chief for plans and preparations, sent a letter in 2017 to commanders and soldiers telling them to cease and desist. "Uninstall all DJI applications, remove all batteries/storage media from devices, and secure equipment for follow on direction."

The US was right to be concerned about cybersecurity. In January 2018, users online noted that the Strava jogging app mistakenly revealed the courses special forces were running on secret bases in Syria, all because users' jogging patterns were open to all. Hackers also got a hold of Predator drone feeds and Reaper plans and put them for sale online.[444] Whoops.

Cheap, Top Secret, and Bizarre

Filling the gaps in the drone war was the name of the game after 2017. The US and other countries now had a wide array of new products to test, and they were also trying to backfill in a whole bevy of vulnerabilities with new technology. The problem was trying to decide how best to do all the different things that could be done. For instance, General Atomics in San Diego wanted to put a 150-kilowatt laser on its Avenger. The lasers were tested at White Sands. But they were at the time too heavy to put on most drones. The Missile Defense Agency (MDA) also liked the idea of jamming new tech onto drones that would let them monitor other drones.[445]

A lot of the drones being built were touch and go. Boeing was building a liquid-hydrogen fueled blimp-like drone with two props on the front that could fly for ten days and carry up to 2,000 pounds. It was called the Phantom Eye.[446] MDA had liked its abilities to conduct long-range sensing and tracking. Meanwhile, at the Dugway Proving Ground in Utah in December 2019, the air force also tested a drone that can fly for two days called the Ultra Long Endurance Aircraft Platform (LEAP).[447] Another experimental albatross called the Zephyr could fly for a month at 75,000 feet. Built by Airbus Defence and Space in 2018, it was called a High Altitude Pseudo Satellite (HAPS).

In March 2019, at the Yuma Proving Grounds, flying over the majestic high desert, another futuristic drone called XQ-58A Valkyrie took flight. It was supposed to be able to penetrate enemy air defense. It was designed to be low-cost and was pushed by the Air Force Research Laboratory at the Wright-Patterson base in Ohio. The plane, which basically looks like a F-117 Stealth with its cockpit cut off, was built by Kratos, a small company that was also making the drone swarm "Gremlins."[448] The XQ-58 would cost only $2 million each. After so much waste, the air force was now looking to develop ideas that were affordable, perhaps drones that could be wingmen or fly more autonomously and conduct missions themselves. The new shoestring budget was called Low Cost Attritable Aircraft Technology.[449]

Another futuristic idea was "Skyborg," which was supposed to fly by 2023. It would be cheap and easy to replace, a kind of flying pod that could accompany aircraft. Acquisition director Will Roper said that Skyborg would take off and land by itself and fly in all weather conditions. These ideas were gaining traction, he said in April 2019, because the new US national security strategy envisioned more great power competition with states such as China, Russia, or Iran. Now was the time to have more diverse options beyond the Predator and Global Hawk line.

This was a positive shift, argued Scharre. He hinted that the US hadn't built new platforms since 2009, noting that they relied on three combat aircraft, the F-35, the F-22, and the future B-21. "Diversity is really helpful to complicate things for the adversary."[450] The real story was probably that the air force was reticent to plow money into new drones when its pilots wanted resources for their planes. Lt.-Gen. Dave Deptula at the Mitchell Institute for Aerospace Studies said the Skyborg wouldn't step on toes. "They have the potential for dramatically changing the game in the conduct of air operations."[451]

Congress was not impressed with the air force plans. Only twelve more Reapers were to be purchased in 2020, with two for the navy, and Congress threw a few dollars at spare parts for the Global Hawks. Suddenly the ridiculously expensive spy aircraft was vulnerable to Iranian missiles. It would be no match for China or Russia. It was a flying whale. Congress allocated just $12 million for the RQ-20B Puma, a small drone, and $100 million at the low cost program.[452]

At the other extreme end of the drone world, DARPA's Squad X idea was supposed to put tiny drones with artificial intelligence in the hands of soldiers. FLIR is usually an abbreviation for Forward Looking Infrared, but a company called FLIR had pitched this idea.[453] The Eighty-Second Airborne looked at them in Afghanistan.[454] By 2020, the US was drawing down soldiers in Afghanistan, its most successful field testing ground for UAVs. The tiniest drones were called "Black Hornets" and could fly for twenty-five minutes. The army hoped these insect-sized drones might one day become "standard."[455]

The air force also wanted more small UAVs. It already had fielded more than 150 Batcam drones for tactical air controllers, and it was looking at more micro drones. The Batcam had the unusual luck of ending up in the air force museum too.[456] But America's pilots still hadn't settled on something that would be as widespread as Predator had been in the past. By 2019, the US wanted to buy another 1,000 combat drones by 2030 and some 43,000 smaller or other surveillance drones.[457]

The US Army also used its Other Transaction Authority, a loophole that lets it grab up new products to meet a need at up to $100 million a pop, to look at smaller drones that are man-packable, hoping to have something versatile to give to soldiers in the field. These drones can be carried in a backpack making them ideal for small units or infantry at the frontline. It wasn't sure what the future would hold, wrapping up operations in Afghanistan and Iraq, but wanted a new range of drones for the next wars.

The Marines, meanwhile, were continually hobbled by the inability to get the drone they wanted. They flew their first Reaper only in March of 2020.[458] Until this point, the Marine Unmanned Aerial Vehicle Squadron had been using Blackjacks. The Marines had been leasing the Reaper from General Atomics and learning to fly it since 2018. US Marines based in Yuma, Arizona, operated the drone.[459] Photos of Marines using the Blackjack and RQ-20 Puma illustrated they needed a larger strike capability.[460]

The Marines were also pushing for a capability for their ships, something called Marine Air-Ground Task Force Unmanned Aerial System Expeditionary, or MUX for short. This word salad of a name first looked like an X-Wing from Star Wars and then a flying "V" with a prop in the front, and was supposed to be ready by 2026.[461] The fact that the Marines predicted this would take most of a decade to fly shows how sluggish US planners were. They had been wanting these systems since 2015, when slide shows the Marines made called it "MQ-X,"[462] but hadn't got them.

A study submitted to Congress had suggested tactical UAVs could move items to the frontline troops, such as blood plasma or communications equipment.[463] For the army, more man-portable platoon-level UAVs were supposed to be rolled out. In 2018, the army decided it wanted to replace its fleet of tactical Shadow drones and put out for ideas for a "Future Tactical Unmanned Aircraft System (FTUAS)." Martin UAV and Northrop came up with one idea, the V-Bat, while Textron AAI made something called the Aerosonde, which looks like an Israeli twin-boom surveillance drone. In fact, it showed not much had changed since the 1980s when it comes to how things look. Throughout 2020, various US Army units, from Kentucky to Washington, Texas, and North Carolina would test and use the drones. They wanted something that didn't need much of a runway and had better optics, less sound, and didn't need much extra stuff lying about to fly and control it.[464] On the positive side, the zoo of new options showed everyone was finally getting access to drones.

The problem for the US military was it didn't really know what it wanted in the future. In an October 2019 meeting, Todd Harrison of the Center for Strategic and International Studies said that the US should assess the possibility of using drones as a low-cost and highly available alternative to manned airplanes. "I think we need a roadmap for RPAs [remote piloted aircraft] in terms of what are the new missions that we can begin to transition over to RPAs and some new operational concepts."[465] Older aircraft, such as the Reaper, may have been jealous of these new concepts. If you're an old dog, you need to learn new tricks: the Reaper took off and landed autonomously for the first time in October 2018.[466]

This was the tip of the iceberg of US problems. In dropping ideas like the futuristic X-47, or keeping them under wraps as classified programs, the navy moved towards creating yet another experiment, a drone tanker MQ-25.[467] It first flew in September 2019.[468] Various countries' air forces kept pushing a Loyal Wingman program, basically a drone mule that would help manned aircraft. In early May 2020, Boeing finally got the go-ahead from the Australian air force to introduce the Airpower Teaming System, which it had unveiled in 2019. Boeing built three aircraft to work with that are thirty-eight-feet long. The plane is sleek and looks like a normal fighter plane if you chopped the top off and kept the wings and half the fuselage. It is paired with fighter aircraft to help carry out some duties. Would it be what pilots wanted, or the worst of both worlds, an unnecessary UAV flying alongside a manned plane that negates the point of unmanned vehicles and distracts the pilot with this new tag-along plane?

Another problem was trying to plan for the future war by uploading the correct data to the drones once they were flying in a crowded airspace. Instead of a war with a few F-15s overhead, the future war would have an airspace that would be crowded like a highway with helicopter drones like the futuristic Bell V-247, swarms of mini-drones, kamikaze drones being fired from tubes on ships, tactical catapult-launched drones by Marines landing on a beach, and drones being flown by special ops soldiers on a hill nearby. All that would be watched by a stealthy flying wing and a combat air patrol of other drones armed with Hellfires. Eventually, they would run into each other. So another acronym had to be invented: Air Space Total Awareness for Rapid Tactical Execution. In 2020, DARPA went looking for a network that could coordinate everything.[469] The Israelis already had it in something called a "glass battlefield" being built for the Germans, which would network all units together on the battlefield. This was part of Rafael's BNET communications system and Fire Weaver that was supposed to digitize units at the frontline so they wouldn't have to rely on cumbersome mountains of radios and different systems to talk to different units.[470]

Secrets

Somewhere in a hangar, maybe in the western deserts of America, are experimental and classified drones. The super-secret models may be operational, but there are just a handful of them. America always had programs designed to develop new drones that might be used secretly. There are numerous flying-wing designs out there, legacies of the Sentinel-like designs that grew out of the 1990s.[471] A photographer claimed to have seen one of these secret flying wings at the Tonopah test range in 2011.[472]

A web of units is reputed to operate these systems. The air force's 645th Aeronautical Systems Group, dubbed "Big Safari," was supposed to support classified programs. The same was the case with the army's Task Force ODIN, which had been given the MQ-1B Warrior Alphas first. The air force's Forty-Fourth Reconnaissance Squadron operates secretive drones, as does another unit called the 732nd Operations Group, Detachment 1, according to research carried out for *The Verge* by Joseph Trevithick and Tyler Rogoway.[473] Speculation is that some secretive new drone was operating over Syria and Afghanistan between 2017 and 2019. The Pentagon also deployed the secretive "ninja" weapon, which includes a munition with swords that carved up terrorist Abu Khayr al-Masri in Idlib in 2017.

The US was retiring aircraft like the B-1 and A-10, and when you retire machines, you need something new. David Axe at *National Interest* speculated that the air force was buying a new secretive RQ-180 drone in February 2020.[474] Air Force Chief of Staff Gen. David Goldfein had already said that the US was buying aircraft in the "classified realm." That means getting Congress to allocate billions and label it secret. There was a lot of buzz about the RQ-180 in 2013, but the hype faded.[475] With an estimated 130-foot wingspan, it was labeled a B-2 or B-21 lookalike, a giant flying wing rumored to be linked to Northrup Grumman, with a sister made by Lockheed Martin dubbed SR-72.[476] The secret flying wing was reportedly tested in Area 51 at Groom Lake, making it seem even more mysterious and alien.

Most of the story of these new products takes place in the US because that is where the funding and technology exist to work on large experimental projects. Israel had already found its feet in terms of drones and was beavering away at platforms that worked. Other countries like Iran were trying to make as many copies of US drones as they could.

To see where the top American commanders believed the future lies, I reached out to Stephen R. Jones, commander of the 432nd Wing at Creech. He said that the most significant challenge facing MQ-9 aircrews in 2020 and beyond were "contested operations," which means places where the drones come under threats from enemies. "We must meet the demands of using MQ-9s in a near peer fight." That's really what drone wars are about: drones and air defense on both sides. "We're exploring a myriad of technologies and tactics to ensure survivability," he said.[477]

The role of drone pilots was also changing. He said that aircrews were working to integrate with manned missions, going beyond Close Air Support (CAP) to have aircrew certified as on-scene commanders and perform search-and-rescue. The Reapers were also incorporating new munitions, such as GBU-38 JDAM with GPS-guidance precision. The numbers tell the tale. The commanders say that during Inherent Resolve fighting ISIS, the Reapers and Predators launched 7 percent of all munitions in 2015 and 18 percent in 2016.[478]

The World Moves On

Other countries often couldn't get their hands on US drones because of reticence to export armed drones abroad. US allies had to build their own or buy from China. The Israelis had drones of their own, and the

UAE unveiled one of its first locally made drones, the Garmousha, an unmanned helicopter. It got a welcome at a local expo in February 2020. The CEO of Edge, the UAE government-owned corporation that built it, said that the technology for drones was "revolutionizing the world."[479] The UAE's Adcom also built a medium-size drone called the Yabhon, which looks like a flying dolphin. It was sold to Algeria.

Iran was moving forward rapidly, as well. Having unveiled night-vision drones and more suicide drones, it developed-long range drones.[480] Tehran claimed a new drone called Kian could fly 600 miles at up to 15,000 feet in September 2019. A second drone called Fotros was shown off in 2013, and Iran said it could fly 2,000 kilometers for up to thirty hours.[481] By the summer of 2020, Iran said it was arming its drones with missiles.

In reality, some of Iran's drones may not have performed as well as the regime said.[482] The Shahed 129, a copy of a US Predator, crashed near the Pakistani border in 2015. Made by HESA, the Iranian company that had taken over a Bell Helicopter factory after the Iranian Revolution, it was produced for the IRGC and was supposed to be armed with Sadid missiles. American F-15s shot down at least two Shahed 129s in Syria in 2017.[483] In early June of that year, one incident saw a Shahed 129 drop "one of several weapons" near US training facilities at Tanf in Syria.[484]

Meanwhile, in Israel, drone pioneers were also pushing new ideas, particularly in kamikaze drones and VTOL drones. By the early 2000s, Israel's IAI was banking $250 million in UAV sales, about a quarter of the global market.[485] In the fall of 2019, I went on a night mission with Israeli Skylark drone operators. The drone is placed in a large backpack that makes the soldier look like a walking skyscraper. I arrived at night near a field not far from the town of Beit Shemesh. It was wet from rains the day before, and I parked in the mud. Two Humvees were purring nearby, and I stood with soldiers in the cold as we waited for the officers' orders.

After more than thirty minutes of waiting, orders came to begin putting the backpack-drones on and to hike into the hills. We walked down a dirt road that snaked its way between two hills. The drill was to test the soldiers' ability to navigate at night. The idea was to practice lugging these drones into a place like Lebanon and then to use them to aid special forces or vehicles in the fields below. After an hour of slow walking, stumbling over rocks and eroded parts of the road, we came to an area where the hills intersected in a small plateau. It was dark, but there was enough moonlight to see dark shapes on the plateau. Here we came across several female soldiers preparing to launch one of the drones with a catapult, basically a giant slingshot. When it was flung into the air, it flew quietly, like a bat, invisible.

It was getting cold. Eventually, a commander's jeep came humming up the road to take several of us back. The soldiers would practice until dawn. For me, at three in the morning, the exercise was over. I did not envy the soldiers in this unit, with these heavy, backpack drones. There had to be a better way to deploy them or a way to make them smaller. Many Israelis were already working on that solution.

IAI's operations consul for UAVs. As drones have increased in their abilities, operators are tasked with less piloting and focusing more on missions. (Courtesy IAI)

At IAI in central Israel, the company that pioneered drones was tweaking its success with systems that had flown some 1.7 million combat hours by 2019. It was adding capabilities to its Heron line of UAVs, the signature twin-tailed long-endurance surveillance aircraft. These machines had helped revolutionize drone warfare in the 1990s, and IAI had sold them worldwide. The company, closely linked to Israel's government and often staffed by former air force officers, added something called a Tactical Heron in 2019 and the Heron MK II in 2020. It also had the "Super Heron," rolled out in 2014, along with a class of small tactical UAVs called Bird Eye.[486] Launched from a truck or mechanism, it was like similar drones such as the American ScanEagle.

What was IAI's vision for the future? Like most companies, it sold UAVs as a system, with several UAVs and a control station.[487] The company had around twenty countries using its Herons and thirty other users worldwide. In contrast to the American way of using "pilots," Israelis were training "operators." This is an important distinction, because modern technology enabled the drones to take off and return to base automatically. The plane can fly itself, so you fly the mission only. This had come a long way from the old Scout, with its 2.5 hours of flying time and range of 150 kilometers, flown with knobs and joysticks. As with most drone manufacturers, the view of the future was not of redesigning the whole airplane but adding more capabilities to it like sensors, optics, and devices. Every maker of big drones was aware that there probably won't be another F-35, so their drones may be called upon to do much of what the F-35s are currently doing.

The Israeli concept of UAVs, focusing more on missions than on pilots and platforms, was clear from a round of interviews I did in the spring and summer of 2020 with all of Israel's major drone manufacturers. At Elbit Systems, a line of Hermes drones were being tailormade for different customers. One, the Elbit StarLiner, would be certified to fly in civilian airspace in Europe. The StarLiner has the same look as a Predator, the bulbous nose with radar and long wings.[488] This was the next drone revolution, to have them everywhere, including at civilian airports, including doing homeland security, or maritime missions to save sailors. Elbit, for instance, is working with Thales in the UK on its Watchkeeper drones, based on the Hermes 450, used in Afghanistan.

"We're not going to replace dogfights," a former Israeli pilot said to me. That's the reality. It's more about integrating more "sensors" into these aircraft. Because Israeli fighter pilots are often involved in work with these drones, they know what needs to go in them.

Aeronautics, which sells to some seventy-five clients in fifty-six countries, also makes a line of Israeli UAVs. I drove to see the factory floor on June 3, 2020. The company is located in an industrial area of an Israeli city close to sand dunes and the ocean. It was a warm day, just prior to the scorching heat of Israel's summers. Like most Israeli drone makers, the lobby was clean, simple and sterile, and had a monitor playing videos of drones flying around and taking off.

Elbit Systems drones come in many sizes and incorporate the latest technology to make some of them prepared to serve in civilian airspace and a conduct a variety of surveillance missions. (Seth J. Frantzman)

From the smaller tactical surveillance drones similar to the American ScanEagle, to the larger "Dominator" which is actually a civilian-style propeller plane converted into a drone, the company excelled at supplying infantry and police forces. Easy to use and launch, the drones are flown with a kind of large tablet and let the user learn quickly, in weeks, and spend 95 percent of their time focusing on the mission while the drone flies itself. The new Orbiter 4 drone can fly for twenty-four hours and lands with a parachute and airbags. Asked about what might come next, the company predicted seeing more in civilian areas.[489] Once again, the technology is here; it's just a matter of regulations and having the vision to use these machines more.

One type of drone was still controversial. Israel's loitering munitions had now become more mainstream. In the early 2000s, the US had tried to restrict Israel from selling upgrades of its Harpy drone to China. The IAI Harpy looked like a kind of giant triangle with a warhead at the front. IAI showed off the Green Dragon, basically a flying missile, in February 2016. It was billed as a loitering missile for use with small groups of infantry or special forces to help protect them. Launched from a canister from a vehicle, its wings fold out as it flies and searches for a target.[490]

"It's an Olympics now," says Yair Dubester. "You want to carry a lot of fuel and also as many payloads as possible on the same platform, communications intelligence, electronic intelligence, radar, etc." But at the same time, air forces want stealth and precision and weapons and less cost.

The goal of all drone developers was to find a new concept that would work best in the future. Lockheed built the Stalker XE, to which it then added vertical take-off and landing (VTOL) rotors too.[491] The need for more VTOL or helicopter drones was apparent to drone pioneers like Kerem. He founded a new company called Frontier Systems and helped on the program that became the Boeing A-160 Hummingbird.[492] It was the first helicopter that could change its speed and still reduce noise. Initially, the US Army had interest, but as with so many ideas, the interest waned. DARPA's Tony Tether thought the idea was good as well, and that it would eventually reappear. Yair Dubester is also enthusiastic about VTOLs.[493] He points to many companies now experimenting with rotors and a wing so you can take off from anywhere and then save energy by flying with a wing once airborne.[494]

The overall picture a quarter-century after the first Predators took flight is that drone makers are trying to put more into their drones while also trying to fill various niches. For instance, that means making drones more stealth-like and wanting both super-small and larger varieties so that there is a kind of menagerie. While some drone styles, such as the Predator or the twin-tailed Israeli Scout, became an origin of species for numerous similar-looking drones that did the same thing, new species have arrived, such as micro- and mini-drones. The original US classification of drones into high-altitude, medium-altitude, and tier-one tactical drones has expanded.

The problem with militaries is that they don't want a menagerie. They want one dependable platform that does many things. They want a drone that is armed and has long endurance. They want a stealthy drone that can penetrate enemy airspace. And they want something troops at the platoon level or special forces can use, packing it into a battlefield and deploying it. Then they want to mass-produce them.

The US problem in its quest for something better was its constantly shifting priorities among the various services and budget battles with Congress, as well as complacency in terms of threats. Laborious work and funding went into numerous canceled programs, at least in part due to quiet pushback from airmen. Despite all the sexy headlines about the future of warfare and tests being carried out with all sorts of apparently cool and hi-tech products, little came out of the stovepipe.

The real name of the game for drone wars may not be the largest, fastest swarms or even the one with the most missiles, but rather something that is a kind of Model T for drones that is usable and cheap.

Lockheed Martin unveiled its Condor drone, a fixed-wing model, at the 2019 Special Operations Forces Industry Conference in May 2019. Labeled a "group 1" drone, it was built with the US Air Force Research Laboratory for tactical ISR missions and had room for a small amount of equipment and endurance of 4.5 hours.[495] Waterproof and weighing eighteen pounds, it had a twelve-foot wingspan and a 720p HD camera.

With so many products now on offer and the US hesitant to settle on any of them, it was unclear if the Americans would continue their dominance in the drone war in the next decades. China, Russia, Turkey, Iran, and other countries were chomping at the bit. Turkey was already showing what it could do in late February and early March 2020, destroying dozens of Syrian regime vehicles and up to eight Pantsir anti-aircraft weapons the Syrians employed, using Turkish drones. It was the first drone Blitzkrieg.[496] It set the scene for what was to come: warfare in which both sides used drones.

CHAPTER 9

THE COMING DRONE WARS: THE NEW BATTLEFIELD

I n the last ninety-six hours of February 2020, Turkish drones hunted Syrian regime fighters in northwest Syria. The landscape here is pretty, with rolling hills and ancient abandoned cities. Alexander the Great, the Crusaders, Romans, Byzantines, and other great empires had fought here. Each had brought new weapons and strategies. Now in the contest between Turkey and the Russian-backed Syrian regime, the drones would show what might be possible in the future of war.

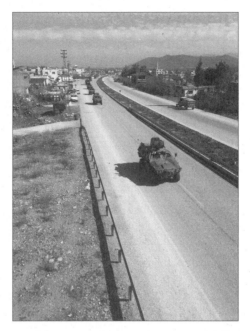

Turkish armed forces on patrol near the border with Syria in 2016.
Turkey pioneered Bayraktar drones and sold them to Azerbaijan, using
them also effectively in Syria and Libya in 2020. (Seth J. Frantzman)

Turkish drones, rolled out in the years before the battle and as yet
mostly untested against armored columns like those the Syrians were
using, made short work of Syria's army. The Syrian regime was overstretched, and its half-fed soldiers, in their battered vehicles, were not
prepared for drone attacks. Ankara boastfully claimed 151 tanks, eight
helicopters, three drones, eighty-six howitzers and one hundred other
armored vehicles were destroyed in Operation Peace Spring in 2020.
Syrian regime media claims that ten Turkish drones were shot down.[497]
This was the first war where drones were used, despite Turkey not controlling the airspace. Turkish drones had to sneak in and attack because
Turkish F-16s couldn't fly in Syria without Russian permission.[498]

The dueling drones in Syria's Idlib and later the use of drones by
Azerbaijan against Armenian forces were a revolution in 2020. While

Syria and Turkey are not the US versus China, the small clash showed what might be coming when drone superpowers fight. Turkey sent in its fleet of Bayraktar TB2s and ANKA-S to fly over Idlib. The Bayraktar, twelve meters long and weighing 650 kilograms, was a simple workhorse, designed to attack and destroy enemies. This was a complex battlefield, with Russians backing the Syrian regime from nearby Latakia but reticent to fight directly against the Turkish army. Similarly, the Syrian regime didn't throw its full weight into the fight. Turkey, too, didn't send its masses of tanks, sitting in Idlib, to crush the regime.

Drones allowed Turkey some plausible deniability. Turkey could show off the videos of drone strikes. There was a kind of dance Turkey had been doing in Syria for years without coming to blows. What matters is not the complex politics but the fact that drones had played a key role in several days of battles and showed that they can help transform a battlefield against armored vehicles.[499]

As Turkey and the Syrian regime tangled near Idlib, Ankara was also sending its drones to Libya to support the Tripoli-based government in a war against the eastern Libya General Khalifa Haftar. Where once Rommel had revolutionized tank warfare in the desert, these warriors were changing the new frontier of drone warfare. Drones had failed to deter terrorists from killing US Ambassador Stevens in 2012. They had returned when the US sent armed drones to target ISIS in 2015 in Libya.[500]

In Libya in 2020, locals were backed by regional powerhouses. The Saudis, Russians, UAE, and French backed Haftar, while Qatar and Turkey backed Tripoli. Drones from China helped Haftar in his offensive, whereas Turkey sent the Tripoli government its own drones. At least two Israeli Orbiter 3 drones, apparently trafficked by Turkey from Azerbaijan, were shot down in July 2019, reports said. An Israeli Harop was also sent by Turkey to Libya. It crashed in the town of Dirj in Libya.[501]

Turkey's drone revolution had happened quickly and quietly, illustrating how a country can build up a drone air force relatively easily with a bit of pluck, copying what works elsewhere. Much as Abe Karem was for the US, a young Turkish innovator named Selcuk Bayraktar became the "dronefather" of Turkey's arsenal. His journey began in 2005, when he applied his engineering background from MIT to interest fellow Turkish politicians in his homemade drone.[502]

Turkey had a handful of drones, such as the Gnat it had acquired from General Atomics, which gives its own drone program an Abe Kerem connection. Later it acquired Israeli Herons. Its Turkish Aerospace Industries built local UAVs. Turkey was moving away from its former close relations with Israel, and it wanted its own program. It was getting intelligence from US drones regarding the PKK, but it wanted armed UAVs. Enter the Anka drone, with its fifty-six-foot wings, in 2010. But it was unarmed.

The Bayraktars, the TB1, and the TB2, rolling off the line in 2014 and after, gave Turkey the killing power it wanted. Soon they were hunting the PKK as the Turkey-PKK ceasefire broke down in 2015. They were flying in Iraq by 2016, conducting their first publicized successful strikes in September 2016. By 2018, the TB2 had flown some 60,000 hours—around 4,500 a month. Using a variety of weapons, primarily the Turkish Roketsan missile, it can strike targets up to eight kilometers away and fly to 25,000 feet for 150 kilometers in range.

The larger Anka-S also came online with missiles in 2018, carrying out a satellite-controlled airstrike. It can fly for up to twenty-four hours and looks like a Predator. At least two, of only sixteen operational, were shot down in Idlib. By contrast, Turkey had around ninety of the Bayraktar TB2s. Turkey's dronefather has gone on to higher things. He married Turkish President Erdoğan's daughter Sümeyye Erdoğan in 2016. His drones are now marketed to Ukraine, Qatar, Tunisia, and other Turkish allies. Now his vision was an even larger drone capable of carrying 1,300 kilograms of missiles called the Bayraktar Akinci, with two turboprops and a sixty-six-foot wingspan.[503] The beast is Turkey's next-generation workhorse armed drone. Turkey can now boast that it is the sixth country to use armed drones alongside the US, Israel, Iran, Pakistan, and China. In truth, its use of drones in Idlib puts it on the cutting edge of using drones as the center of its strategy, which is more than Israel or the US has done.

Dueling drones over the skies of Tripoli and nearby cities remade the battlefield. General Khalifa Haftar, who had fled the Muammar Gadaffi regime and then returned after 2011 to take control of more than half of Libya, was supplied with Chinese-made Wing Loong drones from backers in the UAE. They struck ships and airports.

A source in Haftar's forces said that the Wing Loongs were very effective and highly capable in Libya. He said that they carried out close air support in ways combat aircraft had done in the past. "The drones helped us isolate the enemy in operations against the GNA forces," he said. They used the drones to hunt down GNA supplies and also struck at Turkish drones by targeting their warehouses. This was the first real drone vs. drone war. Each side was using this cheap air force supplied from abroad to conduct operations and try to turn the tide. "We burned their warehouses and their bases," said the Haftar source in April 2020. For Haftar's men, the drones were being used to target "Al Qaeda," whereas Turkey claimed Haftar was a "warlord."

In the battle with the Turkish drones, the LNA fighters said their advantage was that the Turkish Bayraktars have a short range. The battlefield was massive, the same hundreds of miles of desert where German General Erwin Rommel once dueled with the British in the 1940s. The Turks had to add repeating towers to communicate with their drones. Once the LNA grabbed Sirte in January 2020, this frustrated Turkey's maneuvers. Haftar's officers boasted they had shot down fifty Turkish TB2s by April. They used Russian-made air defense and also shoulder-launched missiles. "In one night alone on February 28, we downed six Turkish drones."[504]

Turkey's drones, however, helped the government in Tripoli hold on during a withering offensive by Haftar, who was backed by Moscow, Cairo, and Riyadh. By April 2020, despite the coronavirus pandemic, the Bayraktars were arriving in large numbers. Russian Pantsir air defense systems aided Haftar's men to defend against the threat.[505] This was an issue of prestige for Turkey, especially because the designer of the drone blitz was now part of Erdoğan's family. When a Bayraktar TB2 fell near Nasmah on April 17, it still had its MAM-C missiles. Another Turkish drone was downed days later while trying to bomb a truck.[506] The UAE also lost drones, with one being downed on April 19, 2020.[507] Ankara was still showing its drones could turn the tide in two important conflicts.[508]

The UAE trainers were frazzled. On May 26, a video was surreptitiously recorded inside a Pantsir near Tripoli.[509] Three men sit in front of two screens. On the left is a black and white video. On the right is a video of radar. One man toggles a trigger to decide when to shoot an incoming drone. As it comes in slowly, to just several kilometers, he finally fires and hits it. The men seem confused. Inside the container mounted on a truck, there is no feel for the outside desert heat or the missiles and machine guns mounted on the roof of their container that make up the Pantsir system. The system is a giant box festooned with sets of missiles and guns, with a radar on the roof, like a giant box with sticks on it. It is mounted on a truck chassis. But inside, the users might as well be on the moon. They don't sense the threat of the incoming drone. They laugh and shout "*Allahu Akbar*" when they finally kill the incoming enemy.

On May 18, using Turkish drones, GNA forces struck at Al-Watiya Air Base, a historic base that was full of old Soviet-era equipment Qadafi had once stockpiled. It is southwest of the capital. By 2020, it was a dusty base that was more a museum of Libya's failed history than a modern airbase. But it was a strategic site for the LNA and its operations near Tripoli. Turkish drones swept in and found a Russian-made Pantsir

air-defense system.[510] The drones bombed several hangars, burning the
Pantsir. Then ground forces swept the airbase and took the Pantsir back
to Tripoli on a truck, parading it like war spoils. The next day the LNA
claimed it had downed seven Turkish drones.[511] Libya revealed that
drones could successfully be used against air defense. In pitched battles, drone powers fought each other. Turkey had shown the future of
drone warfare would be using the drones against adversaries with defense
technology, similar to what Iran had proven was possible in attacks on
Saudi Arabia.

The use of drones with ground forces illustrated that even a loose
collection of militias could transform a war with this new technology,
giving it an instant air force. Neither side needed pilots with years of
training. These user-friendly Turkish and Chinese drones showed that
one didn't need billion-dollar price tags or F-35s to fight a drone war
and receive air cover. Libya might be the future, even if it looked like a
chaotic civil war. It was a proxy war for rising powers such as Russia and
Turkey and a testing ground for Chinese technology.

This is exactly the point of drones, Rick Francona says. The veteran
is now a media analyst. He argues drones may not fundamentally change
capabilities, but they complement them and provide the ability to conduct lethal strikes without losing pilots. Neither the UAE nor Turkey
was going to send pilots to Libya. Drones are a unique add-on, he said
in an email.[512]

The drone wars in Libya and Idlib appear small compared to the
American multi-billion-dollar drone programs, but they are important
because they illustrate both the proliferation of drone technology and
how drones are being used today. First, the drones have become a kind
of poor man's air force for countries in a civil war that lack the funds and
stability to build or acquire a real air force. Second, they are easy to ship
and get around arms embargoes. Third, they are an easy way to harass
an enemy without training precious pilots for years. Most soldiers can

learn to fly a sophisticated drone the way they play a video game, because drones do so much of the work autonomously.

Finally, these small wars are a testing ground for new technology and a way for China, Turkey, and others to see if their systems work as well as the "big boys" like America or Israel and their state-of-the-art drones that have dominated since the 1980s. In much the same way that Israel first used drones to powerful effect against the Syrians in the 1980s, so Turkey did once again in Idlib. Is Turkey the new Israel of drones? Probably not. The numbers tell us why Israel and America are still on top. The drone wars in Africa were small but consequential. Near Libya, France was operating drones as part of Operation Barkhane, flying them over Niger and Chad. Armenia and Azerbaijan were also squaring off with drones.

Big Drone

The drone market was estimated to expand to $83 billion between 2019 and 2027, according to Teal Group's World Military Unmanned Aerial Systems market profile.[513] This includes increases from $8.3 billion in spending from 2018 to an estimated $13 billion by 2027. The US was building 1,179 larger drones and medium-sized drones in 2017 and would be building up to 2,500 by 2026. Most money would go into new combat vehicles, and the high- and medium- altitude drones. Less money would be plowed into smaller tactical UAVs.[514] By 2020, estimates put spending at even more, some $98 billion over ten years.[515]

The Drone Databook in 2019 estimated there were some 30,000 military UAVs, with most being smaller types, which they called "Class I," or under 150 kilograms. Eighty-five countries were using these, while only forty-four countries were using drones between 150 kilograms and 600 kilograms, called Class II; thirty-one countries were using large Class III drones over 600 kilograms. Numerous countries were seeking to acquire the larger Class III drones.[516] The number of countries using military drones was rapidly expanding, from around sixty in 2010 to almost one hundred by 2020.

What would they be buying? With the growing popularity of drones comes a mountain of new publications and interest in them, leading to a fascination with ranking and dividing drones into various categories. Among the favorites were the Blackjack, Fire Scout, Triton, Wasp, Shadow, ScanEagle, Reaper, Heron, Hermes, CH-5, Yabhon United 40, Wing Loong II, and Anka.

Who is buying the most drones? A *Jane's* market forecast says that the US will buy another 1,000 larger combat drones by 2029, while China will only buy sixty-eight, Russia forty-eight, India thirty-four, and then fewer by Australia, Egypt, Turkey, Malaysia, Indonesia, and Israel.[517] Meanwhile, the US will buy more than 43,000 lightweight surveillance drones as compared with 8,000 for China, 6,000 for Russia, 5,000 for India, 2,000 for France, and 2,000 for Israel. Because much of the information about the number of missions flown by drones in countries such as Russia, China, or Turkey is secret, and Western countries keep most details classified, there are only some minor points of light out there regarding how many missions drones actually conduct. *The Guardian* points out that the UK flew drones over Iraq and Syria between 2014 and 2018, carrying out 398 airstrikes with Reapers and 2,423 Reaper missions. Drone strikes were around 23 percent of total UK airstrikes and 42 percent of missions in the anti-ISIS campaign in Iraq and Syria. The data reveals that while UAVs might now be flying up to half the missions, they were not conducting the majority of strikes for the UK.[518]

Israel Aerospace Industries Barak air defense system firing at night. The system has been supplied to India and is one of Israel's many air defense systems. (Courtesy IAI)

Despite the massive expansion in the number of countries acquiring drones, the US still was the overwhelming user of armed drones and sophisticated, expensive surveillance drones. However, that monopoly was rapidly weakening in 2020. New America, a non-partisan think tank that focuses on rapid technological and social change in US policy, maintains a list of countries that it says have conducted drone strikes. This includes the US since 2001, Israel since 2004, the UK since 2008, Pakistan in 2015, Iran, Nigeria, Azerbaijan, Iraq, and Turkey in 2016, the UAE in 2018, and Russia and France in 2019. Most countries don't even have armed drones, and if they do, they buy them from only a handful of countries that excel at drone warfare. The drone warrior nations include the US, China, South Africa, and Israel, according to New America.[519] Turkey should be added to that list.

One of the main reasons that most countries don't have armed drones is they don't have the indigenous ability to build them or have not invested in developing them. This isn't that different than other military technology. Most countries don't build their own tanks, submarines, or warplanes. The expansion of drone use was also reduced because the US didn't want to export armed drones and preferred a monopoly on these platforms. That began to change a bit under the Trump administration, but for the most part the world's drone superpower hogged them to itself. There were some exceptions. Italy has armed its Reapers with Hellfire missiles. A few countries are now trying to get in the game, with France, Switzerland, Sweden, Spain, Greece, and Italy investing in a European UCAV project.

The European project involved tests of the futuristic Dassault nEU-ROn, which looks like the US X-45. It was tested between 2012 and 2016 alongside the BAE Systems Taranis, which first flew in 2013. Together, the technology was combined for the Future Combat Air System, which foresaw a carrier-capable UAV that could include swarming technology and work as a "loyal wingman" for the sixth-generation fighter by 2035. The Eurodrone project also foresaw a medium-altitude drone that would be in place by 2025.

Bickering over costs was ever-present. French Defense Minister Florence Parly slammed the project in June 2019 as being too expensive. Europe was not in a hurry. Concepts like Mantis, a large twin-engine drone prototype built by BAE systems in 2009, sat around for a decade with little progress. They would have to continue to rely on US drones. The 2010s were, in some ways, a lost decade in Europe and the US when it came to drones. The UK was nevertheless testing its own armed drones, and the UAE and Turkey were building new drones. For countries that didn't have their own drones in Europe, leasing them from Israel was one option. Israel's IAI sold Greece on a lease deal in early 2020, where a third company supplies the pilots, and Greece gets the surveillance.[520] Subcontracting drones might be the future of surveillance, but not of armed drones. The elephant in the room was obviously China, which has huge potential in building and selling armed drones.

As the glass ceiling of a kind of old boys' network of drone users came crumbling down in 2020, the overall picture was still of a powerful America and a bunch of other countries trying to keep up. For instance, in 2013, the Network for Social Change of the Oxford Research Group commissioned a report for the Remote Control Project. They wanted to focus on unmanned combat air vehicles (UCAV). They identified only six important countries that were building and pioneering sophisticated armed drones. With 200 different UAVs in use at the time by militaries, they found only twenty-nine UCAVs. The vast majority of drones were unarmed and doing surveillance work. But the future is coming, with armed drones carrying and doing more. "China has the most diverse UCAV inventory, though Israel leads the way in terms of technology and export," the report noted.[521]

The study mapped the existing world of drones. For instance, it found Israel had fifty-two types of UAVs, of which four were UCAV. Russia had fifty-four drones and five UCAVs. China had forty-six different UAVs and eleven UCAVs. Iran had seventeen different UAVs, of which six were armed. India had twenty-one UAVs and six UCAVs. By 2019, the Center for the Study of the Drone at Bard found ten countries (Azerbaijan, Iraq, Israel, Iran, Pakistan, Nigeria, Turkey, the UAE, UK, and US) had used drones to carry out strikes. Another thirty countries were acquiring or had drones that could carry out airstrikes.

The International Institute for Strategic Studies concluded in 2019 that the US had 495 "heavy unmanned aerial vehicles." It believed China had twenty-six similar large drones, while France had five, India thirteen, Russia "some," and the UK nine.[522] The Center for the Study of the Drone's 2019 *Drone Handbook* concluded that the UK had ten Reapers. Overall, the IISS study doesn't confirm the *Drone Handbook*'s statistics, which illustrates that in many cases the estimates for the number of large drones or armed drones are unknown or shrouded in some secrecy.

What may be better known is that countries are acquiring masses of smaller drones, such as India seeking to acquire 1,800 smaller tactical drones or the Philippines doing the same with mini-drones. Manila wanted some 1,000 Israeli-made THOR little quadcopters, the catapult-launched Skylark, and medium-sized Hermes 450.[523] The deal is an example of how countries are rapidly trying to acquire a multi-layered drone arm, a kind of instant air force. They piggy-back on decades of development to fill an increasingly clear need to have drones at the ready against enemies. China was about to make sure that would happen.

Soaring Dragon

Sheikh Mohammed bin Zayed, crown prince of the UAE and architect of its foreign policy, was tired of asking. In June 2004, he met with US Brig. Gen. Ronald Yaggi, director of regional affairs for the deputy undersecretary of the US Air Force for international affairs. He had been complaining to the US for years that the UAE needed not only drones but armed Predators to help its mission in Afghanistan, where its special forces were located. It also wanted to use them to project power for the UAE. The US had been saying no, only an unarmed Predator could be sent. This was humiliating.

He reached out to the Department of Defense and State Department. The UAE would not keep begging, he told Yaggi. "There are a lot of offers," he said, to help the UAE develop its own indigenous drones or to sell it other options. With its bustling cities on the Persian Gulf, the emirate, just across from Iran, was already working with the South Africans and their Seeker II UAVs. They had sent those aircraft to Bagram in Afghanistan. They were now willing to work with South Africa, France, Germany, Italy, China, even Israel. "It is under study," he said. The UAE would eventually have the same capabilities as the US, one way or another.[524] While the decision to approach US allies and European countries such as Israel, France, Germany, or Italy was understandable, as was choosing a democracy such as South Africa, the word China stuck out. China might be supplanting the US in the Gulf, where the US Fifth Fleet and CENTCOM are based.

China was coming with drones.

In the 1990s, as China looked to its future needs, it began to acknowledge US and foreign military developments in drone technology. Beijing identified the UAV trend and sought to learn from what was being done abroad to integrate the technology with its own military. This was a multi-pronged effort. China's rapidly growing economy could develop drones for export and also for its own military. It had the industrial might necessary to develop drones, and hundreds, perhaps thousands, of different types could be rolled off the line. In 2004, at an Asian Aerospace convention in Singapore, Yang Ying, the vice president of the China National Aero Technology Import and Export Corporation (CATIC), said that it was the trend of customers in the world to have "reconnaissance, intelligence and long endurance" for UAVs.[525]

China had received types of drones and UAVs over the years from abroad, used for various missions, including as target drones or for mineral surveys. For instance, the Soviet Lavochkin La-17C was reverse-engineered by China to make the Changkong-1, a target drone. The drones China chose to develop were first modeled on foreign successes. Like Israel, China learned from experience of the US Ryan Firebee, building the WZ-5 and Chang Hong (CH-1) in the 1980s. It also modeled the GAIC WZ-9 on the US Global Hawk, which it birthed in the early 2000s.[526] The Chinese versions of the Global Hawk were called Xianglong or Soaring Dragon. With an initial estimated range of 4,000 miles and a length of forty-five feet, it could fly at 460 miles per hour.[527] A model was presented in 2006 at the Zhuhai air show, the usual curtain-raiser for China's drones, and tests were conducted in 2008, with a first flight in 2009.[528] Built by Chengdu and Guizhou, its design changed rapidly from a bizarre quadruple tail and wing with rudders to a sleeker design with an engine mounted near the tail like a Global Hawk.

Deploying drones to the military was another level of sophistication. By 2006, China had deployed for its ground forces several drones labeled ASN or Aisheng, built by Xian Northwestern Polytechnical University UAV Research Institute. Some early ASN drones were based on Israeli Skylarks. ASN-104 was shot off the ground with a rocket and had a wingspan of four meters. It could fly two hours up to 300 kilometers. ASN-105B could fly for seven hours and had GPS, landing with a parachute.[529] Later, the ground forces got an unmanned helicopter called Z-3. The ASN technology would increase rapidly, eventually fielding an advanced UAV ASN-206 that could fly day and night with infrared cameras for up to 150 kilometers and loiter for eight hours up to 6,000 meters.[530] The ASN-206 had a resemblance to other twin-tail drones such as the Hunter. ASN was believed to control 90 percent of China's UAV market through 2013.[531]

Much of China's development followed a similar pattern. Drones would be unveiled at an airshow, and then new models would be developed for export. In 2004, the first design of a Predator lookalike appeared. In 2006, at the Zhuhai International Airshow, China showed off its BZK-005 made by Beijing University of Aeronautics and Astronautics and Harbin aircraft industry, which bore a resemblance to the US Predator. It could fly up to 170 kilometers per hour up to 8,000 meters and could carry up to 150 kilograms in ordnance.[532] It was supposed to be able to fly for up to forty hours.[533] Believed to be operational by 2009, combining China's latest attempt to make it stealthier than the Predator, it was provided to the navy and the PLA air force.[534] It wasn't stealthy enough, though, and when it flew over islands in the South China Sea in April 2018, Japanese aircraft were scrambled to track it and photograph it.[535]

Meanwhile, Beihang University, a descendant of Beijing University of Aeronautics in Beijing, then built on the BZK-005 design to create the TYW-1 in 2017 for export.[536] Wang Jianping of Beihang said he hoped it would tap markets in Southeast Asia and the Middle East. At home,

China also put new technologies on the drone, adding synthetic aperture radar in 2020 to a drone that previously had an EO/IR pod on it.[537]

By 2015, China was estimated to be building 42,000 military drones over the next eight years, including stealth models. One of those models was called the Dark Sword (Anjian), and the technological advances were being noticed abroad. As the US continued to concentrate on fighting terrorists, China sought to outpace the Americans by wooing customers and showing off its new capabilities.[538] It also wanted to muscle around its neighbors. Japan had begun increasing deployment of drones in 2007.[539] China would be coming after it over disputed islands.

A video of the dark blue futuristic flying-wing design called Lijiang, based on the X-47, was put online and then removed, garnering some 250,000 views. Next, a Chinese UAV flew near Japan's airspace in 2013, and Japan scrambled jets to intercept it. China was using drones to show its capabilities over the Diaoyu-Senkaku islands.[540] More island over-flights in May 2017 would lead to another near air-to-air clash. China was also beginning to do armed drone strikes. It had monitored a drug kingpin in Myanmar and considered using drones to kill him.

China then hosted multilateral exercises in Inner Mongolia, where they carried out strikes with the participation of Russia, Kazakhstan, and Kyrgyzstan. It carried out at least fifteen missile strikes using the Wing Loong by 2014. From only an estimated 280 UAVs in 2011, China soon had thousands. Washington was alarmed.[541] Beijing rapidly went from learning from the US to saying its versions of the Reaper, the CH-4, and the CH-5 were better.[542] The CH-5, for instance, could fly for sixty hours, more than twice the Reaper, China said.[543]

Drones were a logical place for China to excel, because they were a new technology. Unlike US dominance at sea, or with tanks, or advanced airplanes like the F-35, China's abilities at mass production and mass experimentation with numerous models gave it an edge. It also didn't have the concerns about budgets or interservice rivalry that seemed to upend US projects, and it had a hunger for new weapons that it wanted to show off. Its pilots also didn't get to lobby the air force against drones. They followed orders. In a system that values the collective over individualism, China was less likely to listen to pilots' griping as a reason not to have as many UAVs. It also wasn't concerned with being accused of copying or reverse engineering existing foreign designs. Lastly, it preferred large numbers of new segmented items, each with its own skill, to jamming everything into one product the way the Americans did with the Global Hawk.

Breakthrough

China was supposed to be so far behind the US in drone development that Washington didn't take it into account. Its spending was far less, with budgets still estimated in the $10 billion range in 2015, and its version of multi-billion dollar US programs costing much less. The Lijiang "stealth" drone, for instance, was said to cost only $1 million. Such low-cost drones couldn't possibly compete or have all the hi-tech of US counterparts.[544]

Much of that began to change after 2010, culminating in a dramatic reveal in 2018. The 2018 Zhuhai airshow featured a large number of Chinese companies that rolled out new stealth drones that appeared to have taken designs the US had partly abandoned, and built on them. The air show illustrated China's emergence as a defense industrial power, commentators argued, all part of President Xi Jinping's overall commitment to transforming China's defense technology.[545]

To complete with the Global Hawk, the Guizhou company built a similar-looking aircraft in the early 2000s.[546] In 2013, China's AVIC tested an armed drone called Sharp Sword (GJ-11) before embarking on an ambitious effort to build numerous armed UAVs.[547] The GJ-11 showed that China could build an armed drone or UCAV in secret. Similar to the Boeing Phantom Ray and European Neuron, it could carry up to 500-kilogram bombs.[548]

The turning point was the CH-7 based on the Northrop X-47 Pegasus. Unveiled in 2018 at Zhuhai, it was considered a stealthy, sub-sonic long-range drone.[549] With a long, sweeping grey wing of twen-ty-two meters, it was unveiled in front of the neon blue billboard of the China Aerospace Science and Technology Corporation banner. It was modern, hi-tech, and sexy.[550] The CH-7 was named after the word for rainbow, *Caihong*, and was built by the state-owned China Aerospace Science and Technology Corporation. The same company was already exporting the CH-4, which looks like the Predator. In 2015, the com-pany said that its total value of contracts was one of the highest in the world, according to Shi Wen, its chief drone designer at the China Academy of Aerospace Aerodynamics in Beijing. The "academy" is part of China Aerospace Science and Technology Corporation. It said it was exporting to ten countries and twenty "users."[551]

In contrast to the US, where complexity was the norm and the air force had wanted to dominate piloting the drones, China's pitch was that anyone could use them: if you can fly a flight simulator, you can fly a drone. The CH line had sold 200 drones by 2014. Customers already included Egypt, Pakistan, Nigeria, the UAE, and countries in South Asia. The company's drones could fire missiles at a stand-off range of ten kilometers and stay in the air for ten hours. By 2015, the drones were flying one hundred hours a month.[552]

The Chengdu Aerospace Corporation also built a fleet of drones that appear like stealthy flying wings, similar to US designs, which it showed off at Zhuhai in 2018. Another similar design was unveiled by the China Aerospace Science and Industry Corporation as part of its Sky Hawk line of drones.[553] Already China's CH series, which look like US Reapers and Predators, had been sold to militaries in ten countries, and the CASC company that built them had become the largest armed drone family China was exporting.[554] Between 2008 and 2018, around half (53 percent) of the country's large military drone exports were Wing

Loongs, and 34 percent were the CH models. ASN models made up only ten percent.[555]

In 2018, the GJ-2 or Wing Loong II, built by Chengdu (CAIG), was also unveiled. It had played a role already in China's "anti-terrorism" fight, China's air-force spokesperson Shen Jinke said.[556] The anti-terror campaign was likely China's increased desire to control Xinjiang, where there was a low-level Uighur insurgency. Like the US in Afghanistan, it appears China modeled its anti-terror operations in the deserts and mountains on a successful campaign across the border. Wing Loong drones were based at Kashi Air Base and conducted operations.[557] China's drone wars were raising eyebrows. The US Department of Defense had believed that Israel, the US, and the UK had the market cornered on drones. But the Chinese were coming.[558] The assumption of American and Israeli dominance was being eroded.

For Washington, the decision not to export armed drones was self-imposed. The US was one of thirty-five signatories to the Missile Technology Control Regime, which sought to impose controls of exports of missiles or drones that could carry 500 kilogram payloads more than 300 kilometers.[559] From 2015, the US began to reexamine the self-imposed exile that the MTCR was placing it in, as China and others sought to sell to US customers such as Egypt, Jordan, the UAE, and others. Iran, China, and other countries were not signatories of the agreement and could skirt it.[560] The State Department hobbled US defense companies by seeking to adhere to strict end-use assurances. Basically, the diplomats didn't want US drones being used in war crimes by allies.[561]

Things began to change for US exports after President Donald J. Trump took office. By April 2018, the administration realized it had to keep up with China on the drone sales frontier.[562] But it wasn't enough. US officials complained that China was "selling the hell" out of drones in February 2019 at an arms fair in the Gulf.[563]

In 2011, attendees at the Zhuhai air show had "swarmed" around a model of a sleek drone targeting what "appeared to be a US aircraft carrier" near an island that looked like Taiwan. The message was clear.[564] The drones were not totally ready, though. A Chinese drone reportedly crashed in a forest in Xingtai, Hebei Province, after takeoff from Shahezhen Airfield in 2011.[565]

In May 2015, California Republican Congressman Duncan Hunter had expressed concern to the Obama administration that China had sent a delegation to Jordan to discuss drone sales. He encouraged leasing US Predators to the Jordanians.[566] China had already sold drones to Iraq, and Iraq said its CH-4s had carried out numerous airstrikes on ISIS. The UAE began purchasing Wing Loongs in 2013, seeking to buy hundreds of Wing Loong IIs in 2018.[567] China would sell more large Wing Loong and CH-series drones to Pakistan, Saudi Arabia, and Serbia by 2019.

The Americans knew that China had been developing drones for years. Reports in 2013 had revealed a hacking operation in Shanghai directed at defense contractors, trying to look for drone technology. The US also knew the Wing Loong had been exported in 2011 with laser-guided missiles.[568] A 2013 study had concluded that Chinese drones didn't have the range to do what the Americans were doing, but that as they increased in abilities, they could be used to guide long-range missiles such as the DF-21D anti-ship missile.[569] A US task-force report in 2012 for the Department of Defense concluded that China's role was a "worrisome trend." It had ramped up research faster than other countries. China was "not constrained by many of the normal political processes found in democratic governments," the US complained. Chinese drones were already probing Japanese ships, including flying a drone between Miyakojima island and Okinawa. The scope and speed of China's development was a "wakeup call."

Washington's military experts were worried what war might bring. The US was not worried about an attack on "CONUS," the term for the contiguous US, but it was more concerned about attacks elsewhere. The US had air defense that could be deployed. But China's new drones could pose the greatest threat since the Soviet-era MiG-25 Foxbat. An enemy like China could use drones to target carriers. "The threat could be extended to rear echelon supply convoys and other combat support assets which have not had to deal with an airborne threat in generations." This kind of instant air force could slaughter US troops in an attrition war and be easily replaceable. The US envisioned an enemy using Global-Hawk-type drones, such as the Chinese variant, to track US ship movements.

A nightmare scenario came into focus. An enemy with large numbers of UAVs would make US planning overly complex. The US also didn't have enough dedicated defensive capabilities to deal with them all, meaning using MANPADs and fighter jets to hunt for them. "It could expose US forces to surprise attack or ambush. To the extent that enemy UAVs presented a credible strike capability, and absent air supremacy, US forces could be forced to disperse and rely on unit-level air defense."[570]

China's rapid development of drones led to a niche industry of spotters trying to find them on the ground and on satellite images. The Soaring Dragon was a favorite because it was big and easy to spot.[571] First found in 2011, in 2018 Bellingcat noted that the Soaring Dragon had been deployed to the Yishuntun Airbase as well as in Tibet at Shigatse and at Lingshui on Hainan Island.[572] Commentators noted how much its design had changed when it was spotted in flight in 2019.[573] It was clearly working by this time because it shadowed the USS *Antietam* in the Taiwan Straits in July 2019.[574] The massive twin-body, twin-tail, monstrous Divine Eagle was spotted first in 2015 and then in May 2018.[575] China knew people were watching and lined up many of its UAVs on a tarmac in Malan in the fall of 2019. Like a kind of petting zoo, these high-altitude monsters could be seen alongside swarms of smaller UAVs and a UAV helicopter as well as several stealth designs such as the Tian Ying, Sharp Sword, and CH-7. The jet-powered Cloud Shadow was also on display.[576]

In October 2019, China decided to put the full might of its drone army on display at celebrations marking the seventieth anniversary of

Communist rule. It showed off a supersonic stealth UAV that could be launched from a plane, such as the twin-engine large bomber H-6.[577] This was the WZ-8, a reconnaissance UAV for the PLAAF's Thirtieth Air Regiment. It was supposed to operate from an airbase in Jiangsu Province called Luhe-Ma'an.[578]

Powered by liquid propellant, which made it cheaper, the vehicle could return to base or be disposable. Also at the parade was a Flying Dragon 1 (Feilong-1) that was built by Zhongtian Feilong Technology and had flown priorly in Shaanxi Province. New antennas were put on the Wing Loong and the Sharp Sword. There seemed no shortage of new drones for China because so many companies were involved in pitching new products. The Nanjing Research Institute for Simulation Techniques has designed a surveillance UAV, while Beijing Wisewell Avionics Science and Technology, which is run by Aviation Industry Corporation of China (AVIC), produces the AW-4 Shark UAV and the AW-12A. The US and Western powers watched with growing angst. A future conflict with China or Russia could now be a two-front UAV drone war against increasingly sophisticated enemies.[579]

Xi Jinping, China's pragmatic leader, was pleased. Having come to office in 2012, he was now able to show off the country's abilities. Not only did it have more types of drones than all its adversaries, it was also on its way to being a leading exporter of military drones, having already become the leading civilian-drone exporter. Where Israel had dominated drone exports in the 1980s and 1990s, China had become the world leader in military-drone exports by 2019.[580] From 2008 to 2017, China exported sixty-eight larger combat drones compared with the US, which only sent sixty-two abroad. Israel sold fifty-six.[581] From 2014 to 2018, the Stockholm International Peace Research Institute said that Beijing became the largest exporter of unmanned combat aerial vehicles. What this meant was that China had sold 153 UCAVs to thirteen countries from 2014 to 2018, while the US sent only five in the same period. Iran sent a few to Syria, while the UAE sold two to Algeria. *Foreign Policy* concluded China had "won" the drone wars by 2018.[582] Everyone seemed to tout China's proclivity in this realm with only a few nagging questions about why Jordan had appeared to want to get rid of the Chinese drones it bought by June 2019.[583]

China's army had embraced drones and wanted to show them off at its 2019 military parade. The potential customers were growing rapidly, from around sixty countries using drones in 2010 to ninety-five countries in 2019.[584] The Center for the Study of the Drone at Bard also concluded in 2019 that China was also working on eleven future development programs, more than other countries.[585] By the summer of 2020, China's drones had helped propel it to be the second biggest arms exporter in the world with some seventy large sales to Saudi Arabia, sixty to Egypt, and twenty-five to Pakistan over the years.[586] From smaller drone swarms to a hypersonic glide missile that was also labeled a UAV, China was now at the forefront in many ways. It had accomplished this without firing a shot. Thousands of miles away, over the misty mountains of Tibet and across the deserts of Central Asia, another drone power was also rising to challenge the West.[587]

The Bear Meets the Drone

A MiG-29 Russian fighter pilot got an order he was not expecting on April 20, 2008. He was to fly over Abkhazia, a disputed area controlled by separatists backed by Russia, and shoot down a surveillance drone that Georgia was using. The drone had crossed a 1990s-era ceasefire line at 9:31 a.m. The Russian was on his way by 9:48 a.m., and the Georgian operator of the drone tried to take evasive action. He turned the drone abruptly toward the south. The MiG-29, flying from Gudauta Airfield, found the drone at a height of 2,800 meters. It fired an AA-11 Archer missile that exploded just fifty feet from the target, destroying it.[588]

After the pilot had downed the Georgian drone, the Russian Ministry of Foreign Affairs said that Abkhazia air defense had shot down an Israeli-built Hermes 450, serial number 553. In March, another Elbit Hermes 450, serial number 551, had been shot down. More Hermes would be shot down in May.[589] The battle over Abhazia eventually led to a full-scale war in August 2008 between Georgia and Russia. Georgia, a much smaller country, was defeated in five days.

Despite Georgia's defeat, its drones had proved indispensable. Russia's UAVs were antiquated and vulnerable. Russia recognized its deficiency and quickly bought twelve drones from Israel's IAI for $53 million. These included the Searcher II, BirdEye, and other models. The Searcher is a stocky-looking drone that builds on the legacy of the Scout with the twin-tail and boxy fuselage. It's not sexy. The BirdEye, by contrast, is a stealthy-looking drone that resembles a boomerang. Launched by catapult, it can fly for several hours and conduct tactical surveillance.

That Russia needed the Israeli drones was an accident of history. The Soviets had built numerous futuristic aircraft. They also built fast rocket-propelled drones like the Tupolev TU-123 and TU-141. These things were basically a giant jet engine with a spear-like body that could do surveillance. It isn't clear how they worked, but they were similar to the machines the US used over Vietnam. However, like the American version, this nascent program never grew into anything, and the drone models were left to rot in fields like the Soviet Union writ large.

After the experiences in 2008, Moscow under Putin got back into UAVs. Soon Russia was buying hundreds of millions of dollars' worth of drones.[590] Russia's deals paid off. Israel reduced its defense ties with Georgia, and Russia began investing up to $13 billion in drones to expand their UAV arm by 2020. Poorer Georgia could only replace its Israeli drones with cheaper local variants.

Russia's drone army grew in fits and starts. Two companies, Sokol and Tanszas, won $33 million in contracts to design a heavy long-distance high-altitude drone and a smaller attack drone called Altius and Inokhodyets (Wanderer) in 2011. Russian Defense Minister Sergei Shoigu got a look at the Altius in 2013 in Tatarstan.[591] It finally publicly flew an Altius-U in 2019, asserting that the large drone with twin propellers could stay in the air for twenty-four hours. Russia also designed a stealth drone that looks like the X-47 and had the uninviting name "Skat."

Russia's drone war strategy got a test in Ukraine in 2014. After protests toppled the pro-Russian president of Ukraine, the country was split by civil war. Separatists in the east were pro-Russian, and Russian drones such as the Orlan-10, a small grey miniature airplane, were deployed to help Russia target the Ukrainian army.[592] The Orlan-10 was similar to the Israeli Skylark. Catapult-launched, it was a small reconnaissance drone that could fly up to 140 kilometers for sixteen hours. The Russians also used the Forpost, which was also modeled on the Israeli IAI Searcher Mark II. It was stronger: with a range of some 250 kilometers, it could carry 100 kilograms and fly up to 20,000 feet. Russia zeroed in on Ukraine's Ninety-Second Mechanized Brigade in August 2014. Using drones to guide the artillery, it ripped apart the Ukrainians.

The Ukrainian army became wary of the buzzing of drones. But Ukraine also wanted drone war revenge, and a bevy of private groups began funding small UAVs to fight the Russian bear.[593] They packed them with the usual video links and infrared cameras. In October 2018, Ukraine's Antonov unveiled a UAV with a seventy-foot wing that could go to 40,000 feet. The war was rapidly becoming, like other conflicts, a testing ground for new technology and fueling innovation.[594] Russia's goal when it began was to slow Ukraine's offensive and cut off parts of eastern Ukraine into new statelets, as it had done in Georgia.

I went to the Donbas frontline in Ukraine in August 2018. Flying into Kiev, I was greeted with a youthful, bustling, and beautiful city. It was pleasant in the summer, and teenagers crowded the streets at night, drinking and having fun. But a grueling war was taking place in the east, in areas once scarred by the great tank battles of the Second World War between Nazism and the Soviet Red Army. Now new technology was transforming this front as T-34 tanks once made the Red Army invincible. The long train ride to the east passed areas the Ukrainian army had retaken from Russian-backed separatists in 2014 and 2015. At the last station before the front, I got off and met a driver who had conducted prisoner negotiation swaps for the Ukrainians during the course of the war.

A Ukrainian Donbas Battalion volunteer cleans his rifle near the frontline in 2018. Like many conflicts, drones became more common in Ukraine even though most soldiers on the front had no protections against them or access to use them. (Seth J. Frantzman)

This part of Ukraine was flat, filled with small cottages and towns that looked little changed from the Soviet era. Ukrainian flags were common. In a store, we stocked up on local processed meats and beer. In the town of Marinka, the houses had sandbags to protect windows from shelling. There were small homes on streets laid out in a grid, with a large brick building marking the old school and government hub. The frontline ran right along one line of civilian homes. Dug in with trench lines and concrete shelters from artillery fire among the houses, the Ukrainians watched the separatists across a kilometer of ground. There was supposed to be a ceasefire, but it didn't seem to cover small arms, mortars, and drones. We could hear the drones buzzing around from time to time at dusk. The Ukrainians had no defense against them, and they could be used to aid separatist artillery to rain fire on us. Our only protection was an earthen bunker with boards and sandbags covering it.

The feeling in Ukraine was like in Mosul. We were exposed and vulnerable. We could hear the drone but not see it or do anything about it. It was a constant little buzzing, coming and going as it traversed the front. Together with two Ukrainian military personnel, one tall with thick hair, the other stocky and bald, we ducked into a covered part of the frontline, earth on one side, sandbags on the other. I stood with them, waiting for the buzzing to pass.

Along hundreds of miles of frontline, the Ukrainians dealt with daily drone flights from the Russian side. In 2018 there had been at least 741 drone flights from the Russian side.[595] Ukrainian officials complained that sanctions against Russia had not dented their drone army. Russia was packing the drones with plenty of dual-use cameras from places like Japan and Sweden, and engines from Germany, as well as parts from China and Israel. Russia used drones for more than just spotting. It also used them to spread misinformation, including text messages telling soldiers to kill their commanding officers. Russia's gamechanger in this case was a Leer-3 RB-341V truck that has provided the Orlan with the ability to disable cell networks and send its own messages. Russia had used it in Syria prior to sending it to Ukraine as well in 2017.[596] Paul Taylor of Enterprise Control Systems said electronic measures could be used against the drones. Ukraine innovated to shoot down the drones, using helicopters and small arms.[597]

Russia's drone experience in Ukraine was relegated mostly to small drones used to harass the Ukrainians. With a ceasefire in place, there wasn't going to be any strategic role for the flying beasts. Back in Moscow, though, things were not going smoothly for the hi-tech part of Russia's drone program. The builders of the Altius high-altitude armed drone were detained by authorities in 2018. Later the project was transferred to the Urals and the Ural Civil Aviation Plant (UZGA). The defense ministry was hot on acquiring new drones. It was developing the Outpost drone, also based on the Israeli Search II. Shoigu, the defense czar, wanted more, though, including up to 4,000 UAVs by the end of 2020.

Winners and Losers

The rapid deployment of drones in war and the expansion of the market for military drones have led to a system of drone alliances. In many ways, this is similar to how US and Soviet military technology was exported to allies during the Cold War. The difference today is that the growth of drone superpowers has largely occurred in the shadow of the US victory in the Cold War. What this means is that the US emerged from the 1990s as a global hegemon, advocating a new world order. That world order was shaped by America's drone wars. The US used drones in the Gulf War, then the Balkans, and during the war on terror. However, relying on this weapon transformed the American way of war. The US's reticence to put boots on the ground and fear of casualties was well suited to drone warfare. At the same time, the controversies that grew out of targeted drone strikes and assassinations caused the US to be wary of exporting its new deadly technology. It had become proficient at killing but didn't want others doing the same.

The result, thirty years after the end of the Cold War, was a group of rising powers that were using drones to challenge American dominance. While Israel is a US ally, Turkey was quickly drifting away from

NATO, signing air defense deals with Russia and challenging US policies in Syria. Turkey used its drones to carve out a sphere of influence in Syria, Iraq, Qatar, and Libya. Its drones were a major tool in challenging the Saudi Arabia-UAE alliance that was involved in isolating Qatar and supporting Haftar in Libya. Drones also helped rip apart the PKK after the Turkey-PKK ceasefire broke down in 2015. After using drones against the PKK inside Turkey, Turkey then used the drones effectively in northern Iraq against PKK bases in the mountains. Ankara used drones again in October 2019 when it invaded eastern Syria and attacked the US-backed Syrian Democratic Forces. This was practice for what Turkey would eventually achieve in the campaign against the Assad regime in February 2020 and in Libya.

China was also filling the US power vacuum, selling its CH-4B and Wing Loong drones to countries where the US had influence, such as Iraq, Jordan, Saudi Arabia, the UAE, and Pakistan. Chinese drones were now spreading their wings around Asia and the Middle East. In the meantime, the US continued to be a drone partner for traditional allies, such as Australia, Japan, South Korea, and European NATO countries. Israel, by contrast, was selling platforms throughout South America, Africa, Europe, and Asia. Turkey and Iran were using their drones as a way to project power.

The export of drones created new drone alliances, mapping out the influence of various countries. As countries and groups clashed, the various drone systems got their first test on battlefields. The results can be seen in at least eleven real "drone wars." They have shaped both the trajectory of drones and also what the future holds. In the drone wars that have already taken place, the outcomes illustrate a mixed bag of success.

Israel successfully used drones against terrorists from the 1980s through the 2020s. They have become the backbone of Israel's surveillance and precision strike capability. Israel's borders are swarming with multiple layers of drones, and Israeli soldiers have at their fingertips a vast array of weapons. Israel also pioneered air defense to confront drone threats. Israeli companies like Rafael are also creating networks that enable drones to operate autonomously alongside unmanned ground robots, with soldiers using point-and-click on a tablet-style computer to guide the machines. Think of a drone and a robot dog entering a building occupied by terrorists and mapping it for special forces prior to a raid. New algorithms and artificial intelligence help the drones identify threats and provide commanders with the best options to take out enemies.

Similarly, the US drone war against terrorists has been effective. The Pentagon pioneered using drones across continents to hunt down militants far from home and to keep the number of boots on the ground minimal. This led to complacency, as well, and the US drone innovation stalled after 2010.

Iran and Turkey became drone innovators around the time the US was stalling in its efforts. This gave both countries an instant air force that could be deployed into contested airspace on their borders and threaten enemies far from home. Smaller states learned from this, and Azerbaijan became a drone sponge, using kamikaze drones to defeat Armenian army units. Azerbaijan's rapid expansion of its drone arm has major ramifications for the drone wars. It acquired masses of Israeli loitering munition drones that it used against Armenian air defenses in the fall of 2020. Turkey also supplied Baku with its Bayraktar drones which were used successfully to decimate Armenian ground forces. When Armenia sued for peace and Russia deployed peacekeepers in early November many countries, such as Ukraine and the UK, looked to the Azerbaijan model as a success. Other countries have had mixed success, such as France's counter-terror strategy in Africa or Russia's attempt to create drones over the years. China is a rising drone superpower, but it has not deployed them in a real conflict yet.

Lessons

The drone wars have shown the drones can be both a game-changer and also a false hope. While they give countries a variety of options, they don't necessarily win wars by themselves because they are often deployed piecemeal. A country has rarely built a whole campaign around drones, instead using them to increase intelligence during a war, or harass enemies, or perform targeted attacks. Drones can't carry many weapons, so they can't decimate enemies. Initially, enemies find them confounding and are fearful of unseen buzzing robots in the air. But with time, they come to accept that drones will monitor them, and they find ways around them, much as ISIS tunneled underground to avoid drone surveillance.

The most important question for soldiers is whether drones are merely a platform with add-ons, such as cameras that can fly or a kind of cruise missile, or whether campaigns will be structured around using drones and the disruption they can cause on the battlefield, a force multiplier like the first tanks or airplanes were. Drones can give poor countries or insurgents and militants an instant air force. They can enable powerful countries to not put boots on the ground and avoid casualties. Between those two extremes is a way of integrating drones into an armed force so that they are used at multiple levels. As armies acquire more tactical, man-packable, loitering munitions, and large drones that act like aircraft, the full power of the drones will be felt. Concepts such as swarms and loyal wingmen, or using drones to transport items are still in the future, even after more than a decade of countries tinkering with them. As stealth drones appear, they will be decisive in wars between powerful countries, but as we have seen with the current drone wars, equal countries rarely wage wars against each other with drones.

This leads to questions about what the vision is for the future of drone warfare.

"The fighter jet era has passed," Elon Musk said during an Air Warfare Symposium in 2020. The SpaceX founder who also pioneered Tesla pre-

dicted that unmanned flight would be the future. He was speaking at the
Air Force Association with Air Force Lt. Gen. John Thompson. Musk
asserted that if an F-35 were put up against a drone fighter augmented
by autonomy, the F-35 would have no chance. The key issue here was
autonomy. An F-35 against a drone piloted by a person is still a person
versus a person. Currently, there isn't a drone fighter that can confront an
F-35, nor is it "autonomous" in making its own decisions.[598] But Musk
was right to prophecy about the future. He was traveling a road many
had gone down.

While many have prophesied the end of manned airpower, the drone
commanders in the US and elsewhere more often predict a world where
manned and unmanned planes fly together. That's what major powers
are actually doing, instead of creating whole masses of drone units, the
way tanks were massed in the Second World War. There is no theory of
"drone blitzkrieg," as it were, where drones overwhelm the enemy and
totally dominate the air. Insofar as we have seen any examples of that,
it was in Iran's attack on Saudi Arabia and in Libya. US commanders
believe drones fundamentally transform the battlefield and provide precision abilities, long endurance, and detailed surveillance, and they can
be sacrificed, whereas pilots cannot.[599]

Drones are a kind of Rashomon, where everyone who sees them sees
something different. Some see killer robots, while others see a unique
platform that can save lives in war by not endangering pilots and ensuring precision strikes can be monitored and guided. Pilots may fear being
replaced, while soldiers on the ground may want more live-feeds to tablets so they can see what drones are seeing in front of them.

While Musk has said that drone warfare is the future, US airpower
experts are more cautious.[600] Writing in *Tomorrow's Air Force* in 2013,
Jeffrey Smith, then commandant and dean of the School of Advanced
Air and Space Studies at Maxwell Air Force Base, noted that while in
the past aircraft were segmented into types, such as fighters and bombers, the new type of mission will not be grounded in these segmenta-

tions. "This transition will be difficult in that the very nature of the Air Force has always been to focus on flying aircraft. However, as history has shown and as technology has advanced, the need for and appropriateness of manned flight as the primary USAF focus has diminished. This long-view transition will require the USAF to force itself out of 'white scarf syndrome,' where the means (flying aircraft) are more important than the ends of providing the nation with the greatest possible amount of airpower options. Unfortunately, if the USAF continues to rationalize its existence under the pretense of decisive operations, continually strives to prove its independence, and views its primary mission in terms of the aircraft it flies, then its future validity and relevance is questionable."[601]

As the battles in Idlib, the Persian Gulf, Syria, and Libya showed, that time was approaching. The race was on now to make drones more autonomous and to add artificial intelligence into them and their targeting systems. To understand how that happened, we need to travel back in time to Israel, as the best and the brightest Israeli youth were preparing themselves for a career in the air force decades ago.

CHAPTER 10

DRONES AND ARTIFICIAL INTELLIGENCE: THE DOOMSDAY SCENARIO

n Israel, long before people are drafted to the army, a government body selects the most talented youth for possible inclusion in a pre-army course. They will study for a degree prior to recruitment, with specialization in physics and other necessities for involvement in advanced military programs. Dubester, the Israeli engineer who pioneered drones in the 1980s and continued to work on new UAVs for decades, recalled speaking to this group of young Israeli geniuses being groomed for sophisticated projects. "I was supposed to be there with the program managers who were trying to convince them to join their projects," he says. This was back in the years when Israel was trying to build its own local warplane called the Lavi.

It was a hot day in central Israel that August, not far from Ben-Gurion International Airport. The group of eighteen-year-olds was waiting to hear about different projects to join. Dubester arrived early to see the pitch that the engineers behind the Lavi were making. "I wanted to wake them up." The heat had made them lethargic. Having heard about the Lavi, the story of working with UAVs would seem positively boring. "Let's together imagine what would happen to the Lavi if we take the pilot out," he said. Suddenly they were interested. "When you design an aircraft, for every kilogram out, it's less wing and engine, it's a formula."[602] If you take the pilot out, you can design the next generation of unmanned attack aircraft.

"I'm not sure it will look like an F-35, you don't need to be like an F-35, but it will be stealthy and it will have better performance than with a pilot, not just supersonic," said Dubester in an interview in 2020. He predicted that the F-35 will last a quarter-century. "A lot of technologies will be developed for an attack aircraft of the future, which I believe will be unmanned. If you look at the manned fighters like the F-35, you can see where aircraft are going, the only thing that limits the capabilities of F-35s is the pilot, because this aircraft could make maneuvers that the human body cannot stand." The F-35 is laden with equipment for the pilot, such as ejectors for their seat, all of which could be replaced to pump it full of more electronics and sensors and weapons. "No one is doing dogfights anymore. You have a missile from two-hundred kilometers with a radar. So why have a pilot there?"[603] Without the pilot, however, you need increasingly intelligent machines.

Researchers at Bar-Ilan University in 2020 explored the connection between neurosciences and machine learning. They wanted artificial intelligence to imitate brain functions, Prof. Ido Kanter said in a recent interview. The problem facing those trying to teach computers to do deep learning like humans is that it is not well understood how people learn to make the right decisions while driving, for instance. Can human learning mechanisms be combined with the speed of computers? theorists asked. "If we were able to implement the slow biological deep-learning mechanism in our brain on a very fast computer, the sky would be the limit," Kanter said.[604]

Artificial intelligence embraces a wide range of issues that might play a role in drone wars. At its base is autonomy, where a drone can perform a mission by optimizing plans and helping solve problems such as allocating resources, analyzing images, and giving the operator the best options.[605] The US Department of Defense viewed autonomy as a set of capabilities that could be provided to unmanned systems to reduce the costs of reaching into distant environments and using that reach to meet mission objectives, according to a task force that looked at the issue. However, despite the potentials of AI, actual human-robot interactions had not been achieved. Robots were not yet planning wars or choosing which drones to use. The concepts were still in their infancy, but with emerging threats, the US needed to catch up. Once again, American planners were worried that China was "moving rapidly to catch up and perhaps ultimately overtake" the West.[606]

To get to autonomy meant different things to different parts of the drone industry. One of the premier examples of what artificial intelligence would bring the unmanned world was embodied in the concept of the "loyal wingman," a drone that would fly alongside a manned aircraft as a kind of Robin to his Batman. This was incredibly complex, to design a flying machine that would not only know how to fly alongside, without crashing into, another plane, but also sponge up data, help with targeting and surveillance, and remove some of the burdens that the primary manned plane would normally have. In combat, it might even be sacrificed or sent on the most dangerous missions, enabling that "stand-off" capability that drones helped with. Boeing rolled out its "loyal wingman" in Australia in May 2020 with Jerad Hayes, the company's senior director of autonomous aviation, heralding the incorporation of artificial intelligence into the unit.[607] This program was at least innovative in comparison to the decision to turn F-16s into unmanned vehicles in 2013 that saw batches of them cannibalized into target drones. A waste of a vehicle that showed how the air force sometimes seemed to not want to realize its own potential.[608]

Thousands of miles away in Israel, another set of programs based on the latest computer algorithms were being created to help confront drone threats. More and more, the drone wars were not just about two unmanned vehicles facing off in the sky to see whose gladiator was best, but about whose computer system was best. The future drone war would be won by the best algorithm and ability to anticipate and respond quickly to a threat, not just whoever could put a bird in the air.

Algorithms: The Human on the Loop

On May 5, I called Meir B., whose name cannot be revealed for security reasons, an expert on air defense at Rafael Advanced Defense Systems. A former colonel in the Israeli Air Force, he remembered back in 2004 when Hezbollah deployed its first Ababil drone. "It was a gamechanger," he says. "We understood we needed to adapt our systems." No longer was the threat just a Soviet MiG from Syria or another neighboring state. Radar at the time was not calibrated to detect drones. It would classify them as a false alarm.

Rafael built a system called Drone Dome to respond to smaller drone threats. Meir says those threats increased rapidly, including Hamas using drones to drop grenades on tanks. Moving from just a small drone threat to proliferation, the threat was now extreme. This includes the swarm technology behind various air displays, using drones for events but with technology that could also be a threat. He says drones are not just a tactical element but a new strategic threat because they can attack strategic targets. To deal with this threat, Israel built its multi-layered defense system that he suggests other countries adopt. It also means using overlapping different types of radar.

A display showing a system for countering drone threats, as threats have proliferates, so have different gadgets for countering them. (Seth J. Frantzman)

A combination of radar with being able to detect and jam the drone's signal and to see it with optics, is employed. You need sensors and effectors to be able to detect and classify and kill the drones rapidly. All of this must be done with algorithms to present the operator with the possibility to decide what to do quickly. "I do believe that drones make game changing in battlefield, such as sensitive sites. There is no unique tool to build a defense area around all your sensitive assets, and the enemy can come and from outside or even inside to attack any assets that they want," says Meir.

"You cannot deal with UAV capabilities to understand all the picture and take the right decisions in a real time scenario. You should use the smart algorithms to recognize the threat and get positive identification and move fast from one target to the next and allocate the right resources between air defense to the relevant targets," says Meir. This means using more futuristic systems, such as lasers, to burn the drones and down them. Israel developed several types of lasers. But what happens when you have to deal with dozens of drones in a swarm?

"Let's say, for example, jamming them. The working assumption point today is that twenty to thirty drones, but it could be one hundred at the same time. If you are using a jammer, all those in the same sector would be defeated, the laser can take out one by one, or high power microwave could deal with all of them at the same time. There is an answer," says Meir. Countries need to be in a hurry to understand the threat, he says.

Meanwhile in the US, a former officer and drone pilot I spoke to said that remote-piloted aircraft, as the air force still liked to call them, were going to need to improve quickly. Facing increased jamming, along with air defenses in places like Iran, it was unclear what the US game plan was. More Reapers and ScanEagles and drones they already had. "In the new budgets, I didn't see anything about new acquisitions; we are comfortable worldwide, there will still be grey zone warfare where [UAVs are] applicable," she said. What she meant was that the US was still focusing on "permissive" environments. A review of US procurement plans for drones confirms this. In 2019 the air force wanted twenty-nine new Reapers.[609] By 2020, the US had around 291 MQ-9 and RQ-4s, and the navy was procuring very few UAVs. It was investing $684 million in the MQ-25 UCALASS program, the tanker UAV.[610]

The former US soldier said we needed to be better prepared. She pointed to AI as the only real revolution. "It's not just four-star generals now saying he needs the 'bird' to go somewhere, they are at the tactical levels, and there are big advances in processing intel."[611]

What this means is that while countries like the US may need an operator to fly the machine, the computers do the rest, such as "counting doorknobs and cars" that the cameras spot. Algorithms digest the data and tell us what is a threat or what has changed. "We want AI to see with machine vision, super accurate high fidelity, but the algorithms were built for humans," she says. Improvements, for instance, for the MQ-9 with full-motion video will free up hundreds of man-hours as sensors get better. The former officer calls it a "human on the loop rather than in one." It's a possible solution for a robot to begin to learn what to look for. Already in Israel, AI was being used to help spot different types of enemy movements and vehicles.

For the former American officer, the comments by Elon Musk rang true. The future would be more drones, fewer F-35s. "We are going there; the Skyborg and Valkyrie have funding lines and will be in a test in April, and that unmanned fighter jet will be looped into open architecture combat clouds, and those are real things. The tech has to mature so we trust the human not being there, and it's not that far off." One reason for this was the Western public not wanting death tolls in future combat. "Why risk thirty pilots' lives when I can send up drones?" Musk's proclaimed future is closer than we think. But it would require a big culture shift.

For those concerned about drone warfare becoming something like Skynet in *Terminator*, taking on a mind of its own to kill people and wage war, the advent of artificial intelligence was worrisome. Stages of autonomy were progressing to places where humans exerted less control "in-the-loop."[612] Would humans soon let the system do most of the work, from taking off to identifying targets? Already the systems could avoid telephone wires and trees using their own sensors.[613] In addition, drone operations were being increasingly subcontracted in 2020, meaning one country like Israel might make the drones and sell to another country, such as Greece or Germany, while someone from a third country pilots the drones.[614] This increased the cobweb of responsibility for their use.

The future war with UAVs was starting to look a lot more like a computer game. Whoever can get to the battlefield first, acquire as much information as possible and feed it back via sensors to provide a controller the options of what to do next, would win. Intelligence has always helped win wars, but modern battlefields were packed with information, using all the latest radars and optics and signals intercepts.

Petraeus agrees that the next step is about confronting more sophisticated adversaries with more sophisticated responses, "keeping in mind that some adversaries already have the capability to launch swarms of drones that do not require remote pilots or GPS links." Strike methods would also improve, he argued. Drones had been used in the past to hit high-value targets when it was difficult to detain them. While interrogation was preferable, the capabilities had evolved now to increasingly precise strikes.[615] The US, for instance, said that in 2019 it had killed no civilians in Yemen with drone strikes.[616]

"I think in the future, the unmanned system will become an organic part of warfare as it's been waged traditionally, and the prospect of it going beyond that I don't see in the next twenty years," says Seth Cropsey, a senior fellow at the Center for American Seapower at the Hudson Institute. With the price of drones decreasing, their use on the battlefield could help keep manned aircraft, like the P-8, out of harm's way as drones talk to unmanned submarines and carry out missions. That means an increased number of smaller platforms that could also be more expendable in a conflict, helping keep larger units safer.[617] Peter Singer, author of *Wired for War*, agrees that there is a coming wave of autonomy. "You went from a human using a joystick to do everything, to do certain functionalities on their own, such as takeoff and landings and mission sets on their own…when I was writing in *Wired for War*, we went into Afghanistan in 2001 had no unmanned ground systems and a handful of unarmed aerial systems, Predator class and that was it. Now I don't have the latest figures, and it was 22,000 [unmanned systems] a few years ago."

He compares the present era to the 1920s and 1930s, when armies sought to incorporate tanks and aircraft. "As late as 1939 the cavalry officer said he wouldn't give up horses for tanks. A second pushback is that this new stuff is great, but [defense departments say], 'I have so many requirements I must satisfy, so in army aviation they think unmanned systems, but I don't have enough manned helicopters I want and then add-on unmanned.'"

This is where AI comes in. It can help with command and control. For instance, Singer says, "We have records of all fire orders from Afghanistan, and AI learns from it and develops ways to improve it, and that is great, a good use, but its pace is Afghanistan, and it learns from fire missions in Afghanistan, and that's different in a US-Russia and US-China scenario."[618] The problem here is a classic military one. We train for future wars by training for the previous war. Yet the future won't look the same. It's like training doctors using the wrong patient pool, Singer notes. Getting things right using UAVs, he concludes, boils down to answering a key question: "What is the vision and doctrine that brings it together?"

Getting things right was on the minds of authors of a RAND study in 2020 that looked at the future of warfare over the ten years that would end in 2030.[619] The study said that AI would continue to play a role in US conflicts with any near-peer competitor, which meant Russia or China. AI was a "disruptor" technology, the authors concluded. States that could develop AI might see it as a way to upend the status quo.[620] Franz-Stephan Gady, a commentator on the future of warfare at IISS, said the study's results were not surprising.[621]

While they were not surprising, the damage that AI systems could potentially do, especially when combined with drones to monitor US forces, was illustrated by US Army Col. Scott Woodward in May 2020, when he showcased the electronic emissions or signature of the Eleventh Armored Cavalry Regiment. The exercise took place at Fort Irwin, California, and his social-media post was designed to show how easy it is using electronic warfare to see a unit's electronic signature, even if the unit is well hidden in the dark. Think of a unit hunkered down with a hillside at its back, vehicles strung out in a semi-circle for defense. Men bed down with camo tarps stretched over them. But the electronics are still humming. All the new sensors and data links and networks that units were using were also making them vulnerable. During these kinds of drills, a massive number of drones could be used.[622] The colonel wondered whether "we trust too much in technology and not enough in human aspects of combat."[623] But clearly, he was showing how weapons systems with electronic warfare could easily pick out an enemy.[624] There were questions about how to maybe use the same electronic signature to fool an enemy, creating a unit that looked bigger than it is.

The US had already fitted MQ-1C Gray Eagles with electronic warfare pods and created a group called the Joint Improvised Explosive Device Defeat Organization (JIEDDO) to explore the jamming of explosive devices such as IEDs. Lockheed Martin was developing a Silent CROW pod, which would increase the electronic and SIGINT cyberwarfare abilities of drones. This Multi-Function Electronic Warfare-Air Large program was being tested in April 2020.[625] The issue with army units pumping out a lot of data because they were more digitized could be both a cost and a benefit. "In an AI empowered environment, he who acts first will have an advantage; there are two competing dynamics, one is for the army to put a lot of data into the Cloud, to create battlefield situational awareness and maximum capability down to lower level like platoons, and this is an issue where there can be tension; if we are in a war with China, then one cannot assume we will have unimpeded flow of data from tactical to central database, if you believe that is the case then it raises concerns; so that [units] have what they need to operate," says Brad Bowman at FDD.[626]

The problem plaguing the US in plans to roll out all this technology were the continuing discussions about how to upgrade existing weapon systems. Although theorists like to discuss ideas like "ghost fleets" of unmanned ships and "autonomous" platforms, evidence was that there was lack of clarity on how best to confront the rising threat of China, Russia, or others.[627]

Christian Brose raised the question of where the US was going with AI and futuristic battle ideas in his book *Kill Chain: Defending America in the Future*.[628] He said many future warfare projects had been suffocated in their cradles by the US, mentioning programs such as the

X-47. The US military needed a redesign, he wrote. The US would have to transition from expensive manned platforms to "large numbers of smaller, low-cost, expendable and highly autonomous machines."[629] Privately, people were suggesting the US build intelligent machines using AI.[630] The "lethal autonomous machines" could be used against a rising China that was already building a vast array of weapons, like drones. He mentioned the Russian advances in drone warfare that had become clear in Ukraine.

The US already knew that China had produced a Defense White Paper of 2019 that foresaw "multi-dimensional, multi-domain unmanned combat weapons system of systems on the battlefield."[631] China's DR-8 supersonic drone and other weapons were freaking the Pentagon out. Fears of intelligent drone swarms should freak people out. The US had once mocked China for plowing money into programs that the US had discarded. But when China unveiled the Gonji-11Sharp Sword, it looked like the X-47 that the US had shown less interest in. China was the real strategic challenge, concluded US planners in 2020. It had rapidly progressed from Deng Xiaoping's era, when it was biding time and hiding capabilities, to using technology to turn the table on enemies. From Hu Jintao to Xi Jingping, the country was moving to push the US aside. Washington moved to increase military pressure on China in May 2020 in the midst of the pandemic.[632] President Trump even boasted of new US missile capabilities, and Secretary of State Mike Pompeo flew to Israel to discuss the overall challenge of China, Russia, and Iran.

Rick Francona, who had seen the capability and success of US drones going back decades, said in early 2020 that America would have to be careful not to allow adversaries to take the lead in UCAV development and deployment. "As long as the Russians and Chinese continue to introduce new and better weapons—and all classes of them, ships, tanks, and aircraft—we will need to keep the pace. Developing and deploying state-of-the-art UCAVs should be a priority."[633]

How drones, reinforced with the latest AI technology, would change this new confrontation with China was as yet untested. Hints of the future were clear, though. On July 11, Elbit in Israel announced it had put its smaller Skylark on an unmanned naval patrol boat called Seagull. With AI, these kinds of systems on top of systems could patrol further and surveil enemies, with one unmanned vehicle deploying other unmanned vehicles, keeping soldiers far away from the battle. Armed, they could swarm and overwhelm adversaries. Imagine a Chinese drone navy launching hundreds of drone aircraft controlled by a supercomputer and acting as one deadly autonomous organism. The US was still theorizing how much AI to put in these systems. Those like Greg Allen, chief of strategy and communications at the Joint Artificial Intelligence Center at the Department of Defense, were working on primers to sort this out. In its final stages, AI would enable machines to gather their own data and improve based on trial and error interactions with the environment, he wrote.[634]

At Lockheed Martin, the engineers and computer experts were drawing on decades of experience to push for more autonomy when the military was ready. The company's Skunk Works that had developed stealth technology for the US in the Cold War eventually had thousands of employees from Palmdale, California, to Marietta, Georgia, and Fort Worth, Texas. Michael Swanson, the chief engineer, told a company podcast that drones are perfect for long missions that are in harm's way. Lockheed was helping design systems to keep humans away from risk.[635] Lockheed packed its aircraft with the latest cameras and radars, lasers, terrain mapping, and day and night cameras. But when it came to autonomy, it was still waiting for policy to catch up to technology. It had built the X-44A in the late 1990s, and then built the larger PoleCat, using a small team at Skunk Works who sought to create a new architecture for UAVs. The X-44 was ahead of its time: tailless, stealthy, and super-maneuverable.[636]

They also wanted a virtual pilot display, which basically means instead of seeing what is outside via a camera, there is a digital overlay. That would mean a lack of visibility wouldn't be an issue.

The company also looked at "flexible autonomy, which has a human on the loop, so the operator will have a part putting the inputs in and can override the system if it makes a decision the operator doesn't agree with, they can stop it and interact with it." The issue here was to enable the computer to fuse data coming into aircraft so as to make autonomous decisions by knowing how to choose among inputs and sensors. "Autonomy is more AI, trained to make decisions that cover a variety, response may be logical but unexpected," the Lockheed experts said in 2019. But they had to wait for policy. "What are we comfortable to allow to happen when the human isn't there at the pointy end of the spear?" one of the voices on the Skunk Works podcast asks. It boils down to trust. While much will be possible to do with AI, people won't be comfortable with it because it reminds them of nightmares from movies and killing machines.

John Clark, vice president of ISR and UAS at Lockheed's Skunk Works, said that one of the major issues they identified in research were problems when the user doesn't know why the technology made a certain decision and stops trusting the system. "We created flexible autonomy, so the user can gain trust over time in missions, so from a long term perspective, AI and machine learning are being introduced, and there is an opportunity to accelerate trust."[637] Lockheed is enthusiastic about AI and the dull, dirty, and dangerous missions that drones do.

For now, the drone war that was unfolding was more prosaic. Drones were not yet learning from their experiences, but surveillance drones were feeding operators more precise information based on recognizing patterns and objects. They were on the cusp of being knitted into a network with soldiers on the ground accessing their information and plotting courses based on data and sensors, becoming a kind of military-industrial organism. The question was how this organism would hold up when forced to fight something similar in the hands of another country. Like the clash of tanks between Germany and Russia in 1941, that would have to wait for fleets of armed US drones to confront China, Russia, or Iran. For now, it was more a matter of combining defenses to jam or down enemy drones and making drones that could avoid enemy radars and missiles.

Stirrup and the Crossbow

On May 15, 2020, a US Reaper drone hammered an ISIS position in the Hamrin Mountains in Iraq. This was still the old-style drone war, but across the Middle East and Asia experts were getting ready for the next round.

As the discussion in Washington continued to revolve around a future war where remote-pilotless aircraft attack the enemy without endangering pilots, there were other points to consider. If the US were to linger much longer on this question, it might find itself playing catch-up, Brad Bowman at FDD said.[638] The ability to send drones into hostile airspace and sacrifice them was a new world of war. "A norm is developing in conflict where shooting down drones is not seen as a big deal. Iran shot down the US drone last year, the Global Hawk. If that had been manned, that would be different, so there are implications for capabilities and thresholds of what is an act of war and what can spark war. So what we see in evolution will affect everything that the US military does and our allies and adversaries do," Bowman said in the spring of 2020.

In his view, twenty years of the war on terror in places like Iraq and Afghanistan had eroded US supremacy. Constrained by budgets, commanders sought to deploy units with the best equipment and postponed modernization. Bad news for America, good news for China, which might be ahead in AI and hypersonic weapons. "If Chinese military analysts think the military balance changed in the Taiwan strait, they might conduct aggression there, and the thing we are trying to avoid might happen," Bowman said.[639]

The relationship with Israel and its advanced technology was key here. "Israel has a unique role to play. It is not a global great power, but I agree with those who argue that it is a technological super-power, and we can learn from Israel and benefit from their agility and sense of urgency. They confront threats on all sides that the US and Pentagon can benefit from and learn from. The relationship is deep and broad."[640] Opportunities were developing for collaboration, not only on air defense like Iron Dome, but directed energy weapons and also continued joint work with the F-35. Learning from Iran's drone threat was also key to learn to counter new drone swarm threats.

On the tactical level, the US and Israel were also looking to bring drones down to the smallest units. As Israel's Momentum war plan went into high gear in 2020, seeking to modernize its forces to make them more precise, lethal, smaller, agile, and to combine all the new technology available, the use of drones like FireFly, which Israel deployed in 2020, would be key. Of course, the problem with giving more technology to smaller units is that enemies such as Russia and China that conduct electronic warfare offensives could try to cut these units off. The US had used Blackhawks and Apaches to decimate Saddam Hussein's Soviet-era technology in the Gulf War, leaving units in trenches blind to the coming American sledgehammer. Now the US could be threatened the same way. Technology helped the US win in 1991, but it was a double-edged sword. Too much reliance on it was a false prophet, and it could make us vulnerable. Drones were a lynchpin in that process.

For some, the 1990s witnessed a revolution in military affairs, sometimes called RMA, but there were concerns the US learned the wrong lessons on how technology would win wars. Then there were concerns the US again learned the wrong lessons about counter-insurgency after 9/11, relying on acronyms such as COIN rather than focusing on near-peer competitors and big-country conflicts. So the US shifted again to confront Russia and China after 2020. But with concerns that not every tech-heavy US weapons system would work against China, this future war was shrouded in fog. Had the US lingered too long and let enemies steal too much information, reverse engineering US equipment as Russia, Iran, and China competed to get ahold of things like US drones or Israeli missiles? "Our pocket has been picked and we need to be awake," said Bowman. Foreign states were stealing information from US suppliers, as well.

Dan Gettinger, the Bard College expert who publishes a yearly drone book, said in 2020 that unlike some who saw the technology as a disruptor, he compared drones to helicopters. They "represent an immense shift in tactical ops, but it's not a strategic shift. One can imagine them as airplanes, they could look different in twenty years, as aircraft changed immensely. We are seeing that," he said. Drones will be smaller, easier to use, and possibly pack more lethal weaponry as industry catches up with technological capabilities. But where were the new larger unmanned planes going? Towards "loyal wingman" programs being developed by European Future Combat Air Systems, or in Australia. It was unclear if these cumbersome "wingmen" would meet the needs that air forces have for them.

While the US was preparing for China and Russia, confronting Iran would be easier. Iran's propaganda about new "stealth" drones and using drones to drop anti-tank missiles, which Iran had copied from Israel's Spike missile, was just talk until they tried to use it. Rawnsley, the expert on Iran's drones, said he expected to see more used if there were a conflict between Hezbollah and Israel. Key mysteries surrounded Iran's drone program, though. Isolated by sanctions, the regime was investing in drones. It had reached a major turning point after 2011, and the secretive nature of the program showed they wanted to guard it from discovery.[641] Iran's use of drones in 2019, from a May 2019 attack that went largely unnoticed, to the Abqaiq attack that damaged a key facility, showed what could come next.

Two Schools: What the Future of War Will Look Like

War on the Rocks, a publication that looks at new topics in war and national security, published a series of pieces looking at the role AI will play in future warfare. At the center of the debate was the degree to which AI would be revolutionary. "A consensus seems to have grown," author Peter Hickman noted in May 2020, that AI and technology "are changing the character of war, if not its nature."[642] The piece nonetheless claimed that human intelligence will win the next war, not technology. They argued that past innovations, such as tanks or machine guns, were supposed to change war, but that "less tech-savvy forces were able to mitigate these advances through tactical innovation." Technological have-nots were able to achieve victory. Robots will not replace humans.

Hickman was looking to the 2035 battlefield like many military planners are. He wrote that he had joined the air force in the early 2000s and that there had been a slow evolution, rather than revolutionary change. "The 1960s era radar systems I first trained on are still our primary ground mobile radar." Indeed, the idea of the "silk scarf" air force has been one of the main issues cited by prophets of drone airpower to explain why things like the F-35 still suck up budgets.

At the heart of Hickman's argument is a 2006 book by Stephen Biddle called *Military Power: Explaining Victory and Defeat in Modern Battle.* In this analysis, a look at sixteen wars fought between 1956 and 1992 concluded that technological superiority only won eight of them. "Those who innovate tactically go on to victory as often as those who possess the most advanced battlefield technology." Tech overmatch is not a necessity if lethality of the tech can be overcome. In short, if you can avoid the machine guns, you'll overcome them.

This discussion revolves around several schools of thought about the war the US needs to train for today. There is resentment in the US about decades of counter-insurgency strategy seemingly wasting training on the Middle East when the US needed to prepare for China and Russia.[643]

The US wanted to get out of the Middle East during the Trump administration and end the "forever wars." Training at places like Kirtland Air Base would shift to battle management platforms in virtual training spaces. Here AI would aid in examining what future partners and enemies would look like.

These two schools of thought, the prophets of unmanned war like Musk and those who saw the man as central to the machine, appeared to present two competing images of the future. But the real question was how much information would the machines be feeding the man. Would they be able to digest it, integrate it with all the available technology, and make effective use of it?

EPILOGUE

The first time I saw a military drone was on the border of Gaza in 2014. Men in a field were holding what looked like a giant model airplane. They had the wings slung over their shoulders. I realized what I was seeing. These men in their green Israeli fatigues were about to launch a drone into Gaza. And sure enough, soon they had thrown it into the air, and it was gone, scanning the border. I was sitting in a field full of Israeli tanks, the former melon patch beneath my feet churned up into a dusty mulch by the tanks. War was on the horizon. We were waiting for the soldiers to go in.

This new drone war came along bit by bit. I recall opening up an old Avalon Hill board game, where little cardboard squares represent military and air-force units. As one plots moves to replay the 1973 war or other Israeli battles, there are no little pieces to represent drones. But on the modern battlefield, there would be. You wouldn't need to waste men and planes. You could send in the drones. Once one thinks of it, the idea is immediately appealing. To understand the developing field, I spent the summer of 2020 visiting drone manufacturers in Israel. I went down to Aeronautics, where I saw their smaller drones, and then to IAI to see the pioneers of Israeli drones.

At Aeronautics, facing the dunes that pour down to the sea around Palmachim Air Base, where Israel has long flown its drones forces from, the manufacturers showed me the factory floor. Composite wings sat stacked in racks, and several drones sat in varying degrees of repair. One, called a Dominator, was just a civilian twin-prop with the cockpit ripped out and sensors packed in. Aeronautics represents the tactical end of smaller and medium drones. They make one loitering munition, but it was unclear what the future for that warhead held.

At IAI, Israel's dronefathers showcased the original Scout hanging from the back of an air-conditioned hangar. Inside were their other drones, including the Herons that Israel pioneered. It was like a menagerie of Israel's flying species. From small to large, from maritime scanning drones to a Heron destined for Germany and then to be used in Mali against extremists. In the summer of 2020, the European countries were still buying Israeli but were keen on developing their own high-altitude, long-endurance drones. The European concept is the "EuroMALE," expected to be delivered in 2024 and be operational by 2028 in Germany.

What was next? I wondered. Every day brought news of new drone innovations. France was working on a new drone helicopter. Iran announced new drone and radar technology in the summer of 2020. The UAE and Israel signed an agreement to create diplomatic relations, potentially paving the way for technological cooperation. In February 2021, Israel's defense giants attended IDEX—a major defense exhibition in Abu Dhabi—where drones and counter-drone technology are a major attraction. Drone swarming technology and kamikaze drones both received a lot of attention in the spring of 2021, with militaries from China to the US all expressing interest in how these types of weapons could be added successfully to existing arsenals. The range of drones from Iran to China also increased in the spring of 2021, while user interface—such as using a tablet computer screen to point and click where the drone should go—made operating drones increasingly easy for average soldiers. More autonomous systems, automatically recognizing targets, were also demonstrated as Israel's Rafael showcased at a bucolic house on the coast of Israel in late December 2020.

At Spear UAV in Israel, a new canister-launched drone that could be fired from a tank or grenade launcher was in the works. VTOLs and more tactical drones seemed to be the answer to many problems. Classified systems, like loyal wingmen programs, or stealthy super-secret drones, are also in the air. The F-35 is supposed to be the last manned system, one expert told me. That means we had better get moving quickly on providing the drone solutions to replace it. However, a lot of the work of drones was more boring. Whereas once Israel needed manned aircraft to scan the sea for enemy ships or smugglers, now Heron drones could stay aloft for fifty hours. Drones can perform a multiplicity of tasks. But overall, the platforms have remained the same. It's just about putting more optics and radar and other data and sensors into them. No one wants to change their appearance. It works, so why change it? Just like F-16s and F-15s continue to be updated, keeping the essential shape of the aircraft the same, or U-2 planes still flying after sixty-five years, there is little desire to change what appears to be working. Techology has rapidly advanced, but the airframes aren't changing as quickly, partly because there is no incentive to change them. The drones are getting smarter, though, at taking off on their own or doing most of their mission without needing someone to control them.

The options that drones offer become immediately apparent when you start playing with civilian models. I bought a small Tello drone for my son, and we started taking it out to fiddle with. We photographed vineyards and took it on hikes. Every infantry unit should have things like this, dozens of them with a dedicated drone operator. UAVs can solve all sorts of problems. They give you an instant long lens to peer around bushes, and over fields, and get a sense of the battlefield from above. They can carry small payloads, and they are expendable. The issue with drones was not that the technology wasn't there; it was that people were not ready for them. Terrorists and armies hadn't thought of how to employ them effectively. Drones can wreak havoc, slamming into powerlines or sensitive areas *en masse*. There is no limitation to what they can do. The limitation is the operator. That is why artificial intelligence is trying to help drones do most of the flying, and humans do most of the mission. That means the drone detects other drones and doesn't fly into them. It takes off and lands. The user just decides where it should go and what it should do.

At Israel's drone manufacturers, the quiet disdain for the concept of having "pilots" fly these birds was clear. You don't need a pilot in a storage container using pedals and a stick. You just need an operator. The drone will return to base if it encounters bad weather or loss of signal. It can even self-destruct. There are no people on board, so you're not risking lives, as long as it doesn't crash in an urban area. On the other hand, some larger drones are so expensive, into the tens of millions of dollars, that many countries can only buy or lease a small number of them.

Huge resources are plowed into them. In the summer of 2020, for instance, the UK was still working on its armed MQ-9 SkyGuardian, called Protector, with Paveway IV bombs and Brimstone missiles. The Protector program envisioned just sixteen drones for a cost of half a billion dollars.[644] Trainees would spend six weeks in Nevada learning to fly with elements of the 39 and 54 Reaper squadrons.[645] If you have just a few, you can't afford to lose them. The result is that countries often put resources in the wrong places, investing in irreplaceable drones to replace manned aircraft. Considering the huge losses in manned aircraft in past wars, the drones seem even more sensitive, like large flying endangered species. This is not helpful when it comes to strategy. Like all military systems, that problem will become apparent when these platforms are thrown up against one another.

The limitation of the US armed-drone program was apparent two decades after its inception in the wake of 9/11. The Reapers couldn't fly in contested airspace against S-300s and air defense. Before embarking on a mission, pilots and crews were shown a map with a circle drawn around areas where enemy air defense exists, warning them off. Only under rare circumstances would they venture into the enemy's sights and risk losing the drones. Some drones were too expensive to be lost. Others, the secretive spy drones like Sentinel, could fly over enemy radar and missile installations, but there weren't that many of them, and they were not heavily armed.

Nevertheless, everyone who has worked with drones sees them as revolutionary. Their ability to stay over targets basically forever and then strike when ready is a new way of waging war. Col. Jones, the Creech commander who had been with drones since they were first armed, believes no other platform can provide anything near the level of endurance or detailed surveillance, and few can provide the degree of prevision. So would the future be just precision strikes? No. It doesn't mean the era of mass combat is over. Drones will be massed into swarms to defeat enemies. There will be a discussion of quality versus quantity, with Western countries preferring quality and others preferring quantity and attrition. Investment in artificial intelligence, and the first country that truly trusts its drone force to use AI, may prevail. That could be China.

The arms race in artificial intelligence is all about figuring out how much human you want in the loop. The public doesn't want machines choosing when to shoot missiles, but militaries seek to use artificial intelligence to sort through mountains of information, identify targets, and choose the right weapons, giving the operator choices, rather than burdening them with too much information. Prophets of the AI revolution see it as becoming operational in the 2020s. That isn't about teaching planes to land and take off or to avoid collisions. It is about teaching them to process data and learn and adjust and perform most of the functions that pilots and others would have had to do before. The point where the machines begin to function more like an organism, and humans can rely on them in war, is certainly a fundamentally concerning thought because it conjures up post-apocalyptic horror movies where machines are hunting down people. That's not necessarily what the future holds. But will the future showcase two AI-empowered systems fighting each other, and if so might one of the systems just choose to stand down, knowing it won't win? Not likely either.

The problem with predicting future wars is that since the time of Leonardo Da Vinci, people have been drawing futuristic concepts about what war will look like, and they have almost always been wrong. There are no clean wars, no way of getting war right, and the nature of conflict is that what seems like even the best military system can be defeated. Drones have taught us that, by humiliating Russian air defenses in Syria as well as Saudi air defenses. The US learned that lesson when its Sentinel was brought down. Conversely, drones haven't really led groups like ISIS, the Houthis or Hezbollah to win battles, but instead they became more a tool of harassment than of winning wars. Even the Reapers didn't win wars; they enabled wealthy Western countries to wage war far from home without too many questions from legislators, surrendering wide swaths of the globe to ungoverned terrorist-run areas where the only consolation prize was that the terrorists were always looking over their shoulders for drones. There's no evidence that since the advent of armed drones they have successfully policed all these areas from the Sahel to the Philippines where terrorist cells operate. There aren't enough drones to do that. They seek targets of opportunity, high-value targets, not random guys with AK-47s. So the jihadist knows, if he is just one guy with an AK, the drones won't do anything.

Drones still act primarily in their own bubble of military operations. They don't do close-air support for infantry and tanks. This leaves several possibilities for their future. Combining them with manned aircraft is one vision. Using them as a separate "drone force" is another. A multi-layered drone approach is a third option, integrating them into operations of all branches of the military. Using them in massive swarms as a disposable weapon system to achieve dominance is a fourth concept.

I recall in 1998, during a summer trip to Martha's Vineyard, I went to the Bunch of Grapes book shop in Vineyard Haven and saw a new book called *The Future of War*. It described the early UAVs that were already successful. "The UAV holds out the greatest promise over the next twenty years. It is relatively inexpensive so its loss is not a disaster, it is small and unobtrusive, it can shift position and in due course it will be able to carry multiple sensors and even weapons."[646] I was only a teenager then, but already these flying machines were preparing to transform our world. We have now seen how this prophecy came true. The sensor and weapon revolution did take place, but the overall revolution of the drones remains like a colossus in the cradle. It is like the 1943 Salvador Dali painting *Geopoliticus Child Watching the Birth of the New Man,* which was an allegory for the US being "born" out of the world. The bizarre painting predicts a world dominated by America. Today's drone wars tell us something else.

The drones developed by Israel and then revolutionized by America have now proliferated everywhere. Activists who hoped to stop armed drones from being used are behind the curve. Armed drones are here to stay, no matter how many UN reports express concern about their use in killings like the strike on Iran's Soleimani. The real question is how many drones armies will have, how much artificial intelligence will be jammed into them, and if they will be high-end expensive drones whose development precludes sacrificing them, or whether they will be masses of drone swarms used more like smart bombs and cruise missiles.

At the apex of the question is the new frontier of drone conflict between the US and China as well as other countries, such as Turkey and Russia in Libya. The world is rapidly shifting from the international world order put in place in 1990 with the fall of the Soviet Union, to a new global chaos as the US retreats from leadership and other countries step in. With this change in the kind of international rules-based world order, drones will be called upon more to do the dull, dirty, and dangerous work they are known for. They offer plausible deniability, the ability to strike anywhere and then disappear without risking lives. Soon the use of more stealth drones will transform battlefields. But we should be careful about the prospect of drones replacing airplanes. More likely, they will enable countries to have an instant air force and not invest in as many expensive planes.

The first country to fully vertically integrate drones into every operation and every service will have an advantage. Countries that experiment with drone strikes, like Iran, will also be able to present stronger enemies with a real threat. This is the threat of being able to attack anywhere against national infrastructure and sensitive sites that don't have enough defenses. Like the ironclad ships, the tank, or even the first plane that sank a ship, drones present this disruptive military technology to armies. However, like the painting, we are still in the growing pains of this revolution, waiting for it to fully materialize. When it does, with its swarms and artificial intelligence and full vertical integration, countries that are not prepared may find themselves on the losing end of a new world order.

ACKNOWLEDGMENTS

would like to thank David Hazony for supporting this project, along with Adam Bellow, David Bernstein, and Heather King at Post Hill Press, as well as Monique Happy who edited the manuscript. John Rigsbee, Scarlett Trujillo, Leah Garton, Stephen Jones, and others at the US Air Force and Creech Air Base, US Central Command. Erica Tierney and others at Lockheed Martin. Peter Singer, Mike Giglio, Sean Durns, Richard Kemp, Adam Rawnsley, Dan Gettinger, and the Center for the Study of the Drone, Seth Cropsey, Brad Bowman, Jonathan Schanzer, Behnam Ben Taleblu, and the staff at the Foundation for Defense of Democracies, David Ishai at Rafael, Yael Zafrir-Levi, the International Institute for Strategic Studies, David Petraeus, Kevin McDonald, Douglas Feith, Yair Dubester, Elbit Systems, Dan Bichman, and Israel Aerospace Industries, Rafael Advanced Defence Systems, UVision, Adam Tiffen, Rick Francona, as well as anonymous sources and numerous others whose assistance was integral to the creation of this book. Foremost I want to thank my family, especially my wife Kasaey Damoza, for their support.

ENDNOTES

1   Bernard Gwertzman, "Weinberger to visit three Middle East Nations," *New York Times*, August 28, 1982, accessed June 23, 2020, https://www. nytimes.com/1982/08/28/world/weinberger-will-visit-threee-mideast-na-tions.html; Micah Zenko, "What else we don't know about drones," Council on Foreign Relations, February 27, 2012, accessed January 2, 2021, https://www.cfr.org/blog/what-else-we-dont-know-about-drones.

2   Hedrick Smith, "Weinberger says pact with Israel could be restored," *New York Times,* June 15, 1983, accessed June 23, 2020, https://www.nytimes. com/1983/06/15/world/weinberger-says-pact-with-israel-can-be-restored. html.

3   Israel Air Force Squadrons, IAF webpage, accessed June 23, 2020.

4   "Israeli drones keep an electronic eye on the Arabs," *New York Times*, May 23, 1981, accessed June 23, 2020, https://www.nytimes.com/1981/05/23/ world/israeli-drones-keep-an-electronic-eye-on-the-arabs.html;   The Q-2c Firebee cost $100,000 in 1962 and hundreds were built, see Military Procurement Authorizations; United States Senate, Washington, 1961, p. 456.

5   Israel Air Force Squadrons, IAF, accessed June 23, 2020, https://www.iaf. org.il/4968-33518-en/IAF.aspx.

6   Carl A. Schuster, "Lightning Bug War Over Vietnam," History.Net, accessed March 20, 2020, Originally appeared in Feb. 2013 issue of *Vietnam*, https://www.historynet.com/lightning-bug-war-north-vietnam.htm.

7   Rudolph Herzog, "Rise of the Drones," *Lapham's Quarterly*, Accessed June 11, 2020, https://www.laphamsquarterly.org/spies/rise-drones.

8   Israel Drori, Shmuel Ellis, Zur Shapira, *The Evolution of a New Industry*, Stanford, Stanford Business Books, 2013. 56.

9   "Israeli drones keep an electronic eye on the Arabs," *New York Times*, May 23, 1981, accessed June 23, 2020, https://www.nytimes.com/1981/05/23/world/israeli-drones-keep-an-electronic-eye-on-the-arabs.html; The Scout looked like a miniature version of existing planes used for spotting enemies, such as the Cessna 0-2 Skymaster, used by the US for operations in Vietnam.

10   Yaakov Lappin, "1970s platform offers reminder of Israeli drones," *The Jerusalem Post*, Sept 7, 2015, Accessed June 23, 2020, https://www.jpost.com/Business-and-Innovation/1970s-platform-offers-reminder-on-origins-of-Israeli-drone-revolution-at-exhibition-415529.

11   Carl Conetta, Charle Knight and Lutz Unterseher, "Toward Defensive Restructuring in the Middle East, research monograph," Feb. 1991, Accessed June 23, 2020, http://comw.org/pda/9703restruct.html.

12   Emily Goldman, The Diffusion of Military Technology, p. 187, accessed June 23, 2020.

13   Robert Frank Futrell, Ideas, Concepts, Doctrine, Basic thinking in the US air force 1964-84, vol. II, Alabama, 1989, p. 556. "Air Power in the 1991 war" chapter online, accessed June 23, 2020, http://hdl.handle.net/10603/14933.

14   See also *The Sword of David*, p. 125.

15   Yair Dubester, The Combat in the Bakaa Valley, "Transforming joint air power," accessed June 23, 2020, http://www.japcc.org/wp-content/uploads/japcc_journal_Edition_3.pdf.

16 Don McCarthy, *The Sword of David*, p. 125.

17 PBS Frontline, "Drones," Weapons of the Gulf War, accessed May 23, 2020, https://www.pbs.org/wgbh/pages/frontline/gulf/weapons/drones.html.

18 Yair Dubester, "30 Years of Israeli UAV Experience," JAPCC, 2006. http://www.japcc.org/wp-content/uploads/japcc_journal_Edition_3.pdf.

19 Yair Dubester, "30 Years of Israeli UAV Experience," JAPCC, 2006. http://www.japcc.org/wp-content/uploads/japcc_journal_Edition_3.pdf.

20 The YF-12, for instance, flew against drones. Steve Pace, "Projects of Skunk Works," Voyager Press, p. 115.

21 Steve Pace, "Projects of Skunk Works," Voyager Press, p. 115-23.

22 The French Nord Aviation made something called the CT-20 and Saab made the RB-08

23 Newcomb, *Unmanned Aviation: A History*, p. 83.

24 Hearings on National Defense Authorization Act 1997, p. 832.

25 Ibid.

26 The Hunters used two engines, originally German-made, but later Italian-made and eight of them were bought by the US.

27 Laurence Newcome, *Unmanned Aviation: A Brief History*; Emily Goldman, Lesle Eliason, *The Diffusion of Military Technology and Ideas.*

28 Vector Site, Pioneer Entry, accessed June 24, 2020, https://web.archive.org/web/20110908060052/http:/www.vectorsite.net/twuav_07.html#m4.

29 Dubester interview; Richard Haillon, *Storm over Iraq: Air Power and the Gulf War.*

30 Grover Alexander, Aquila Remotely Pilot Vehicle, Lockheed, Sunnyvale California, Report April 1979, https://apps.dtic.mil/dtic/tr/fulltext/u2/a068345.pdf.

31 Hearings on National Defense Authorization, 1996, p. 832; Unmanned Aerial Vehicles, Dod Acquisition Efforts, April 9, 1997, https://fas.org/irp/gao/nsi97138.htm; At Federation of American Scientists website, accessed June 24, 2020.

32 Hearings on Military Posture, H.R 3689, House of Representatives, Washington, 1976, https://babel.hathitrust.org/cgi/pt?id=umn.31951d03 556686k&view=1up&seq=255.

33 Hearings Before the Special Reports Committee on Unmanned Aerial Vehicles, Washington, 1976, p. 3964.

34 Vector Site, Aquila entry, accessed June 24, 2020, https://web.archive.org/ web/20110908060052/http:/www.vectorsite.net/twuav_07.html#m4. It was tested in 1983 in Fort Huachuca, Arizona where Dubester had also showcased Israeli drones.

35 Entry on PQM-149 at Designation Systems, Accessed June 24, 2020, http://www.designation-systems.net/dusrm/m-149.html. It lived on as a machine designated R4E-40 used in Central America.

36 "The Dronefather," *The Economist,* December 1, 2012, Accessed June 24, 2020, https://www.economist.com/technology-quarterly/2012/12/01/the-dronefather.

37 Ibid. The history of Aquila is similar to the history of the Bradley Fighting Vehicle.

38 Emily Goldman, Leslie Eliason, *Diffusion,* p. 187.

39 "New footage shows Niger attack," *The Guardian,* May 18, 2018, https://www.theguardian.com/world/2018/may/18/drone-footage-us-forces-desperately-trying-escape-niger-ambush.

40 Gen. John P. Abizaid (US Army, Ret.) and Rosa Brooks, "Recommendations and Report of The Task Force on US Drone Policy," Stimson, April 2015, https://www.stimson.org/wp-content/files/file-attachments/recommendations_and_report_of_the_task_force_on_us_drone_policy_second_edition.pdf.

41 They could scan an area up to 60 miles away. Mark Bowden, "How the Predator changed the character of war," *Smithsonian Magazine,* November 2013,https://www.smithsonianmag.com/history/how-the-predator-drone-changed-the-character-of-war-3794671/.

42 PBS Frontlines, Gulf War episode, weapons, PBS, https://www.pbs.org/wgbh/pages/frontline/gulf/weapons/drones.html.

43 UAV procurement report to Congress, 1997, https://fas.org/irp/gao/nsi97138.htm.

44 PBS Frontlines, Gulf War episode, weapons, PBS, https://www.pbs.org/wgbh/pages/frontline/gulf/weapons/drones.html.

45 Ibid.

46 Colin Clark, *Must Read Tale of Predator's Torturous Ride to Fame* and Rick Whittle's *Predator: The Secret Origins of the Drone Revolution.*

47 Frank Strickland, "The Early Evolution of the Predator Drone," CIA Center for the Study of Intelligence, March 2013, https://www.cia.gov/resources/csi/studies-in-intelligence/volume-57-no-1/the-early-evolution-of-the-predator-drone/.

48 Steve Coll, *Ghost Wars.*

49 Global Perspectives, YouTube video interview with Thomas Twetten, March 7, 2011, Accessed June 24, 2020, https://www.youtube.com/watch?v=egF2tuHWL5M&feature=youtu.be.

50 A third crashed. Curtis Peebles, *Dark Eagles: A History of Secret US Aircraft Programs.* Random House, NY, 1997, p. 208. Karem sold Amber to General Atomics.

51 Bill Sweetman, "Drones Developed and Forgotten," *Popular Science,* September 1994; see also Richard Whittle, "The Man Who Invented the Predator," *Air and Space Magazine,* April 2013, accessed July 11, 2020, https://www.airspacemag.com/flight-today/the-man-who-invented-the-predator-3970502/?page=3. For more on the Scarab see Tyler Rogoway and Joseph Trevithick, "The US sold this spy drone to Egypt," The Drive, Nov. 17, 2018, accessed July 11, 2020, https://www.thedrive.com/the-war-zone/24966/the-united-states-sold-egypt-this-unique-stealth-recon-drone-called-scarab-in-the-1980s. It seemed the UAV market would be

dominated by Teledyne Ryan's Scarab and Development Sciences Sky Eye or other ideas that were percolating around at the time.

52 Unit cost was estimated at $16 million a drone. Overall 286 were built with 100 still flying by 2018, see Deniz Cam and Christopher Helman, "The Quiet Billionaires Behind America's Predator Drone," *Forbes*, Jan. 7, 2020, accessed July 11, 2020, https://www.forbes.com/sites/denizcam/2020/01/07/the-quiet-billionaires-behind-americas-predator-drone-that-killed-irans-soleimani/?sh=4fb6c6895cb0.

53 Frank Strickland, "The Early Evolution of the Predator Drone," CIA Center for the Study of Intelligence, March 2013, https://www.cia.gov/resources/csi/studies-in-intelligence/volume-57-no-1/the-early-evolution-of-the-predator-drone/.

54 "To be effective as a persistent surveillance platform, however, the UAV also had to be able to receive instructions and deliver its data from places far from its ground control site," *Studies in Intelligence* 57, March 2013, p. 3.

55 Newcombe, *Unmanned Aircraft*.

56 Taylor Baldwin Kiland, *Strategic Inventions of the War on Terror*, New York: Cavendish, 2017 p. 25.

57 Rick Francona to author, email interview, May 20, 2020.

58 Frank Strickland, "The Early Evolution of the Predator Drone," CIA Center for the Study of Intelligence, March 2013, https://www.cia.gov/resources/csi/studies-in-intelligence/volume-57-no-1/the-early-evolution-of-the-predator-drone/.

59 Richard Whittle, "The Man Who Invented the Predator," *Air and Space Magazine*, 2013, https://www.airspacemag.com/flight-today/the-man-who-invented-the-predator-3970502/?page=4.

60 See David Axe, *Shadow Wars*, p. 19.

61 Coll, *Ghost Wars*.

62 See Axe, *Shadow Wars*, p. 42.

63   Testimony to Congress, 1996, *Hearings on National Defense Authorization Act*, p. 836.

64   Hasik, *Arms and Innovation*.

65   Coll, *Ghost Wars*.

66   Coll, *Ghost Wars, p.* 300.

67   Perry Memo, 1996, https://nsarchive2.gwu.edu/NSAEBB/NSAEBB484/ docs/Predator-Whittle%20Document%202%20-%20Air%20Force%20 assigned%20as%20Predator%20lead%20service%209%20April%20 1996.pdf.

68   Interview with Brad Bowman, March 2, 2020.

69   Clark Memo, https://nsarchive2.gwu.edu/NSAEBB/NSAEBB484/docs/ Predator-Whittle%20Document%203%20-%20Snake%20Clark%20 Taszar%20trip%20report%20%2028%20April%201997.pdf.

70   This particular UAV concept died out in October of the same year. Testimony on US UAV efforts to Congress, 1997, https://fas.org/irp/gao/nsi97138.htm.

71   Deutsch Memo, July 12, 1993, https://nsarchive2.gwu.edu/NSAEBB/ NSAEBB484/docs/Predator-Whittle%20Document%201%20-%20 Deutch%20Endurance%20UAV%20Memo%2012%20July%201993.pdf.

72   Axe, *Shadow Wars*, p. 42.

73   "Predator" Memo, Department of the Air Force, April 28, 1997, https:// nsarchive2.gwu.edu/NSAEBB/NSAEBB484/docs/Predator-Whittle%20 Document%203%20-%20Snake%20Clark%20Taszar%20trip%20 report%20%2028%20April%201997.pdf.

74   Clark Memo, https://nsarchive2.gwu.edu/NSAEBB/NSAEBB484/docs/ Predator-Whittle%20Document%203%20-%20Snake%20Clark%20 Taszar%20trip%20report%20%2028%20April%201997.pdf.

75   Richard Whittle, *Predator: The Secret Origins of the Drone Revolution*; Document list at website on history of the Predator, accessed June 24, 2020, https://nsarchive2.gwu.edu/NSAEBB/NSAEBB484/.

76   Ibid.

77 US Air Force Bio, Joseph Ralston, https://www.af.mil/About-Us/Biographies/Display/Article/105866/general-joseph-w-ralston/.

78 *Air Force Magazine*, December 1995, p. 27.

79 "The Term 'CINC' is Sunk," *Afterburner: News for Retired USAF Personnel*, Vol. 45, no. 1, January 2003, page 4, https://www.retirees.af.mil/Portals/53/documents/AFTERBURNER-ARCHIVE/Afterburner-January%202003.pdf?ver=2016-08-16-133713-257.

80 Ralston, *Air Force Magazine*, December 1995.

81 Ronald Wilson, "Eyes in the Sky," *Military Intelligence Professional*, Volume 22, 1996, p. 16.

82 This is called C4i. Ibid.

83 Charles Thomas, Vantage Point, *Military Intelligence Professional Bulletin*, Volume 22, p. 2.

84 Ibid.

85 Testimony on US UAV efforts to Congress, 1997, https://fas.org/irp/gao/nsi97138.htm.

86 FAS details website backup. "Outrider Tactical UAV," FAS Intelligence Resource Program, https://fas.org/irp/program/collect/outrider.htm.

87 Vector Site web archive, accessed June 24, 2020, https://web.archive.org/web/20110908060052/http:/www.vectorsite.net/twuav_07.html#m6.

88 Testimony to Congress on UAV procurement, 1997, https://fas.org/irp/gao/nsi97138.htm.

89 Tim Ripley, *The Air War*, London: Pen and Sword, 2004. p. 50.

90 Bill Sweetman, "Drones: Invented and Forgotten," *Popular Science*, September 1994.

91 *US Air Force Magazine*, Volumes 79-80, May 1997.

92 Major Keith E. Gentile, "The Future of Airborne Reconnaissance," FAS, March 27, 1996, https://fas.org/irp/eprint/gentile.htm.

93 *US Air Force Magazine*, Volumes 79-80, May 1997, p. 189.

94 Hearings on National Defense Authorization, 1996, p. 833.

95 Stephen Trimble, "Lockheed's Skunk Works Reveals Missing Link in Secret UAV History," Flight Global, March 26, 2018, https://www.flightglobal. com/civil-uavs/lockheeds-skunk-works-reveals-missing-link-in-secret-uav-history/127509.article.

96 Vector Site Web Archive, accessed June 24, 2020, https://web.archive.org/web/20110907171245/http:/www.vectorsite.net/twuav_13.html#m5.

97 Andrew Tarantola, "Why Did Lockheed Blow Up Its Own Prototype UAV Bomber?" Gizmodo, March 20, 2014, https://gizmodo.com/why-did-lockheed-blow-up-its-own-prototype-uav-bomber-1532210554; Also "Lockheed Confirms P-175 Polecat UAV Crash," Flight Global, March 20, 2007, https://www.flightglobal.com/lockheed-confirms-p-175-pole-cat-uav-crash/72561.article.

98 Hearings on National Defense Authorization, 1996, p. 833.

99 Ibid.

100 Hearings on National Defense Authorization, 1996, p. 840.

101 Ibid.

102 Dr. Daniel L. Haulman, "U.S. Unmanned Aerial Vehicles in Combat, 1991-2003," June 9, 2003, accessed May 23, 2020, https://apps.dtic.mil/dtic/tr/fulltext/u2/a434033.pdf.

103 "Defying the years, Global Hawk Goes from Strength to Strength," Shepherd Media, November 27, 2019, https://www.shephardmedia.com/news/uv-online/defying-years-global-hawk-goes-strength-strength/.

104 "Teledyne Ryan Rolls Out Global Hawk UAV," Aviation Week Network, February 21, 1997, https://aviationweek.com/teledyne-ryan-rolls-out-global-hawk-uav; "Teledyne Ryan Plans First Engine Runs of Global Hawk," Flight Global, December 18, 1996, https://www.flightglobal.com/teledyne-ryan-plans-first-engine-runs-of-global-hawk-reconnaissance-uav/4878.article. The company used ideas from its Cope-R and Compass Arrow designs.

105   Testimony to Congress on UAV procurement, 1997, https://fas.org/irp/gao/nsi97138.htm.

106   "Northrop Grumman Celebrates 20th Anniversary of Global Hawk's First Flight," Northup Grumman, February 28, 2018, accessed June 24, 2020, https://news.northropgrumman.com/news/releases/northrop-grumman-celebrates-20th-anniversary-of-global-hawks-first-flight.

107   Ibid.

108   Bill Kanzig, Global Hawk Systems Engineering Case Study, Air Force Center for Systems Engineering, 2010.

109   "Defying the Years: Global Hawk Goes from Strength-to-Strength (Studio)," Shephard Media, November 27, 2019, https://www.shephardmedia.com/news/uv-online/defying-years-global-hawk-goes-strength-strength/.

110   Bill Kanzig, MacAulay-Brown, Inc., "Global Hawk Systems Engineering Case Study, Air Force Center for Systems Engineering," Air Force Center for Systems Engineering, Wright-Patterson AFB, 2010, https://www.lboro.ac.uk/media/wwwlboroacuk/content/systems-net/downloads/pdfs/GLOBAL%20HAWK%20SYSTEMS%20ENGINEERING%20CASE%20STUDY.pdf. AV-3 also had an accident in December 1999, driving off the runway and crushing its nose gear. That air vehicle continued flying until 2008 when it was put on display at the Air Force Museum at Wright-Patterson.

111   "RQ-4A Global Hawk (Tier II+ HAE UAV)," FAS Intelligence Resource Program, https://fas.org/irp/program/collect/global_hawk.htm.

112   "Prototype Global Hawk Flies Home after 4,000 Combat Hours," Tech. Sgt. Andrew Leonard, 380th Air Expeditionary Wing Public Affairs, Air Force Link, 14 February 2006.

113   "Defying the Years: Global Hawk Goes from Strength-to-Strength (Studio)," Shephard Media, November 27, 2019, https://www.shephardmedia.com/news/uv-online/defying-years-global-hawk-goes-strength-strength/.

114   Northup Grumman Aeorspace Systems, "Global Hawk Turns 20," Edwards Air Force Base, February 28, 2018, https://www.edwards.af.mil/News/ Article/1453679/global-hawk-turns-20/.

115   Bill Kanzig, MacAulay-Brown, Inc., "Global Hawk Systems Engineering Case Study, Air Force Center for Systems Engineering," Air Force Center for Systems Engineering, Wright-Patterson AFB, 2010, https://www. lboro.ac.uk/media/wwwlboroacuk/content/systems-net/downloads/ pdfs/GLOBAL%20HAWK%20SYSTEMS%20ENGINEERING%20 CASE%20STUDY.pdf.

116   "RQ-4A 'Global Hawk'," Museum of Aviaton Foundation, accessed June 24, 2020, https://museumofaviation.org/portfolio/rq-4a-global-hawk/.

117   Bill Kanzig, MacAulay-Brown, Inc., "Global Hawk Systems Engineering Case Study, Air Force Center for Systems Engineering," Air Force Center for Systems Engineering, Wright-Patterson AFB, 2010, https://www. lboro.ac.uk/media/wwwlboroacuk/content/systems-net/downloads/ pdfs/GLOBAL%20HAWK%20SYSTEMS%20ENGINEERING%20 CASE%20STUDY.pdf.

118   Ibid.

119   Ibid.

120   "RQ-4A 'Global Hawk'," Museum of Aviaton Foundation, accessed June 24, 2020, https://museumofaviation.org/portfolio/rq-4a-global-hawk/.

121   Bill Kanzig, MacAulay-Brown, Inc., "Global Hawk Systems Engineering Case Study, Air Force Center for Systems Engineering," Air Force Center for Systems Engineering, Wright-Patterson AFB, 2010, https://www. lboro.ac.uk/media/wwwlboroacuk/content/systems-net/downloads/ pdfs/GLOBAL%20HAWK%20SYSTEMS%20ENGINEERING%20 CASE%20STUDY.pdf.

122   Ibid, p. 76.

123   Ibid.

124   Jeffrey Richelson, *The US Intelligence Community*.

125 Greg Goebel, "Modern US Endurance UAVs," TUAV, March 1, 2010, https://web.archive.org/web/20110907171245/http:/www.vectorsite.net/twuav_13.html#m5.

126 Kara Platoni, "That's Professor Global Hawk," *Air and Space Magazine*, May 2011, https://www.airspacemag.com/flight-today/thats-professor-global-hawk-433583/.

127 Department of Defense procurement testimony 1997, https://fas.org/irp/gao/nsi97138.htm.

128 Testimony to Congress on procurement, https://fas.org/irp/gao/nsi97138.htm.

129 "The Northrop Grumman MQ-4 Triton is the Naval Equivalent of the Land-Based RQ-4 Global Hawk UAV with Notable Changes to Suit the Maritime Role," Military Factory, Last Edited November 3, 2020, https://www.militaryfactory.com/aircraft/detail.asp?aircraft_id=983.

130 Greg Goebel, "Modern US Endurance UAVs," TUAV, March 1, 2010, https://web.archive.org/web/20110907171245/http:/www.vectorsite.net/twuav_13.html#m5.

131 Jeffrey Richelson, *The US Intelligence Community*.

132 David Axe, "The U.S. Drone Shot Down by Iran is $200 Million Prototype Spy Plane," *The Daily Beast*, June 20, 2019, https://www.the-dailybeast.com/bams-d-drone-shot-down-by-iran-is-a-dollar200-million-prototype-spy-plane.

133 "CENTCOM Releases Video of US Navy BAMS-D Shoot Down Over Straight of Hormuz," *Naval Today*, June 21, 2019, https://www.navaltoday.com/2019/06/21/centcom-releases-video-of-us-navy-bams-d-shoot-down-over-strait-of-hormuz/.

134 Patrick Tucker, "How the Pentagon Nickel-and-Dimed Its Way Into Losing a Drone," Defense One, June 20, 2019, https://www.defense-one.com/technology/2019/06/how-pentagon-nickel-and-dimed-its-way-losing-drone/157901/.

135 "Tracked and Killed," Middle East Eye, Jan 4, 2020. Accessed June 25, 2020.

136 TOI Staff, "Four Hellfire Missiles and a Severed Hand: The Killing of Qassem Soleimani," *The Times of Israel,* Jan. 3, 2020, Accessed June 25, 2020, https://www.timesofisrael.com/four-hellfire-missiles-and-a-severed-hand-the-killing-of-qassem-soleimani/.

137 Reuters Staff, "Trump Gives Dramatic Account of Soleimani's Death: CNN," Reuters, January 18, 2020, Accessed August 30, 2020, https://www.reuters.com/article/us-usa-trump-iran/trump-gives-dramatic-account-of-soleimanis-last-minutes-before-death-cnn-idUSKBN1ZH0G3.

138 "As Iran Missiles Battered Iraq Base, US Lost Eyes in the Sky," *Bangkok Post*, January 15, 2020, https://www.bangkokpost.com/world/1836219/as-iran-missiles-battered-iraq-base-us-lost-eyes-in-sky.

139 Interview with Douglas Feith, March 15, 2020.

140 P.W. Singer, *Wired for War.*

141 Headquarters Air Combat Command, Cable, "RQ-1, Predator, Program Direction," May 1, 2000; Richard Whittle, *Predator: The Secret Origins of the Drone Revolution*; Document list at website on history of the Predator, accessed June 24, 2020, https://nsarchive2.gwu.edu/NSAEBB/NSAEBB484/.

142 Department of the Air Force, Emails, "Predator Weaponization and INF Treaty," September 2000; Richard Whittle, *Predator: The Secret Origins of the Drone Revolution*; Document list at website on history of the Predator, accessed June 24, 2020, https://nsarchive2.gwu.edu/NSAEBB/NSAEBB484/.

143 Richard Whittle, *Predator: The Secret Origins of the Drone Revolution*; Document list at website on history of the Predator, accessed June 24, 2020, https://nsarchive2.gwu.edu/NSAEBB/NSAEBB484/.

144 Ibid; Clarke Memo, https://nsarchive2.gwu.edu/NSAEBB/NSAEBB147/clarke%20attachment.pdf.

145   Christopher J. Fuller, "The Origins of the Drone Program," Lawfare, February 18, 2018, https://www.lawfareblog.com/origins-drone-program.

146   Richard Whittle, *Predator: The Secret Origins of the Drone Revolution*; Document list at website on history of the Predator, accessed June 24, 2020, https://nsarchive2.gwu.edu/NSAEBB/NSAEBB484/.

147   Ibid.

148   Christopher J. Fuller, "The Origins of the Drone Program," Lawfare, February 18, 2018, https://www.lawfareblog.com/origins-drone-program.

149   Christopher Westland, *Global Innovation Management*, p. 264. At the time there were only forty-two Predators in service and four had been lost in Kosovo operations. Overall, eleven had been lost due to other reasons. Each Predator system consisted of four vehicles, one ground control station, and satellite link. By 2001 there were eighty vehicles under contract and twelve ground control stations. While ten Predators were in use, the rest were with the 11th and 15th Reconnaissance Squadrons. See 2001 Congressional testimony, Department of Defense appropriations hearngs, p. 247, accessed July 11, 2020.

150   P.W Singer, *Wired for War*.

151   Laurence Newcome, *Unmanned Aviation: A Brief History of Unmanned Aerial Vehicles*, p. 83.

152   Mark Bowden, "How the Predator Drone Changed the Character of War," *Smithsonian Magazine*, November 2013, https://www.smithsonianmag.com/history/how-the-predator-drone-changed-the-character-of-war-3794671/.

153   Ibid. Predators fired at 115 targets in their first year in Afghanistan.

154   150 were put to production in the following years. Singer, *Wired for War*.

155   David Glade, UAVs: Implications for Military Operations. 2000.

156   Daniel McGrory, Michael Evans, and Elaine Monaghan, "Robotic Warfare Leaves Terrorists No Hiding Place," *The Times*, November 6, 2002, https://www.thetimes.co.uk/article/robotic-warfare-leaves-terrorists-no-hiding-place-0srcfhq7nq5.

157 His full name was Qaed Salim Sinyan Al-Harethi; James Hasik, *Arms and Innovation: Entrepreneurship and Innovation in the 21st Century.*

158 Avery Plaw, "The Legality of Targeted Killing as an Instrument of War: The Case of the US Targeting Qaed Salim Sinan al-Harethi," *The Metamorphisis of War*, p. 55-72.

159 Philip Smucker, "The Intrigue Behind the Drone Strike," *The Christian Science Monitor,* November 12, 2002, https://www.csmonitor.com/2002/1112/p01s02-wome.html.

160 Ibid.

161 Christopher J. Fuller, "The Origins of the Drone Program," Lawfare, February 18, 2018, https://www.lawfareblog.com/origins-drone-program.

162 Some proposed arming the drones with AIM-92 Stinger missiles. War is Boring, "Yes, America Has Another Secret Spy Drone—We Pretty Much Knew That Already," *Medium,* December 6, 2013, https://medium.com/war-is-boring/yes-america-has-another-secret-spy-drone-we-pretty-much-knew-that-already-41df448d1700.

163 James Hasik, *Arms and Innovation: Entrepreneurship and Innovation in the 21st Century.*

164 Ibid.

165 Singer, *Wired for War.*

166 Senior Airman James Thompson, "Sun Setting the MQ-1 Predator: A History of Innovation," Nellis Air Force Base, February 14, 2018, accessed June 25, 2020, https://www.nellis.af.mil/News/Article/1442622/sun-setting-the-mq-1-predator-a-history-of-innovation/.

167 Singer, *Wired for War.*

168 Singer, *Wired for War.*

169 K. Valavanis and George J. Vachtsevanos (Eds.), *Handbook of Unmanned Aerial Vehicles.*

170 "Transforming Joint Air Power," *The Journal of the JAPCC,* 2006, http://www.japcc.org/wp-content/uploads/japcc_journal_Edition_3.pdf.

[171] Steve Linde, "50 Years Later, Ammunition Hill Hero Recalls Key Battle for Jerusalem," *The Jerusalem Post*, February 6, 2017, https://www.jpost.com/israel-news/50-years-later-ammunition-hill-hero-recalls-key-battle-for-jerusalem-480727.

[172] Interview with Gal Papier at Rafael, May 4, 2020.

[173] Interview with Richard Kemp, March 2, 2020.

[174] Interview with Kevin McDonald, April 27, 2020.

[175] "Transforming Joint Air Power," *The Journal of the JAPCC*, Edition 3, p. 24, 2006, http://www.japcc.org/wp-content/uploads/japcc_journal_Edition_3.pdf.

[176] David Mets, *Airpower and Technology*.

[177] Rudolph Herzog, "Rise of the Drones," *Lapham's Quarterly*, accessed June 11, 2020, https://www.laphamsquarterly.org/spies/rise-drones.

[178] Dan Hawkins, "RPA Training Next Transforms Pipeline to Competency-Based Construct," U.S. Air Force, June 3, 2020, Accessed July 7, 2020, https://www.af.mil/News/Article-Display/Article/2207074/rpa-training-next-transforms-pipeline-to-competency-based-construct/.

[179] Interview with unidentified drone operator, July 4, 2020.

[180] See also Tony Guerra, "Rank & Job Description of Air Force Drone Pilots," Chron, Accessed July 7, 2020, https://work.chron.com/rank-job-description-air-force-drone-pilots-20092.html; See also job description for "Remote Piloted Aircraft Pilot," U.S. Air Force, accessed July 7, 2020, https://www.airforce.com/careers/detail/remotely-piloted-aircraft-pilot.

[181] Brett Velicovich, *Drone Warrior*, page 10.

[182] Joseph Trevithick, "USAF Reveals Details," The Drive, July 13, 2018, https://www.thedrive.com/the-war-zone/22158/usaf-reveals-details-about-some-of-its-most-secretive-drone-units-with-new-awards; See also 432nd Wing/432nd Air Expeditionary Wing Public Affairs, "Air Force Awards First Remote Device: Dominant Persistent Attack Aircrew Recognized," Air Combat Command, July 11, 2018, accessed July 7, 2020, https://www.

acc.af.mil/News/Article-Display/Article/1572831/air-force-awards-first-remote-device-dominant-persistent-attack-aircrew-recogni/.

183 Greg Goebel, "Modern US Endurance UAVs," TUAV, March 1, 2010, https://web.archive.org/web/20110907171245/http:/www.vectorsite.net/twuav_13.html#m5.

184 James Hasik, *Arms and Innovation: Entrepreneurship and Innovation in the 21st Century.*

185 See *Permanent War: Rise of the Drones, The Washington Post,* August 13, 2013.

186 Christopher Fuller, See it/shoot it, p. 127.

187 "The Drone War in Pakistan," New America Foundation, https://www.newamerica.org/international-security/reports/americas-counterterrorism-wars/the-drone-war-in-pakistan/.

188 Ibid.

189 Interview with anonymous former drone pilot.

190 Alice Ross, Chris Woods, and Sarah Leo, "The Reaper Presidency: Obama's 300th Drone Strike in Pakistan," The Bureau of Investigative Journalism, December 3, 2012, https://www.newamerica.org/international-security/reports/americas-counterterrorism-wars/the-drone-war-in-pakistan/.

191 Ibid.

192 Ibid.

193 Christian Brose, *Kill Chain: Defending America in the Future,* p. 138.

194 Christopher J. Fuller, "The Eagle Comes Home to Roost: The Historical Origins of the CIA's Lethal Drone Program," *Intelligence and National Security,* p. 769-792, May 1, 2014, https://www.tandfonline.com/doi/abs/10.1080/02684527.2014.895569.

195 Reapers, flown from Creech in Nevada, and run by the 9th Attack Squadron at Holloman in New Mexico. Jeffrey Richelson, *The US Intelligence Community.*

196 Ibid.

197 Ibid.

198 WikiLeaks, "Scenesetter: Turkey's CHOD and Minister of Defense Travel to Washington," Public Library of US Diplomacy, May 28, 2009, https://wikileaks.org/plusd/cables/09ANKARA756_a.html.

199 "US Terminates Secret Drone Programme with Turkey: US Officials," Middle East Eye, February 5, 2020, https://www.middleeasteye.net/news/us-terminates-secret-drone-program-turkey-us-officials.

200 WikiLeaks, "Pakistan Media Reaction: February 03, 2010," Public Library of US Diplomacy, February 3, 2010, https://wikileaks.org/plusd/cables/10ISLAMABAD265_a.html.

201 Fuller, *See it, shoot it,* p. 236.

202 Christopher Fuller argues that it likely reduced US casualties in Afghanistan. Fuller, p. 237.

203 Gen. John P. Abizaid (US Army, Ret.) and Rosa Brooks, "Recommendations and Report of The Task Force on US Drone Policy," Stimson, April 2015, https://www.stimson.org/wp-content/files/file-attachments/recommendations_and_report_of_the_task_force_on_us_drone_policy_second_edition.pdf.

204 James Clark, ISR innovation director at the Air Force said ninety percent of missions were in combat. Senior Airman James Thompson, "Sun Setting the MQ-1 Predator: A History of Innovation," Nellis Air Force Base, February 14, 2018, accessed June 25, 2020, https://www.nellis.af.mil/News/Article/1442622/sun-setting-the-mq-1-predator-a-history-of-innovation/.

205 Ibid. For details on the life of the pilots, see Senior Airman Christian Clausen, "Flying the RPA Mission," U.S. Air Force, March 22, 2016, accessed July 7, 2020, https://www.af.mil/News/Article-Display/Article/699974/flying-the-rpa-mission/.

206 In 1965, for instance, the US had flown 55,000 sorties in Vietnam during Operation Rolling Thunder. Michael Clodfetter, *Warfare and Armed Conflict*, New York: 2017, Accessed June 27, 2020.

[207] Joseph Trevithick and Tyler Rogoway, "Shedding Some Light on the Air Force's Most Shadowy Drone Squadron," The Drive, April 25, 2018. Accessed June 27, 2020, https://www.thedrive.com/the-war-zone/19318/uncovering-the-air-forces-most-mysterious-drone-squadron.

[208] For details see the US Air Force website, 432nd list of articles, https://www.acc.af.mil/News/Tag/84014/432nd-wing432nd-air-expeditionary-wing/; 15th Attack Squadron, https://www.acc.af.mil/News/Tag/89078/15th-attack-squadron/; 11th Attack Squadron, https://www.acc.af.mil/News/Tag/84124/11th-attack-squadron/; and Senior Airman James Thompson, "Sun Setting the MQ-1 Predator: A History of Innovation," Nellis Air Force Base, February 14, 2018, accessed June 25, 2020, https://www.nellis.af.mil/News/Article/1442622/sun-setting-the-mq-1-predator-a-history-of-innovation/.

[209] Stephen Jones to author, interview, June 28, 2020.

[210] US Air Force biography sent to author by US Air Force.

[211] Ibid.

[212] *Accidents Will Happen*, Drone Wars UK, p. 14.

[213] Micah Zenko, "What Was That Drone Doing in Benghazi?" Council on Foreign Relations, November 2, 2012, https://www.cfr.org/blog/what-was-drone-doing-benghazi.

[214] Mark Thompson, "Why the U.S. Military Can't Kill the Benghazi Attackers With a Drone Strike," *TIME*, February 2, 2014, https://time.com/3316/why-the-u-s-military-cant-kill-the-benghazi-attackers-with-a-drone-strike/.

[215] See screenshot of testimony. Mark Thompson, "Why the U.S. Military Can't Kill the Benghazi Attackers With a Drone Strike," *TIME*, February 2, 2014, https://time.com/3316/why-the-u-s-military-cant-kill-the-benghazi-attackers-with-a-drone-strike/.

[216] Christopher J. Fuller, "The Origins of the Drone Program," Lawfare, February 18, 2018, https://www.lawfareblog.com/origins-drone-program.

217 Inside the rescue operations. David Axe, "8,000 Miles, 96 Hours, 3 Dead Pirates: Inside a Navy Seal Rescue, *Wired*, October 17, 2012, https://www. wired.com/2012/10/navy-seals-pirates/.

218 Tanya Somanader, "The President Addresses the Nation on a U.S. Counterterrorism Operation in January," The White House: President Barack Obama, April 23, 2015, https://obamawhitehouse.archives.gov/ blog/2015/04/23/president-addresses-nation-us-counterterrorism-opera-tion-january.

219 Alice Ross, Chris Woods, and Sarah Leo, "The Reaper Presidency: Obama's 300th Drone Strike in Pakistan," The Bureau of Investigative Journalism, December 3, 2012, https://www.newamerica.org/interna-tional-security/reports/americas-counterterrorism-wars/the-drone-war-in-pakistan/; For Pakistan, see "The Drone War in Pakistan," New America Foundation, https://www.newamerica.org/international-security/reports/ americas-counterterrorism-wars/the-drone-war-in-pakistan/.

220 Gen. John P. Abizaid (US Army, Ret.) and Rosa Brooks, "Recommendations and Report of The Task Force on US Drone Policy," Stimson, April 2015, https://www.stimson.org/wp-content/files/file-attachments/recommen-dations_and_report_of_the_task_force_on_us_drone_policy_second_ edition.pdf.

221 Christopher J. Fuller, "The Origins of the Drone Program," Lawfare, February 18, 2018, https://www.lawfareblog.com/origins-drone-program.

222 Jeremy Scahill, "Find, Fix Finish: For the Pentagon, Creating an Architecture of Assasination Meant Navigating a Turf War with the CIA," *The Intercept*, October 15, 2015, https://theintercept.com/drone-papers/find-fix-finish/.

223 Joseph Trevithick, "USAF reveals details about some of its most secretive units," The Drive, July 12, 2018, accessed June 27, 2020.

224 See document by *The Intercept* on TF 84-4 operations, https://theintercept. com/document/2015/10/14/small-footprint-operations-5-13/#page-5.

225   Nick Turse, "Target Africa: The U.S. Military's Expanding Footprint in East Africa and the Arabian Peninsula," *The Intercept,* October 15, 2015, https://theintercept.com/drone-papers/target-africa/; See document by *The Intercept* on TF 84-4 operations, https://theintercept.com/document/2015/10/14/small-footprint-operations-5-13/#page-5.

226   Amnesty International, "Will I Be Next?: US Drone Strikes in Pakistan," Amnesty International Publications, 2013, https://www.amnestyusa.org/files/asa330132013en.pdf.

227   Ibid.

228   Ibid.

229   Micah Zenko, "Redefining the Obama Administration's Narrative on Drones," Council on Foreign Relations, June 13, 2013, accessed June 27, 2020, https://www.cfr.org/blog/refining-obama-administrations-drone-strike-narrative.

230   Amnesty International, "Will I Be Next?: US Drone Strikes in Pakistan," Amnesty International Publications, p. 19, 2013, https://www.amnestyusa.org/files/asa330132013en.pdf.

231   Ibid.

232   ACLU, "Al-Aulaqi v. Panetta—Constitutional Challenge to Killing of Three U.S. Citizens," June 4, 2014, https://www.aclu.org/cases/al-aulaqi-v-panetta-constitutional-challenge-killing-three-us-citizens.

233   Ibid.

234   Jon Shelton, "Court Hears Case on Germany's role in US Drone Deaths in Yemen," DW, March 14, 2019, https://www.dw.com/en/court-hears-case-on-germanys-role-in-us-drone-deaths-in-yemen/a-47921862.

235   "UN Rights Experts Call for Transparency in the Use of Armed Drones, Citing Risks of Illegal Use," UN News, October 25, 2013, https://news.un.org/en/story/2013/10/453832-un-rights-experts-call-transparency-use-armed-drones-citing-risks-illegal-use.

236   Dana Hughes, "US Drone Strikes in Pakistan Are Illegal, Says UN Terrorism Official," ABC News, March 16, 2013, https://abcnews.

go.com/blogs/politics/2013/03/us-drone-strikes-in-pakistan-are-illegal-says-un-terrorism-official/.

237 Ibid.

238 Don McCarthy, *The Sword of David*, p. 125.

239 See for instance, "Armed Drones in the Middle East," RUSI, accessed June 27, 2020, https://drones.rusi.org/countries/israel/; Michael R. Stolley, *Unmanned Vanguard: Leveraging the Israeli Unmanned Aircraft System Program*, April 2012, p. 5, https://apps.dtic.mil/dtic/tr/fulltext/u2/1022968.pdf; João Ferreira, "Parliamentary Questions: EU Agencies' Relationships with Companies Violating Human Rights," European Parliament, April 12, 2020, accessed June 27, 2020, https://www.europarl.europa.eu/doceo/document/E-9-2020-002217_EN.html; also the website https://whoprofits.org/company/elbit-systems/.

240 *Israel's Drone Wars: An Update*, Drone Wars UK, p. 5-6, November, 2019.

241 Aurora Intel, @AuroraIntel, "#IDF Hermes 450 UAV captured on video over #Lebanon earlier today. #Israel," May 19, 2020. Tweet accessed May 19, 2020, https://twitter.com/AuroraIntel/status/1262684924177534976.

242 "UAV Crash in Lebanon Reveals Secret Israeli Weapon," South Front, April 1, 2018, Accessed May 19, 2020, https://southfront.org/uav-crash-in-lebanon-reveals-secret-israeli-weapon/.

243 "European Parliament Resolution of 27 February 2014 on the Use of Armed Drones," European Parliament, February 27, 2014, Strasbourg, https://www.europarl.europa.eu/doceo/document/TA-7-2014-0172_EN.html?redirect.

244 Ibid.

245 See for instance, WikiLeaks, "(Enemy Action) Direct Fire RPT (RPG, Small Arms) TF Red Currahee (Reaper 7)," July 27, 2008, https://wikileaks.org/afg/event/2008/07/AFG20080727n1367.html; "Counting Drone Strike Deaths," Human Rights Clinic at Columbia Law School, October 2012, https://web.law.columbia.edu/sites/default/files/microsites/human-rights-institute/files/COLUMBIACountingDronesFinal.pdf; The

Center for the Study of the Drone at Bard College, https://dronecenter. bard.edu/; *The Intercept's* "The Drone Papers," https://theintercept.com/ drone-papers/; "Pakistan: Reported US Strikes 2010," The Bureau of Investigative Journalism, https://www.thebureauinvestigates.com/drone-war/data/obama-2010-pakistan-strikes; Peter Bergen, Melissa Salyk-Virk, and David Sterman, "World of Drones," July 30, 2020, New America, https://www.newamerica.org/international-security/reports/world-drones/.

246 Gen. John P. Abizaid (US Army, Ret.) and Rosa Brooks, "Recommendations and Report of The Task Force on US Drone Policy," Stimson, April 2015, https://www.stimson.org/wp-content/files/file-attachments/recommen-dations_and_report_of_the_task_force_on_us_drone_policy_second_edition.pdf.

247 Ibid.

248 Ibid.

249 See SOCOM Aspen Institute. Benjamin Wittes, "More Videos from the Aspen Security Forum: A Look Into SOCOM," July 27, 2015. https://www.lawfareblog.com/more-videos-aspen-security-forum.

250 Jeremy Scahill, "Find, Fix Finish: For the Pentagon, Creating an Architecture of Assasination Meant Navigating a Turf War with the CIA," *The Intercept*, October 15, 2015, https://theintercept.com/drone-papers/find-fix-finish/.

251 "Statement of General Raymond A. Thomas, III, U.S. Army Commander, United States Special Operations Command Before the House Armed Services Committee Subcommittee on Emerging Threats and Capabilities," February 15, 2018, https://docs.house.gov/meetings/AS/AS26/20180215/106851/HHRG-115-AS26-Wstate-ThomasR-20180215.pdf; also Cora Currier and Peter Maass, "Firing Blind: Flawed Intelligence and the Limits of Drone Technology," *The Intercept*, October 15, 2015, https://theintercept.com/drone-papers/firing-blind/.

252 Gen. John P. Abizaid (US Army, Ret.) and Rosa Brooks, "Recommendations and Report of The Task Force on US Drone Policy," Stimson, April 2015, https://www.stimson.org/wp-content/files/file-attachments/recommendations_and_report_of_the_task_force_on_us_drone_policy_second_edition.pdf.

253 Christopher J. Fuller, "The Origins of the Drone Program," Lawfare, February 18, 2018, https://www.lawfareblog.com/origins-drone-program.

254 Wim Zwijnenburg, interview, March 3, 2020.

255 James Hasik, *Arms and Innovation: Entrepreneurship and Innovation in the 21st Century.*

256 Valerie Insinna, "US Air Force Relaunches Effort to Replace MQ-9 Reaper Drone," *Defense News*, June 4, 2020, https://www.defensenews.com/air/2020/06/04/the-air-force-is-looking-for-a-next-gen-replacement-to-the-mq-9-reaper-drone/.

257 Gordon Lubold and Warren P. Strobel, "Secret U.S. Missile Aims to Kill Only Terrorists, Not Nearby Civillians," *The Wall Street Journal,* May 9, 2019, https://www.wsj.com/articles/secret-u-s-missile-aims-to-kill-only-terrorists-not-nearby-civilians-11557403411.

258 Thomas Barnett, *The Pentagon's New Map*, New York: Putnam, 2004.

259 The company was later purchased by Northrop.

260 For one list see "Non-State Actors with Drone Capabilities," New America, https://www.newamerica.org/international-security/reports/world-drones/non-state-actors-with-drone-capabilities/.

261 Terrorists develop UAVs, December 6, 2005; http://www.armscontrol.ru/UAV/mirsad1.htm.

262 Syrian intelligence aided Hezbollah drone incursion, US diplomatic cable; WikiLeaks, "MGLE01: Syrian Intelligence May Have Worked with Hizballah on UAV Launchings," Public Library of US Diplomacy, April 25, 2005, https://wikileaks.org/plusd/cables/05BEIRUT1322_a.html.

263 US Dialogue, WikiLeaks, "U.S./IS Dialogue on Lebanon: Support Moderates, But Disagreement Over How," Public Library of US Diplomacy, September 29, 2008, https://wikileaks.org/plusd/cables/08TELA-VIV2247_a.html.

264 Congressional Research on Iran: Kenneth Katzman, "Congressional Research Service Report RL32048, Iran: U.S. Concerns and Policy Responses," WikiLeaks Document Release, December 31, 2008, Released February 2, 2009, https://file.wikileaks.org/file/crs/RL32048.pdf.

265 Milton Hoenig, "Hezbollah and the Use of Drones as a Weapon of Terrorism," *Public Interest Report* (67) no. 2, Spring 2014, https://fas.org/wp-content/uploads/2014/06/Hezbollah-Drones-Spring-2014.pdf; Arthur Holland Michel, Dan Gettinger, "A Brief History of Hamas and Hezbollah's Drones," Need to Know, July 14, 2014, https://dronecenter.bard.edu/hezbollah-hamas-drones/.

266 "Iranian-Made Ababil-T Hezbollah UAV Shot Down by Israeli Fighter in Lebanon Crisis," FlightGlobal, August 15, 2006, https://www.flightglobal.com/iranian-made-ababil-t-hezbollah-uav-shot-down-by-israeli-fighter-in-lebanon-crisis/68992.article.

267 WikiLeaks, "U.S./IS Dialogue on Lebanon: Support Moderates, but Disagreement Over How," Public Library of US Diplomacy, September 29, 2008, https://wikileaks.org/plusd/cables/08TELAVIV2247_a.html.

268 Stratfor email: https://wikileaks.org/gifiles/docs/66/66411_-insight-in-sight-lebanon-hez-preparations-me1-.html.

269 Congressional Research on Iran: Kenneth Katzman, "Congressional Research Service Report RL32048, Iran: U.S. Concerns and Policy Responses," WikiLeaks Document Release, December 31, 2008, Released February 2, 2009, https://file.wikileaks.org/file/crs/RL32048.pdf.

270 See Critical Threats Iran Tracker: Michael Adkins, "Iran-Lebanese Hezbollah Relationship Tracker," Critical Threats, March 19, 2010, https://www.criticalthreats.org/briefs/iran-lebanese-hezbollah-relationship-tracker/

iran-lebanese-hezbollah-relationship-tracker-2010#_edn96b5b263bb-f1e4493514627b8fb9e5bf51.

[271] Yaakov Katz, "IDF Encrypting Drones after Hezbollah Accessed Footage," *The Jerusalem Post,* October 27, 2010, https://www.jpost.com/israel/idf-encrypting-drones-after-hizbullah-accessed-footage.

[272] WikiLeaks, "Re: S3/G3 – Israel/Lebanon/Syriamil – Hizbullah Has Drones, Israeli Officer Warns: We Will Strike Syria if it Continues Its Support," *The Global Intelligence Files,* August 25, 2013, https://wikileaks.org/gifiles/docs/11/1194067_re-s3-g3-israel-lebanon-syriamil-hizbullah-has-drones.html.

[273] Adam Rawnsley, "Iran's Drones Are Back in Iraq," *War is Boring,* January 24, 2015, Accessed June 15, 2020, https://medium.com/war-is-boring/irans-drones-are-back-in-iraq-ed60bb33501d.

[274] David Donald, "Israel Shoots Down Hezbollah's Iranian UAV," AIN Online, October 12, 2012, https://www.ainonline.com/aviation-news/defense/2012-10-12/israel-shoots-down-hezbollahs-iranian-uav.

[275] Mariam Karouny, "Hezbollah Confirms it Sent Drone Downed Over Israel," Reuters, October 11, 2012, https://www.reuters.com/article/us-lebanon-israel-drone/hezbollah-confirms-it-sent-drone-downed-over-israel-idUSBRE89A19J20121011.

[276] Belen Fernandez, "Meet Ayoub: The Muslim Drone," Al Jazeera, October 18, 2012, https://www.aljazeera.com/opinions/2012/10/18/meet-ayoub-the-muslim-drone.

[277] Avery Plaw and Elizabeth Santoro, "Hezbollah's Drone Program Sets Precedents for Non-State Actors," Jamestown Foundation, November 10, 2017, https://www.refworld.org/docid/5a0d7eb94.html.

[278] "Hezbollah Drone Airstrip in Lebanon Revealed," Ynet, April 25, 2015, https://www.ynetnews.com/articles/0,7340,L-4650361,00.html.

[279] Rosana Bou Mouncef, "Hezbollah Drone Another Example of Iran Exerting Regional Influence," Al-Monitor, October 16, 2012, https://www.al-mon-

itor.com/pulse/security/01/10/hezbollah-drone-shows-irans-regional-influence-undimmed.html.

280 *The Associated Press,* "Israel Uses Patriot Missile to Shoot Down Drone," *Defense News,* November 13, 2017, https://www.defensenews.com/land/2017/11/13/israel-uses-patriot-missile-to-shoot-down-drone/.

281 Amos Harel, "Air Force: Hezbollah Drone Flew Over Israel for Five Minutes," *Haaretz,* August 11, 2004, https://www.haaretz.com/1.4752200.

282 David Kenner, "Why Israel Fears Iran's Presence in Syria," *The Atlantic,* July 22, 2018, https://www.theatlantic.com/international/archive/2018/07/hezbollah-iran-new-weapons-israel/565796/.

283 Roi Kais, "Hezbollah Has Fleet of 200 Iranian-Made UAVs," Ynet, November 25, 2013, https://www.ynetnews.com/articles/0,7340,L-4457653,00.html.

284 David M. Halbfinger, "Israel Says It Struck Iranian 'Killer Drones,'" *The New York Times,* August 24, 2019, https://www.nytimes.com/2019/08/24/world/middleeast/israel-says-it-struck-iranian-killer-drones-in-syria.html.

285 Ronen Bergman, "Hezbollah Stockpiling Drones in Anticipation of Israeli Strike," Al-Monitor, February 15, 2013, https://www.al-monitor.com/pulse/security/01/05/the-drone-threat.html.

286 Agencies, "Lebanese Man Pleads Guilty in US to Buying Drone Parts for Hezbollah," *The Times of Israel,* March 11, 2020, https://www.timesofisrael.com/lebanese-man-pleads-guilty-in-us-to-buying-drone-parts-for-hezbollah/.

287 Arthur Holland Michel, Dan Gettinger, "A Brief History of Hamas and Hezbollah's Drones," Need to Know, July 14, 2014, https://dronecenter.bard.edu/hezbollah-hamas-drones/.

288 David Cenciotti, "Hamas Flying an Iranian-Made Armed Drone Over Gaza," *The Aviationist,* July 14, 2014, https://theaviationist.com/2014/07/14/ababil-over-israel/; See also Steven Stalinsky and R. Sosnow, "A Decade of Jihadi Organizations' Use of Drones," MEMRI, February 21, 2017, Accessed June 27, 2020, https://www.memri.org/

reports/decade-jihadi-organizations-use-drones-%E2%80%93-early-experiments-hizbullah-hamas-and-al-qaeda.

[289] Yoav Zitun, "Watch: Israeli Air Force Shoots Down Hamas Drone," Ynet, September 20, 2016, https://www.ynetnews.com/articles/0,7340,L-4857327,00.html.

[290] Reuters Staff, "Israel Shoots Down Hamas Drone from Gaza Strip: Military," Reuters, February 23, 2017, https://www.reuters.com/article/us-israel-palestinians-uav/israel-shoots-down-hamas-drone-from-gaza-strip-military-idUSKBN1621TL.

[291] "Egyptian Military Shoots Down 'Hamas Drone' from Gaza," The New Arab, September 25, 2019, https://english.alaraby.co.uk/english/news/2019/9/25/egypt-shoots-down-hamas-drone-from-gaza.

[292] "US Navy Seizes Illegal Weapons in Arabian Sea," U.S. Central Command, February 13, 2019, https://www.centcom.mil/MEDIA/PRESS-RELEASES/Press-Release-View/Article/2083824/us-navy-seizes-illegal-weapons-in-arabian-sea/#.XkWiDE6gzoo.twitter.

[293] Lisa Barrington and Aziz El Yaakoubi, "Yemen Houthi Drones, Missiles Defy Years of Saudi Air Strikes," Reuters, September 17, 2019, https://www.reuters.com/article/us-saudi-aramco-houthis/yemen-houthi-drones-missiles-defy-years-of-saudi-air-strikes-idUSKBN1W22F4.

[294] "Drone Attack by Yemen Rebels Sparks Fire in Saudi Oil Field," Al Jazeera, August 17, 2019, https://www.aljazeera.com/economy/2019/8/17/drone-attack-by-yemen-rebels-sparks-fire-in-saudi-oil-field.

[295] In May 2019, Houthis claimed they attacked oil pumping stations in Saudi Arabia. It later emerged those drones might have been flown from Iraq by Iranian-backed Kataib Hezbollah. Laurie Mylroie, "US Says Drones from Iraq Were Fired at Saudi Pipeline, As Military Build Up Continues," Kurdistan 24, June 29, 2019, https://www.kurdistan24.net/en/news/416f57dc-f3a5-454b-aa14-8e6eea71f4fa.

296   Dhia Muhsin, "Houthi Use of Drones Delivers Potent Message in Yemen War," IISS, August 27, 2019, https://www.iiss.org/blogs/analysis/2019/08/houthi-uav-strategy-in-yemen.

297   Almasdar link to photos: https://cdn.almasdarnews.com/wp-content/uploads/2017/02/1-25.jpg.

298   Jon Gambrell, *The Associated Press*, "How Yemen's Rebels Increasingly Deploy Drones," *Defense News*, May 21, 2019, https://www.defensenews.com/unmanned/2019/05/21/how-yemens-rebels-increasingly-deploy-drones/.

299   Jon Gambrell, *Associated Press,* "Devices Found in Missiles, Yemen Drones Link Iran to Attacks," ABC News, February 19, 2020, https://abcnews.go.com/International/wireStory/devices-found-missiles-yemen-drones-link-iran-attacks-69064032.

300   For an image of the Shahed-123 see: https://twitter.com/jeremybinnie/status/1110933643499921412; For details on the Hermes 450, see Bill Yenne's *Drone Strike!*; For details on Hermes 450s crashing, see Drone Wars 2019 publication *Accidents Will Happen*, p. 19, https://dronewars.net/wp-content/uploads/2019/06/DW-Accidents-WEB.pdf.

301   "Evolution of UAVs Employed by Houthi Forces in Yemen," Conflict Armament Research, February 19, 2020, https://storymaps.arcgis.com/stories/46283842630243379f0504ece90a821f.

302   Ibid, p. 21.

303   *Iran's Networks of Influence in the Middle* East, International Institute for Strategic Studies, p. 170.

304   James Reinl, "Middle East Drone Wars Heat Up in Yemen," The New Arab, April 30, 2019, https://english.alaraby.co.uk/english/indepth/2019/4/30/middle-east-drone-wars-heat-up-in-yemen.

305   "Evolution of UAVs Employed by Houthi Forces in Yemen," Conflict Armament Research, February 19, 2020, https://storymaps.arcgis.com/stories/46283842630243379f0504ece90a821f.

306 "Timeline of Houthis' Drone and Missile Attacks on Saudi Targets," Al Jazeera, September 14, 2019, https://www.aljazeera.com/news/2019/9/14/timeline-houthis-drone-and-missile-attacks-on-saudi-targets; For more details see Thomas Harding, "The Houthis Have Built Their Own Drone Industry in Yemen," *The National,* June 13, 2020, https://www.thenationalnews.com/world/mena/the-houthis-have-built-their-own-drone-industry-in-yemen-1.1032847.

307 Jamie Prentis, "Houthi Drone Power Increasing with Iranian Help: The Key Takeaways," *The National,* February 19, 2020, https://www.thenationalnews.com/world/mena/houthi-drone-power-increasing-with-iranian-help-the-key-takeaways-1.981603.

308 "Suicide Drones…Houthi Strategic Weapon," Abaad Studies & Research Center, https://abaadstudies.org/print.php?id=59795.

309 "Yemeni Army Unveils New Indigenous Combat, Reconnaissance Drones," Press TV, February 26, 2017, https://www.presstv.com/Detail/2017/02/26/512188/Yemeni-army-combat-reconnaissance-drone-Qasef-Hudhud-Borkan-ballistic-missile.

310 Aaron Stein, "Low-Tech, High-Reward: The Houthi Drone Attack," Foreign Policy Research Institute, January 11, 2019, https://www.fpri.org/article/2019/01/low-tech-high-reward-the-houthi-drone-attack/.

311 "Report: Yemen's Houthis Developing Deadlier, More Accurate Drones," Middle East Monitor, February 19, 2020, https://www.middleeastmonitor.com/20200219-report-yemens-houthis-developing-deadlier-more-accurate-drones/.

312 Howard Altman, "Tale of Two Drones: ISIS Wreaked Havoc Cheaply, Tampa Meeting Showcases State of the Art," *Tampa Bay Times,* May 17, 2017, https://www.tampabay.com/news/military/tale-of-two-drones-isis-wreaked-havoc-cheaply-tampa-meeting-showcases/2324138/.

313 Gary Sheftick, "Innovative Agencies Partner to Counter Drone Threat," Army News Service, November 18, 2015, https://www.army.mil/arti-

cle/158748/innovative_agencies_partner_to_counter_drone_threat; John Kester, "Darpa Wants Mobile Technologies to Combat Small Drones," *Foreign Policy*, October 5, 2017, https://foreignpolicy.com/2017/10/05/darpa-wants-mobile-technologies-to-combat-small-drones/#:~:text=The%20U.S.%20military%20needs%20better%20tech%20to%20fight%20store%2Dbought%20drones.&text=U.S.%20military%20convoys%20in%20dangerous,about%20three%20to%20four%20years.

314 James Lewis, "The Battle of Marawi: Small Team Lessons Learned for the Close Fight," The Cove, November 26, 2018, Accessed May 27, 2020, https://cove.army.gov.au/article/the-battle-marawi-small-team-lessons-learned-the-close-fight.

315 Oriana Pawlyk, "New Pentagon Team Will Develop Ways to Fight Enemy Drones," *Defense News,* January 15, 2020, https://www.military.com/daily-news/2020/01/15/new-pentagon-team-will-develop-ways-fight-enemy-drones.html.

316 Kyle Rempfer, "Did US Drones Swarm a Russian Base? Probably Not, but That Capability Isn't Far Off," Military Times, October 29, 2018, https://www.militarytimes.com/news/2018/10/29/did-us-drones-swarm-a-russian-base-probably-not-but-that-capability-isnt-far-off/.

317 Kelsey D. Atheron, "If This Rocket is So 'Dumb,' How Does it Ram Enemy Drones Out of the Sky?" C4ISRNET, April 23, 2019, https://www.c4isrnet.com/unmanned/2019/04/23/russian-robot-will-ram-drones-out-of-the-sky/.

318 "Russia Repels Drone Attack on Base in Syria's Latakia," Tasnim News Agency, January 20, 2020, https://www.tasnimnews.com/en/news/2020/01/20/2185986/russia-repels-drone-attack-on-base-in-syria-s-latakia.

319 Clay Dillow, "The 'Beast of Kandahar' Stealth Aircraft Quietly Resurfaces in New Pics," *Popular Science,* January 25, 2011, https://www.popsci.com/technology/article/2011-01/beast-kandahar-quietly-resurfaces-new-pics/.

320 Bill Yenne, *Area 51-Black Jets: A History of the Aircraft Developed at Groom Lake;* See also Joseph Trevithick and Tyler Rogoway, "Details Emerge About the Secretive RQ-170 Stealth Drone's First Trip to Korea," January 28, 2020, https://www.thedrive.com/the-war-zone/31992/exclusive-details-on-the-secretive-rq-170-stealth-drones-first-trip-to-korea.

321 WikiLeaks, "Iran Military Shoots Down U.S. Drone-State TV," Huma Abedin to Hillary Clinton, December 4, 2011, https://wikileaks.org/clinton-emails/emailid/24991.

322 "Video: Iran Shows Off Captured U.S. Drone, Swears It's No Fake," *Wired,* December 8, 2011, https://www.wired.com/2011/12/iran-drone-video/.

323 WikiLeaks, "AP Sources: Drone Crashed In Iran on CIA Mission (AP)," Huma Abedin to Hillary Clinton, December 6, 2011, https://wikileaks.org/clinton-emails/emailid/12828.

324 AP, "Iran Says Downed US Drone Was Deep In Its Airspace," *Egypt Independent,* December 7, 2011, https://www.egyptindependent.com/iran-says-downed-us-drone-was-deep-its-airspace/.

325 Andrew Tarantola, "Why Did Lockheed Blow Up Its Own Prototype UAV Bomber?" Gizmodo, March 20, 2014, https://gizmodo.com/why-did-lockheed-blow-up-its-own-prototype-uav-bomber-1532210554.

326 WikiLeaks, "Pilot Error May Have Caused Iran Drone Crash (Reuters)," Huma Abedin to Hillary Clinton, December 16, 2011, https://wikileaks.org/clinton-emails/emailid/12818.

327 Adam Rawnsley, *Wired,* December 8, 2011; Part of a Wikileaks digest on the drone downing: WikiLeaks, "[OS] Iran/US/MIL/CT/TECH – Tech Websites' Coverage of the Iranian RQ-170 Footage," *The Global Intelligence Files,* December 9, 2011, https://wikileaks.org/gifiles/docs/60/60475_-os-iran-us-mil-ct-tech-tech-websites-coverage-of-the.html.

328 Zachary Wilson, "Airmen Demonstrate Unmanned Aircraft Systems Not Merely 'Drones,'" DVIDS, March 25, 2009, https://www.dvid-

shub.net/news/31579/airmen-demonstrate-unmanned-aircraft-systems-not-merely-drones.

329 WikiLeaks, "Analysis for Edit – 3 – Iran/MIL – UAV Rumors – Short – ASAP," Stratfor emails, *The Global Intelligence Files,* December 5, 2011, https://wikileaks.org/gifiles/docs/18/1850711_analysis-for-edit-3-iran-mil-uav-rumors-short-asap-.html.

330 Justin Fishel, "Panetta Says Drone Campaign Over Iran Will Continue," *Fox News,* December 13, 2011, https://www.foxnews.com/politics/panetta-says-drone-campaign-over-iran-will-continue.

331 Lockheed had used a fail-safe option to down the Polecat in December 2006. "Iran Warns Afghanistan About U.S. Drones," *The Daily Beast,* December 15, 2011, https://www.thedailybeast.com/cheats/2011/12/15/iran-warns-afghanistan-about-u-s-drones.

332 Heather Maher, "Iran Shows Footage Of Captured U.S. Drone," RFERL, December 8, 2011, https://www.rferl.org/a/iran_airs_footage_of_us_drone/24416107.html.

333 Adam Stone, "How Full-Motion Video is Changing ISR," C4ISR, March 23, 2016, https://www.c4isrnet.com/intel-geoint/isr/2016/03/23/how-full-motion-video-is-changing-isr/. For more see "What Is Full Motion Video (FMV)?" GISGeography.com, https://gisgeography.com/full-motion-video-fmv/.

334 See *The Future of Air Force Motion Imagery Exploitation.* February 23, 2013, Rand.

335 David Donald, Israel Shoots Down Hezbollah's Iranian UAV," AIN Online, October 12, 2012, https://www.ainonline.com/aviation-news/defense/2012-10-12/israel-shoots-down-hezbollahs-iranian-uav. "The vehicle shot down appears to be in the class of a Scan Eagle."

336 "Did Iran Release a Video of Hacked American UAVs in Syria and Iraq?" SOFREP, February 26, 2019, https://sofrep.com/fightersweep/did-iran-release-a-video-of-hacked-american-uavs-in-syria-and-iraq/.

337   Ariel Ben Solomon, "Did Iran Stage 'Dowing' of Israeli Drone?" *The Jerusalem Post,* September 1, 2014, https://www.jpost.com/middle-east/did-iran-stage-downing-of-israeli-drone-373045.

338   S. Tsach, *et. al.,*"History of UAV Development in IAI & Road Ahead," 24th ICAS 2004, http://www.icas.org/ICAS_ARCHIVE/ICAS2004/PAPERS/519.PDF.

339   "The First UAV Squadron," Israeli Air Force, Accessed May 10, 2020, https://www.iaf.org.il/4968-33518-en/IAF.aspx.

340   Reuters, "Iranian Revolutionary Guard Unveils New Attack Drones," *The Jerusalem Post,* October 1, 2016, https://www.jpost.com/israel-news/iranian-revolutionary-guard-unveils-new-attack-drones-469235.

341   Wim Zwijnenburg, "Sentinels, Saeqehs and Simorghs: An Open Source Survey of Iran's New Drone in Syria," Bellingcat, February 13, 2018, https://www.bellingcat.com/news/mena/2018/02/13/sentinels-saeqehs-simorghs-open-source-information-irans-new-drone-syria/.

342   Wam/Ridyadh, "Saudi Foils Houthi Drone Attack Bid on Abha Airport," *Khaleej Times,* May 27, 2018, https://www.khaleejtimes.com/region/saudi-arabia/Saudi-foils-drone-attack-bid-on-Abha-airport-.

343   "How Did the Supreme Leader's Strategic Recommendation to the IRGC/Iran Airspace Become the Owner of the Largest Fleet of Combat Drones in the Region?" FARS, Accessed June 7, 2020, https://www.farsnews.ir/news/13981011001126/.

344   It was similar to a German V-1.

345   Dan Gettinger, "Drone Activity in Iran," Offizier.ch, June 4, 2016, https://www.offiziere.ch/?p=27907; Gettinger's latest product is a weekly Drone Bulletin: https://dronebulletin.substack.com/.

346   The Seeker 2000 had a range of 200km and speed of 120km/hr. Forecast International: https://www.forecastinternational.com/fic/loginform.cfm.

347   "Seeker II UAV Shot Down in Yemen," defenceWeb, July 8, 2015, https://www.defenceweb.co.za/aerospace/aerospace-aerospace/seeker-ii-uav-shot-

down-in-yemen/; Denel Dynamics also built an armed Seeker 400 called Snyper. "Weaponised Seeker 400 Debuts at IDEX," defenceWeb, February 24, 2015, https://www.defenceweb.co.za/aerospace/aerospace-aerospace/ weaponised-seeker-400-debuts-at-idex/.

348   Cal Pringle, "5 Times in History Enemies Shot Down a US Drone," C4ISRNET, August 22, 2019, https://www.c4isrnet.com/ unmanned/2019/08/23/5-times-in-history-enemies-shot-down-a-us-drone/.

349   Ibid; Benjamin Minick, "ScanEagle Drone Shot Down by Yemeni Rebels, But Do The Saudis Fly Them?" *International Business Times*, November 1, 2019, https://www.ibtimes.com/scaneagle-drone-shot-down-yemeni-rebels-do-saudis-fly-them-2858390.

350   See a blueprint of the IAI Scout here: https://www.the-blueprints.com/ blueprints/modernplanes/modern-i/81182/view/iai_scout/.

351   See Aeronautics website: https://aeronautics-sys.com/home-page/page-systems/page-systems-aerostar-tuas/.

352   See Galen Wright's Arkenstone site Mohajer: http://thearkenstone.blog-spot.com/2011/02/ababil-uav.html.

353   Ibid.

354   Wright, ibid.

355   The army also unveiled killer robots in October 2019. Kelsey D. Atherton, "Beetle-Like Iranian Robots Can Roll Under Tanks," C4ISRNet, October 8, 2019, https://www.c4isrnet.com/unmanned/2019/10/08/ beetle-like-iranian-robots-roll-under-tanks/.

356   "Iran's Defense Ministry Makes Mass Delivery of New Drones to Army," PressTV, April 18, 2020, https://www.presstv.com/Detail/2020/ 04/18/623293/US-militants-defect-Syria-Tanf-base.

357   See footage at this twitter link: https://twitter.com/BabakTaghvaee/ status/1251599587774775296.

358 John Drennan, *Iranian unmanned systems*, International Institute for Strategic Studies, 2019, p.3.

359 Adam Rawnsley, February 28, 2020 inerview.

360 Thomas Donnelly, "Drones: Old, New, Borrowed, Blue," AEI, February 6, 2014, https://www.aei.org/articles/drones-old-new-borrowed-blue/.

361 David Hambling, "The Predator's Stealthy Successor is Coming," *Popular Mechanics,* December 15, 2016, https://www.popularmechanics.com/military/aviation/a24311/air-force-new-drone/.

362 For a map see Dan Gettinger, "Drone Activity in Iran," Offizier.ch, June 4, 2016, https://www.offiziere.ch/?p=27907.

363 Barbara Starr, "Iranian Surveillance Drone Flies Over U.S. Aircraft Carrier in Persian Gulf," CNN Politics, January 29, 2016, https://edition.cnn.com/2016/01/29/politics/iran-drone-uss-harry-truman/index.html.

364 Ahmad Majidyar, "Iranian Drone Allegedly Spotted Flying Over Western Afghanistan," MEI@75, August 29, 2017, https://mei.edu/publications/iranian-drone-allegedly-spotted-flying-over-western-afghanistan.

365 This followed the Velayat 94 drills. Seth J. Frantzman, "50 Iranian Drones Conduct Massive 'Way to Jerusalem' Exercise – Report," *The Jerusalem Post,* March 14, 2019, https://www.jpost.com/Middle-East/50-Iranian-drones-conduct-massive-way-to-Jerusalem-exercise-report-583387.

366 Ron Ben-Yishai, "The Race is On To Retrieve the U.S. Spy Drone Brought Down By Iran," Ynet, June 20, 2019, https://www.ynetnews.com/articles/0,7340,L-5529508,00.html.

367 Bill Chappell and Tom Bowman, "USS Boxer Used Electronic Jamming to Take Down Iranian Drone, Pentagon Sources Say," NPR, July 19, 2019, https://www.npr.org/2019/07/19/743444053/u-s-official-says-government-has-evidence-iran-drone-was-destroyed.

368 Patrick Tucker, "How the Pentagon Nickel-and-Dimed Its Way Into Losing a Drone," Defense One, June 20, 2019, https://www.defenseone.com/

technology/2019/06/how-pentagon-nickel-and-dimed-its-way-losing-drone/157901/.

369 "Photo Release – Northrop Grumman Conducts First Fligth of Modernized, Multi-Mission Hunter UAV," Northrop Grumman, August 9, 2005, https://news.northropgrumman.com/news/releases/photo-release-northrop-grumman-conducts-first-flight-of-modernized-multi-mission-hunter-uav.

370 James Hasik, *Arms and Innovation: Entrepreneurship and Innovation in the 21st Century.*

371 David Axe, "The Secret History of Boeing's Killer drone," *Wired*, June 6, 2011, https://www.wired.com/2011/06/killer-drone-secret-history/.

372 Ibid.

373 "Russia's Latest Attack Drone Performs 1st Joint Flight with Su-57 Fifth-Generation Plane," TASS, September 27, 2019, https://tass.com/defense/1080201#:~:text=Russia's%20latest%20Okhotnik%20(Hunter)%20heavy,Defense%20Ministry%20announced%20on%20Friday.&text=%22The%20Okhotnik%20unmanned%20aerial%20vehicle,plane%2C%22%20the%20ministry%20said.

374 "Army Takes Another Step in Warrior UAV Development," Military & Aerospace Electronics, March 9, 2006, https://www.militaryaero-space.com/unmanned/article/16722199/army-takes-another-step-in-warrior-uav-development.

375 Nathan Hodge, "Army's Killer Drone Takes First Shots in Combat," *Wired*, March 5, 2009, https://www.wired.com/2009/03/armys-new-drone/.

376 "Sky Warrior ERMP UAV System," Defense Update, December 5, 2008, https://defense-update.com/20081205_warrioruav.html.

377 In 2019 and 2020 Israel also scrambled F-15s to shoot down drones from Gaza. Israel shoots down Gaza drone off enclave's coast: "IDF Shoots Down Gaza Drone Off the Enclave's Coast," i24 News, February 27, 2020, https://www.i24news.tv/en/news/israel/diplomacy-defense/1582795868-

idf-shoots-down-gaza-drone-over-coastal-enclave; Yaniv Kubovich and Almog Ben Zikri, "Israel Intercepts High Flying UAV Over Gaza," *Haaretz,* October 29, 2019, https://www.haaretz.com/israel-news/.premium-israeli-army-intercepts-drone-flying-at-an-unusual-height-over-the-gaza-1.8055230.

378 Kyle Mizokami, "A Reaper Drone Shot Down Another Drone in First Unmanned Air-to-Air Kill," *Popular Mechanics,* September 19, 2018, Accessed May 25, 2020, https://www.popularmechanics.com/military/aviation/a23320374/reaper-drone-first-unmanned-air-to-air-kill/. The incident was done by the 432 Air Expeditionary Wing at Creech. It used an infrared guided air-to-air missile.

379 Judah Ari Gross, "Unmanned Subs, Sniper Drones, Gun That Won't Miss: Israel Unveils Future Weapons," *The Times of Israel,* September 5, 2017, https://www.timesofisrael.com/unmanned-subs-and-sniper-drones-israel-unveils-its-weapons-of-the-future/.

380 Barbara Opall-Rome, "Pentagon Eyes US Iron Dome to Defend Forward-Based Forces," Defense News, August 26, 2016, https://www.defensenews.com/smr/space-missile-defense/2016/08/08/pentagon-eyes-us-iron-dome-to-defend-forward-based-forces/.

381 Shawn Snow, "The Marine Corps Has Been Looking at Israel's Iron Dome to Boost Air Defense," *Marine Corps Times,* May 7, 2019, https://www.marinecorpstimes.com/news/your-marine-corps/2019/05/07/the-marine-corps-has-been-looking-at-israels-iron-dome-air-defense-system/.

382 Jason Sherman, "US Army Scraps $1B. Iron Dome Project, After Israel Refuses to Provide Key Codes," *The Times of Israel,* March 7, 2020, https://www.timesofisrael.com/us-army-scraps-1b-iron-dome-project-after-israel-refuses-to-provide-key-codes/.

383 Adam Chandler, "Israel Shoots Down Hamas' First Combat Drone With $1M Missile," *The Atlantic,* July 14, 2014, https://www.theat-

lantic.com/international/archive/2014/07/israel-shoots-down-hamas-first-combat-drone-with-1m-missile/374368/.

384 Judah Ari Gross, "IDF: Patriot Missile Fired at Incoming UAV from Syria, Which Retreats," *The Times of Israel,* June 24, 2018, https://www.timesofisrael.com/patriot-interceptor-reportedly-fired-in-northern-israel-circumstances-unclear/; Judah Ari Gross, "IDF Intercepts Syrian Drone That Penetrated 10 Kilometers Into Israel," *The Tims of Israel,* July 11, 2018, https://www.timesofisrael.com/idf-patriot-missile-fired-toward-incoming-drone-from-syria/.

385 Anna Ahronheim, "Patriot Missile Intercepts Drone on Israel's Border with Syria," *The Jerusalem Post,* November 11, 2017, https://www.jpost.com/arab-israeli-conflict/patriot-missile-intercepts-drone-on-israels-border-with-syria-513968.

386 Yaakov Lappin, "Israeli Fighters Jet, Patriots, Miss Suspicious Drone That Intruded From Syria," *The Jerusalem Post,* July 17, 2016, https://www.jpost.com/Arab-Israeli-Conflict/Rocket-alert-sirens-sounded-in-Golan-Heights-460643.

387 David Hambling, "How did Hezbollah's Drone Evade a Patriot Missile?" *Popular Mechanics,* July 29, 2016, https://www.popularmechanics.com/flight/drones/a22114/hezbollah-drone-israel-patriot-missile/.

388 Chris Baraniuk, "Small Drone 'Shot with Patriot Missile,'" BBC News, March 15, 2017, https://www.bbc.com/news/technology-39277940; Kyle Mizokami, "A Patriot Missile Shot Down a Quadcopter in an Impressive But Wildly Expensive Shot," *Popular Mechanics,* March 15, 2017, https://www.popularmechanics.com/military/weapons/news/a25694/patriot-shot-down-quad-expensive/.

389 PAC-2 was the upgrade rolled out in 1990 while PAC-3 was rolled out after 2003: http://www.military-today.com/missiles/patriot_pac2.htm.

390 Zachary Keck, "Why America Is Ramping Up Its Production of Patriot Missiles," *National Interest*, December 14, 2019, https://nationalinterest.org/blog/buzz/why-america-ramping-its-production-patriot-missiles-103952.

391 Russ Read, "'They Can't Be Everywhere at Once': Why Patriot Missile Interceptors Were Not Used During Iran Missile Strike," *Washington Examiner*, January 8, 2020, https://www.washingtonexaminer.com/policy/defense-national-security/they-cant-be-everywhere-at-once-why-patriot-missile-interceptors-were-not-used-during-iran-missile-strike.

392 Seth J. Frantzman, "Why the US Can't Move Patriot Missiles to Iraq," *The Jerusalem Post*, February 6, 2020, https://www.jpost.com/middle-east/why-the-us-cant-move-patriot-missiles-to-iraq-616674.

393 Gary Sheftick, "Patriot Force Halfway Thru Major Modernization," U.S. Army, August 22, 2019, https://www.army.mil/article/225044/patriot_force_halfway_thru_major_modernization.

394 C-RAM is a Northrop Grumman system. The company got a $122 million contract to supply the system to forward operating bases in Iraq and Afghanistan in 2012. "U.S. Army Awards Northrop Grumman $122 Million Counter-Rocket Artillery and Mortar (C-RAM) Contract," Northrop Grumman, January 30, 2012, https://news.northropgrumman.com/news/releases/u-s-army-awards-northrop-grumman-122-million-counter-rocket-artillery-and-mortar-c-ram-contract.

395 Warrior Scout, "How the Army Plans to Counter Massive Drone Attacks," We Are the Mighty, February 5, 2020, https://www.wearethemighty.com/tech/how-the-army-plans-to-counter-massive-drone-attacks/.

396 Kris Osborne, "Army C-Ram Adds Drones to List of Threats to Kill," Real Clear Defense, July 26, 2017, https://www.realcleardefense.com/2017/07/26/army039s_c-ram_adds_drones_to_list_of_threats_to_kill_295255.html.

397 C-RAM, Missile Defense Advocacy Alliance, C-RAM page: https://missiledefenseadvocacy.org/defense-systems/counter-rocket-artillery-mortar-c-ram/.

398 Kris Osborn, "Army C-RAM Base Defense Will Destroy Drones," Warrior Maven, November 28, 2017, https://defensemaven.io/warrior-maven/land/army-c-ram-base-defense-will-destroy-drones-iERxJDqgm-kuuz67ZO4y4ZA.

399 "Special Report: 'Time To Take Out Our Swords' - Inside Iran's Plot To Attack Saudi Arabia," Reuters, November 25, 2019, https://www.reuters.com/article/us-saudi-aramco-attacks-iran-special-rep/special-report-time-to-take-out-our-swords-inside-irans-plot-to-attack-saudi-arabia-idUSKBN1XZ16H.

400 Humeyra Pamuk, "Exclusive: US Probe of Saudi Oil Attack Shows It Came from North," Reuters, December 19, 2019, https://www.reuters.com/article/us-saudi-aramco-attacks-iran/exclusive-u-s-probe-of-saudi-oil-attack-shows-it-came-from-north-report-idUSKBN1YN299.

401 Pini Yungman interview with Seth J. Frantzman, September 18, 2019. See also Seth J. Frantzman, "Are Air Defense Systems Ready to Confront Drone Swarms?" Defense News, September 26, 2019, https://www.defensenews.com/global/mideast-africa/2019/09/26/are-air-defense-systems-ready-to-confront-drone-swarms/.

402 Kenenth McKenzie at Middle East Institute discussion about CENTCOM, June 10, 2020. See full clip on YouTube, minute 57:00: https://www.youtube.com/watch?v=fsXcWLDNTcE&feature=youtu.be.

403 "Ben-Gurion U Team Unveils Laser Drone Kill System," Globes, March 5, 2020, https://en.globes.co.il/en/article-ben-gurion-u-team-unveils-laser-drone-defense-system-1001320876.

404 Yoav Zitun, "The Next Generation of Reconnaissance Drones," Ynet, June 12, 2019, https://www.ynetnews.com/business/article/Sy11m5jbar.

405 "RAFAEL's Drone Dome Intercepts Multiple Maneuvering Targets with LASER Technology," RAFAEL, February 16, 2020, https://www.rafael.co.il/press/rafaels-drone-dome-intercepts-multiple-maneuvering-targets-with-laser-technology/.

406 "Could the Iron Dome Protect You One Day?" IDF, May 22, 2015, https://www.idf.il/en/articles/military-cooperation/could-the-iron-dome-protect-you-one-day/.

407 Seth J. Frantzman, "Countering UAVs, An Inside Look at IAI's Elta Drone Guard," Defense News, January 28, 2019, https://www.defensenews.com/unmanned/2019/01/28/countering-uavs-an-inside-look-at-iai-eltas-drone-guard/.

408 Sébastien Roblin, "Why U.S. Patriot Missiles Failed to Stop Drones and Cruise Missiles Attacking Saudi Oil Sites," NBC News, September 23, 2019, https://www.nbcnews.com/think/opinion/trump-sending-troops-saudi-arabia-shows-short-range-air-defenses-ncna1057461.

409 Yoav Zitun, "Israel's New Answer to Drone Threats: Laser Beams," Ynet, February 12, 2020, https://www.ynetnews.com/business/article/SyEfY00bmU.

410 Seth J. Frantzman, "Israel is Developing Lasers to Kill Drones and Rockets," Defense News, January 9, 2020, https://www.defensenews.com/industry/techwatch/2020/01/09/israel-is-developing-lasers-to-kill-drones-and-rockets/.

411 MDAA website: https://missiledefenseadvocacy.org/defense-systems/iron-beam/.

412 "USS Portland Conducts Laser Weapon System Demonstrator Test," Commander, U.S. Pacific Fleet, May 22, 2020, Accessed May 23, 2020, https://www.cpf.navy.mil/news.aspx/130628.

413 Kris Osborn, US Army website. "Army Lasers Will Soon Destroy Enemy Mortars, Artillery Drones and Cruise Missiles," USA ASC, June 9, 2016, https://asc.army.mil/web/news-army-lasers-will-soon-de-stroy-enemy-mortars-artillery-drones-and-cruise-missiles/#:~:text=No%20menu%20assigned-,Army%20Lasers%20Will%20Soon%20Destroy%20Enemy,Artillery%2C%20Drones%20and%20

Cruise%20Missiles&text=Laser%20Weapons%20Will%20Protect%20 Forward,as%20missiles%2C%20mortars%20and%20artillery.

414 Interview with Lockheed Martin, July 1, 2020.

415 Interview with Doug Graham, July 2, 2020.

416 Nick Waters, "Has Iran Been Hacking U.S. Drones?" Bellingcat, October 1, 2019, https://www.bellingcat.com/news/2019/10/01/has-iran-been-hacking-u-s-drones/.

417 Brett Velicovich, *Drone Warrior*, p. 104.

418 David Axe, "The Secret History of Boeing's Killer drone," *Wired*, June 6, 2011, https://www.wired.com/2011/06/killer-drone-secret-history/.

419 See video at this link: https://twitter.com/PressTV/status/125253240 1873522689.

420 Valerie Insinna, "US Air Force's Next Drone to be Driven by Data," Defense News, September 6, 2017, https://www.defensenews.com/smr/defense-news-conference/2017/09/06/air-forces-next-uav-to-be-driven-by-data/.

421 Joseph Trevithick and Tyler Rogoway, "Pocket Force of Stealthy Avenger Drones May Have Made Returning F-117s to Service Unnecessary," The Drive, March 5, 2019, https://www.thedrive.com/the-war-zone/26791/pocket-force-of-stealthy-avenger-drones-may-have-made-returning-f-117s-to-service-unnecessary.

422 Singer, *Wired for War*, p. 140.

423 See "US Air Force Unmanned Aircraft Systems Flight Plan 2009-2047," FAS, May 18, 2009, https://fas.org/irp/program/collect/uas_2009.pdf.

424 Perdix Drone demonstration video: https://www.youtube.com/watch?v=D-jUdVxJH6yI&feature=youtu.be.

425 Thomas McMullan, "How Swarming Drones Will Change Warfare," BBC News, March 16, 2019, https://www.bbc.com/news/technology-47555588.

426 Kyle Mizokami, "Gremlin Drone's First Flight Turns C-130 Into a Flying Aircraft Carrier," *Popular Mechanics,* January 21, 2020, https://www.popular-mechanics.com/military/aviation/a30612943/gremlin-drone-first-flight/.

427 "Watch the Navy's LOCUST Launcher Fire a Swarm of Drones," *Business Insider,* YouTube, April 20, 2017: https://www.youtube.com/watch?v=qW77hVqux10&feature=youtu.be.

428 "Mind of the Swarm," Raytheon Missiles & Defense, https://www.raytheonmissilesanddefense.com/news/feature/mind-swarm.

429 Anam Tahir, *et. al.* "Swarms of Unmanned Aerial Vehicles—A Survey," *Journal of Industrial Information Integration,* Volume 16, December 2019, https://www.sciencedirect.com/science/article/pii/S2452414X18300086.

430 There would also be issues involving jamming or GPS-denied environments and use of new 5G technology. Mitch Campion, Prakash Ranganathan, and Saleh Faruque, *A Review and Future Directions of UAV Swarm Communication Architectures,* 2018, https://und.edu/research/rias/_files/docs/swarm_ieee.pdf.

431 "NASC TigerShark-XP UAV Receives FAA Experimental Certification," UAV News, Space Daily, April 29, 2019, https://www.spacewar.com/reports/NASC_TigerShark_XP_UAV_Receives_FAA_Experimental_Certification_999.html; See NASC website for more info: https://www.nasc.com/pages/defense/uas/tigershark.html.

432 David Hambling, "The Predator's Stealthy Successor Is Coming" *Popular Mechanics,* December 15, 2016, https://www.popularmechanics.com/military/aviation/a24311/air-force-new-drone/.

433 Mike Ball, "DARPA Successfully Tests UAV Swarming Technologies," Unmanned Systems News, March 25, 2019, https://www.unmannedsystemstechnology.com/2019/03/darpa-successfully-tests-uav-swarming-technologies/.

434 Shawn Snow, "The Corps Just Slapped a Counter-Drone System on an MRZR All-Terrain Vehicle," *Marine Corps Times,* September 19, 2018,

https://www.marinecorpstimes.com/news/2018/09/19/the-corps-just-slapped-a-counter-drone-system-on-an-mrzr-all-terrain-vehicle/.

435 Andrew Liptak, "A US Navy Ship Used a New Drone-Defense System to Take Down an Iranian Drone," The Verge, July 21, 2019, https://www.theverge.com/2019/7/21/20700670/us-marines-mrzr-lmadis-iran-drone-shoot-down-energy-weapon-uss-boxer.

436 Not to be confused with Israel's tactical THOR drone. Andrew Liptak, "The Air Force Has a New Weapon Called THOR That Can Take Out Swarms of Drones," The Verge, June 21, 2019, https://www.theverge.com/2019/6/21/18701267/us-air-force-thor-new-weapon-drone-swarms.

437 Russell Brandom, "The Army is Buying Microwave Cannons to Take Down Drones in Mid Flight," The Verge, August 7, 2018, https://www.theverge.com/2018/8/7/17660414/microwave-anti-drone-army-weapon-lockheed-martin.

438 See for instance the book *Swarm Troopers* by David Hambling.

439 Petraeus to author, March 14, 2020.

440 Ibid.

441 Drdrone.ca website, accessed April 11, 2020: https://www.drdrone.ca/blogs/drone-news-drone-help-blog/timeline-of-dji-drones.

442 Wang Ying, "Drone Maker DJI to Develop More Industry Applications," *China Daily*, January 27, 2018, https://www.chinadaily.com.cn/a/201801/27/WS5a6bd252a3106e7dcc1371b0.html.

443 Ben Watson, "The US Army Just Ordered Soldiers to Stop Using Drones from China's DJI," Defense One, August 4, 2017, https://www.defenseone.com/technology/2017/08/us-army-just-ordered-soldiers-stop-using-drones-chinas-dji/139999/.

444 Taylor Hatmaker, "US Air Force Drone Documents Found for Sale on the Dark Web for $200," Tech Crunch. July 11, 2018, https://techcrunch.com/2018/07/11/reaper-drone-dark-web-air-force-hack/.

445 MDAheadJamesSyringwasenthusiasticabouttheideain2017.PatrickTucker, "DronesArmedWithHigh-EnergyLasersMayArriveIn2017," DefenseOne, September 23, 2015, https://www.defenseone.com/technology/2015/09/ drones-armed-high-energy-lasers-may-arrive-2017/121583/.

446 It was apparently a bust even though some variants kept being tinkered with in 2013 and 2014. See Boeing website, Phantom Eye: https://www. boeing.com/defense/phantom-eye/.

447 A previous version had flown some 18,000 combat hours in Afghanistan with a small number of operators and low mishap rate. The Air Force put this program into its Center for Rapid Innovation. 88th Air Base, "AFRL Successfully Completes Two and a Half-Day Flight of Ultra Long Endurance Unmanned Air Platform (LEAP)," Wright-Patterson AFB, December 12, 2019, https://www.wpafb.af.mil/News/Article-Display/ Article/2038921/afrl-successfully-completes-two-and-a-half-day-flight-of-ultra-long-endurance-u/.

448 Kyle Rempfer, "Air Force Offers Glimpse of New, Stealthy Combat Drone During First Flight," Air Force Times, March 8, 2019, https://www.airforcetimes.com/news/your-air-force/2019/03/08/ air-force-offers-glimpse-of-new-stealthy-combat-drone-during-first-flight/.

449 88th Air Base, "AFRL XQ-58A UAV Completes Second Successful Flight," U.S. Air Force, June 17, 2019, https://www.af.mil/News/Article-Display/ Article/1877980/afrl-xq-58a-uav-completes-second-successful-flight/.

450 Rachel S. Cohen, "Meet the Future Unmanned Force," Air Force Magazine, April 4, 2019, https://www.airforcemag.com/meet-the-future-unmanned-force/.

451 Ibid.

452 Rachel S. Cohen, "Congress Looks to Bolster USAF Dront Development in 2020," Air Force Magazine, January 3, 2020, https://www.airforcemag. com/congress-looks-to-bolster-usaf-drone-development-in-2020/.

453 "FLIR Systems Awarded $39.6 Million Contract for Black Hornet Personal Reconnaissance Systems for US Army Soldier Borne Sensor Program," FLIR, January 24, 2019, https://www.flir.com/news-center/press-releases/flir-systems-awarded-$39.6-million-contract-for-black-hornet-personal-reconnaissance-systems-for-us-army-soldier-borne-sensor-program/.

454 Jay Peters, "Watch DARPA Test Out a Swarm of Drones," The Verge, August 9, 2019, https://www.theverge.com/2019/8/9/20799148/darpa-drones-robots-swarm-military-test.

455 They weigh 32 grams. Vidi Nene, "US Army Testing FLIR Infrared Drones In Afghanistan," DroneBelow.com, July 2, 2019, https://dronebelow.com/2019/07/02/us-army-testing-flir-infrared-drones-in-afghanistan/.

456 See US Air Force Museum: https://www.nationalmuseum.af.mil/.

457 Dan Sabbagh, "Killer Drones: How Many Are There And Who Do They Target?" The Guardian, November 18, 2019, https://www.theguardian.com/news/2019/nov/18/killer-drones-how-many-uav-predator-reaper.

458 "USMC Makes First Operational Flight in the Middle East with an MQ-9A," ABG Strategic Consulting, April 17, 2020, https://www.abg-sc-portal.com/2020/04/17/17-4-2020-usmc-makes-first-operational-flight-in-the-middle-east-with-an-mq-9a/.

459 Gina Harkins, "In First, Marine Corps Crew Flies MQ-9 Reaper Drone in the Middle East," Military.com, April 22, 2020, https://www.military.com/daily-news/2020/04/22/first-marine-corps-crew-flies-mq-9-reaper-drone-middle-east.html.

460 See US Marine Corps website, "Modernization and Technology," Accessed May 23, 2020, https://www.candp.marines.mil/Programs/Focus-Area-4-Modernization-Technology/Part-5-Aviation/UAS/.

461 USMC Unmanned Assets, https://www.monch.com/mpg/news/unmanned/4214-usmcuas.html; Ben Werner, "Marine Corps wants Mux to Fly by 2026," USNI News, May 7, 2019, https://news.usni.org/2019/05/07/marine-corps-wants-mux-to-fly-in-2026; See also a mock-up design

of the Marines concept: "USMC Wants Ship-Based Unmanned AEW, EW, ISR Platform," Alert 5 Military Aviation News, March 13, 2018, accessed May 23, 2020, https://alert5.com/2018/03/13/usmc-wants-ship-based-unmanned-aew-ew-isr-platform/.

462 See slide show pasted online in 2015, accessed May 23, 2020, https://www.slideshare.net/tomlindblad/usmc-uas-familyofsystems.

463 WikiLeaks, "Military Aviation: Issues and Options for Combating Terrorism and Counterinsurgency," FAS Document, CRS Report for Congress, January 7, 2006, https://file.wikileaks.org/file/crs/RL32737.txt.

464 Arcuturus pushed the Jump-20 and L-3 Harris a bird called the FVR-90. The drones were tossed around at the Dugway Proving Ground in Utah in 2019. Jen Judson, "First Candidate for US Army's Future Tactical Drone Gets First Soldier-Operated Flight," Defense News, April 10, 2020, https://www.defensenews.com/land/2020/04/09/first-candidate-for-armys-future-tactical-unmanned-aircraft-gets-first-soldier-operated-flight/.

465 Valerie Insinna, "Unmanned Aircraft Could Provide Low-Ccost Boost for Air Force's Future Aircraft Inventory, New Study Says," Defense News, October 29, 2019, https://www.defensenews.com/air/2019/10/29/unmanned-aircraft-could-provide-low-cost-boost-for-air-forces-future-aircraft-inventory-new-study-says/.

466 The RQ-11B Raven was exported to Ukraine after being in use by the US for more than a decade. Joseph Trevithick, "America is Still Training Ukrainian Troops to Fly a Drone They Hate," The Drive, April 4, 2017, https://www.thedrive.com/the-war-zone/8921/america-is-still-training-ukrainian-troops-to-fly-a-drone-they-hate.

467 Patrick Tucker, "How the Pentagon Nickel-and-Dimed Its Way Into Losing a Drone," Defense One, June 20, 2019, https://www.defenseone.com/technology/2019/06/how-pentagon-nickel-and-dimed-its-way-losing-drone/157901/. See Navy website requirement for UAV tanker 2016: https://www.navysbir.com/n16_1/N161-003.htm.

468 See "US Air Force Unmanned Aircraft Systems Flight Plan 2009-2047," FAS, May 18, 2009, https://fas.org/irp/program/collect/uas_2009.pdf.

469 Harry Lye, "DARPA Looks to AI, Algorithms to De-Conflict Airspace," Airforce Technology, April 9, 2020, https://www.airforce-technology.com/features/darpa-looks-to-ai-algorithms-to-de-conflict-airspace/.

470 Amanda Harvey, "UAV ISR Payloads Demand Lighter Weight, Faster Processing," Military Embedded Systems, April 24, 2014, http://mil-embedded.com/articles/uav-weight-faster-processing/.

471 See "RQ-170 Sentinel Origins Part II: The Grandson of 'Tacit Blue,'" Aviation Intel, January 12, 2012, http://aviationintel.com/rq-170-origins-part-ii-the-grandson-of-tacit-blue/; See also @mmissiles2 on Twitter. June 29, 2020 tweet, accessed June 30, 2020, https://twitter.com/MMissiles2/status/1277691975391641602.

472 War is Boring, "Yes, America Has Another Secret Spy Drone—We Pretty Much Knew That Already," *Medium,* December 6, 2013, https://medium.com/war-is-boring/yes-america-has-another-secret-spy-drone-we-pretty-much-knew-that-already-41df448d1700.

473 Joseph Trevithick and Tyler Rogoway, "Pocket Force of Stealthy Avenger Drones May Have Made Returning F-117s to Service Unnecessary," The Drive, March 5, 2019, https://www.thedrive.com/the-war-zone/26791/pocket-force-of-stealthy-avenger-drones-may-have-made-returning-f-117s-to-service-unnecessary.

474 David Axe, "It's a Safe Bet the US Air Force is Buying Stealth Spy Drones, *National Interest*, February 28, 2020, https://nationalinterest.org/blog/buzz/it%E2%80%99s-safe-bet-us-air-force-buying-stealth-spy-drones-127767.

475 See blog posts such as this: Mark Collins, "RQ-180: Stealthy New USAF/CIA Black Drone," Mark Collins 3Ds Blog, December 6, 2013, https://mark3ds.wordpress.com/2013/12/06/mark-collins-rq-180-stealthynew-usafcia-black-drone/.

476 Richelson, US Intelligence, p. 140.

477   June 28, 2020 interview with Stephen R. Jones, USAF Commander 432nd Wing.

478   Ibid, Jones interview.

479   Agnes Helou, "Meet Garmousha: A New Rotary-Wing Drone Made in the UAE," Defense News, February 25, 2020, https://www.defensenews.com/unmanned/2020/02/25/meet-garmousha-a-new-rotary-wing-drone-made-in-the-uae/.

480   See Michael Rubin, "Iran Unveils Night Vision Drone," AEI, July 1, 2014, https://www.aei.org/articles/iran-unveils-night-vision-drone/; "Iran Unveils Kamikaze Drones," AEI, April 3, 2013, https://www.aei.org/articles/iran-unveils-kamikaze-drones/.

481   It may have been a second generation Hamaseh UAV, with the classic twin-tail design. Built by HESA, the Hamaseh it first appeared in 2013. FAS document on Hezbollah: Milton Hoenig, "Hezbollah and the Use of Drones as a Weapon of Terrorism," Hezbollah's Drones, https://fas.org/wp-content/uploads/2014/06/Hezbollah-Drones-Spring-2014.pdf.

482   "Iran Unveils 'Indigenous' Drone with 2,000km Range," BBC News, September 26, 2012, https://www.bbc.com/news/world-middle-east-19725990.

483   Kyle Mizokami, "U.S. F-15 Shoots Down Yet Another Iran-Made Drone," Popular Mechanics, June 20, 2017, https://www.popularmechanics.com/military/aviation/a27001/syria-iran-drone-shaheed-129/.

484   "U.S. Downs Pro-Syrian Drone that Fired at Coalition Forces," Reuters, June 8, 2017, https://www.reuters.com/article/us-mideast-crisis-usa-syria/u-s-downs-pro-syrian-drone-that-fired-at-coalition-forces-spokesman-idUSKBN18Z2CP.

485   James Hasik, Arms and Innovation: Entrepreneurship and Innovation in the 21st Century.

486   The Bird Eye came with electrical or gas engines and a flying time up to fifteen hours and rang of 150km Interview at IAI, June 11, 2020.

487   "Tens of millions of dollars" in price tag.

488   Elbit visit and interviews, June 18, 2020.

489   Aeronautics vist and interview, June 3, 2020.

490   See IAI website: https://www.iai.co.il/p/green-dragon.

491   Lockheed website: https://www.lockheedmartin.com/en-us/products/stalker.html.

492   See Richard Whittle, "The Man Who Invented the Predator," *Air & Space Magazine,* April 2013, https://www.airspacemag.com/flight-today/the-man-who-invented-the-predator-3970502/?page=4; See also: "Mr. Abe Karem, Aeronatutics Innovator and Pioneer, is Navigator Award Winner, Potomac Institute for Policy Studies, March 20, 2012, https://www.prnewswire.com/news-releases/mr-abe-karem-aeronautics-innova-tor-and-pioneer-is-navigator-award-winner-143494356.html.

493   Yair Dubester of UVision interview, April 7, 2020.

494   IAI in Israel was also working on a VTOL idea according to discussion in May 2020, a solution that would be best suited for the sea or tactical units where one doesn't want to use runways or catapults IAI interview with Dan Bichman, June 10, 2020.

495   Andrew White, "Lockheed Martin Unveils Condor UAS," Jane's 360, May 27, 2019, https://www.crows.org/news/453240/Lockheed-Martin-unveils-Condor-UAS.htm.

496   Ali Bakeer, "The Fight For Syria's Skies: Turkey Challenges Russia With New Drone Doctrine," MEI@75, March 26, 2020, https://www.mei.edu/publications/fight-syrias-skies-turkey-challenges-russia-new-drone-doctrine.

497   "Syrian Army Shoots Down Turkish Drone in Idlib, 10th in 3 Days," Al-Masdar News, March 4, 2020, https://www.almasdarnews.com/article/syrian-army-shoots-down-turkish-drone-in-idlib-10th-in-3-days-photo/.

[498] Merve, Aydogan, "Turkey Neutralizes 3,000+ Regime Elements in Idlib, Syria," Anadolu, April 3, 2020, https://www.aa.com.tr/en/middle-east/turkey-neutralizes-3-000-regime-elements-in-idlib-syria/1754130.

[499] Alex Gatopoulos, "Battle for Idlib: Turkey's Drones and a New Way of War," Al Jazeera, March 3, 2020, https://www.aljazeera.com/news/2020/3/3/battle-for-idlib-turkeys-drones-and-a-new-way-of-war.

[500] Gordon Lubold, "Italy Quietly Agrees to Armed U.S. Drone Missions Over Libya," *The Wall Street Journal*, February 22, 2016, https://www.wsj.com/articles/italy-quietly-agrees-to-armed-u-s-drone-missions-over-libya-1456163730; Adam Entous and Gordon Lubold, "U.S. Wants Drones in North Africa to Combat Islamic State in Libya," *The Wall Street Journal*, August 11, 2015, https://www.wsj.com/articles/u-s-wants-drones-in-north-africa-to-combat-islamic-state-in-libya-1436742554.

[501] Anna Ahronheim, "Is an Israeli Air Defense System Shooting Down Israeli Drones in Libya?" *The Jerusalem Post*, April 12, 2020, https://www.jpost.com/middle-east/is-an-israeli-air-defense-system-shooting-down-israeli-drones-in-libya-624413.

[502] Umar Farooq, "The Second Drone Age," *The Intercept*, May 14, 2019, https://theintercept.com/2019/05/14/turkey-second-drone-age/.

[503] See video of it published by Selcuk Bayraktar on May 23, 2020. Tweet, accessed May 23, 2020: https://twitter.com/Selcuk/status/1263537819261251584.

[504] Interview with anonymous source in the UAE with knowledge of Haftar's operations, April 22, 2020.

[505] Samer Al-Atrush and Mohammed Abdusamee, "Beseiged Airbase Shows Turkey Turning Tide in Libya's War," Bloomberg, April 17, 2020, https://www.bloomberg.com/news/articles/2020-04-17/besieged-airbase-shows-turkey-turning-the-tide-in-libya-s-war; See tweet @LAN2019M, April 18 2020: https://twitter.com/LNA2019M/status/1253311464251625472.

506 Al-Ain, "A Turkish 'March' Was shot Down Before the Bombing of Trucks in Western Libya," Al Ain News, April 22, 2020, https://al-ain.com/ article/1587502834.

507 Walid Abdullah, "Libya: UN-Recognized Government Downs UAE Drone," Anadolu, April 19, 2020, https://www.aa.com.tr/en/middle-east/ libya-un-recognized-government-downs-uae-drone/1810336.

508 See tweet: https://twitter.com/aatilow/status/1310554418530725888.

509 See the footage on Twitter at this link @Oded121351, June 9, 2020: https://twitter.com/ddsgf9876/status/1270265825950343168.

510 ImageSat International, tweet, May 18, 2020: https://twitter.com/ ImageSatIntl/status/1262371291195211780; "Al-Watyah base," accessed May 19, 2020: https://twitter.com/emad_badi/status/1270107380739641344.

511 Khaled Mahmoud, "Libyan National Army Prepares for Air Battle by Destroying 7 Turkish Drones," Asharq al-Awsat, May 23, 2020, https:// english.aawsat.com/home/article/2298086/libyan-national-army- prepares-air-battle-downing-7-turkish-drones.

512 Rick Francona to author, email interview, May 20, 2020.

513 Dee Ann Davis, "Military UAV Market to Top $83B," Inside Unmanned Systems, April 25, 2018, https://insideunmannedsystems.com/military- uav-market-to-top-83b/.

514 Ibid.

515 Joe Harper, "$98 Billion Expected for Military Drone Market," Real Clear Defense, January 7, 2020, https://www.realcleardefense.com/ 2020/01/07/98_billion_expected_for_military_drone_market_ 311539.html.

516 The classification, based on NATO, was a bit confusing because the US Department of Defense used a different classification, referring to "groups" one through five. In their view group 1, drones under 20 pounds and groups 2, drones under 55 lbs were separate. The next group 3 was from 55 to 1,320 lbs, which included Class II. The US included group 4 and

5, what NATO calls Class 3. "The *Databook* found 171 types of UAVs in active inventories," the authors noted. Dan Gettinger, *Drone Data Book*, Center for the Study of the Drone at Bard College, 2020.

[517] Dan Sabbagh, "Killer Drones: How Many Are There And Who Do They Target?" *The Guardian*, November 18, 2019, https://www.theguardian.com/news/2019/nov/18/killer-drones-how-many-uav-predator-reaper.

[518] See Drone Wars website, Accessed June 30, 2020, https://dronewars.net/uk-drone-strike-list-2/.

[519] "Who Has What: Countries That Have Conducted Drone Strikes," New America, Accessed June 30, 2020, https://www.newamerica.org/international-security/reports/world-drones/who-has-what-countries-that-have-conducted-drone-strikes/.

[520] Seth J. Frantzman, "Greece And Israel Deal Spotlight Leasing Model for Military UAVs," Defense News, May 8, 2020, https://www.defense-news.com/global/europe/2020/05/08/greece-and-israel-deal-spot-light-leasing-model-for-military-uavs/#:~:text=JERUSALEM%20%E2%80%94%20Greece's%20Hellenic%20Ministry%20of,-pricey%20acquisitions%20amid%20budgetary%20constraints.&text=Greece%20will%20have%20an%20option,term%20ends%20in%20three%20years.

[521] Gorman and Abbott, *Remote Control War*, p. 2.

[522] IISS 2019 annual report: https://www.iiss.org/publications/the-military-balance/military-balance-2020-book/comparative-defence-statistics.

[523] Seth J. Frantzman "Israel's Elbit Sells Over 1,000 Mini-Drones to Southeast Asian Country," Defense News, October 9, 2018, https://www.defensenews.com/unmanned/2019/10/09/israels-elbit-sells-over-1000-mini-drones-to-southeast-asian-country/.

524 WikiLeaks, "Shaykh Mohamed Bin Zayed Rejects Unarmed Predator Proposal," Public Library of US Diplomacy, June 27, 2004, https://wikileaks.org/plusd/cables/04ABUDHABI2113_a.html.

525 Roxana Tiron, "China is Pursuing Unmanned Tactical Aircraft," *National Defense*, May 1, 2004, https://www.nationaldefensemagazine.org/articles/2004/5/1/2004may-china-is-pursuing-unmanned-tactical-aircraft.

526 See Reborn Technology post on history and development of Chinese UAVs: http://reborn-technology.blogspot.com/2008/06/history-development-of-chinese-uavs.html.

527 Brian Wang, "China Building 42000 Military Drones Over Next Eight Years and Many are Copies of US Designs," Next Big Future, June 13, 2015, https://www.nextbigfuture.com/2015/06/china-building-42000-military-drones.html.

528 See initial description here. "Chinese UAV Unmanned Aerial Vehicle Global Hawk Could Be in Service in the Chinese Air Force 0407113," Army Recognition, July 4, 2011, https://www.armyrecognition.com/july_2011_news_defense_army_military_industry_uk/chinese_uav_unmanned_aerial_vehicle_global_hawk_could_be_in_service_in_the_chinese_air_force_0407113.html.

529 Dennis Blasko, *The Chinese Army Today*, 2006, p. 139.

530 See FAS link: https://fas.org/irp/world/china/sys/an-206.htm.

531 Blasko, *The Chinese Army Today*, 2013, p. 166.

532 See details at Wautum blog here: https://www.wautom.com/2013/04/harbin-bzk-005-uav/.

533 See drone blog Dragon Drone: https://dragondron.wordpress.com/drones/.

534 "BZK-005 Giant Eagle is Operational," Defense Studies, October 14, 2009, http://defense-studies.blogspot.com/2009/10/bzk-005-giant-eagle-is-operational.html.

535 See Aviationist blog April 2018 tweet: https://twitter.com/aircraftspots/status/986713289101996032?lang=he.

536 Zhao Lei, "Expert: Drone to Soar on Market," ChinaDaily.com, April 5, 2017, https://www.chinadaily.com.cn/china/2017-04/05/content_28793243.htm.

537 "Beijing University Promoted Firm Developing Missile-Carrying Drones," DefenseWorld.net, April 7, 2017, https://www.defenseworld.net/news/18941/Beijing_University_Promoted_Firm_Develops_Missile_carrying_Drone.

538 Brian Wang, "China Building 42000 Military Drones Over Next Eight Years and Many are Copies of US Designs," Next Big Future, June 13, 2015, https://www.nextbigfuture.com/2015/06/china-building-42000-military-drones.html; Rick Joe, "China's Growing High-End Military Drone Force," *The Diplomat*, November 27, 2019, https://thediplomat.com/2019/11/chinas-growing-high-end-military-drone-force/.

539 WikiLeaks, "Japanese Morning Press Highlights," Public Library of US Diplomacy, August 20, 2007, https://wikileaks.org/plusd/cables/07TOKYO3820_a.html.

540 Ivan Willis Rasmussen, "Everyone Loves Drones, Especially China," November 9, 2014, Working paper, http://web.isanet.org/Web/Conferences/ISSS%20Austin%202014/Archive/b429b86f-27b8-4341-9372-a28ca52ee6df.pdf.

541 Mark McDonald, "The Pentagon is 'Alarmed' by China's Big Move Into Drones," *Business Insider*, November 28, 2012, https://www.businessinsider.com/us-china-drones-2012-11.

542 Ivan Willis Rasmussen, "Everyone Loves Drones, Especially China," November 9, 2014, Working paper, http://web.isanet.org/Web/Conferences/ISSS%20Austin%202014/Archive/b429b86f-27b8-4341-9372-a28ca52ee6df.pdf.

543 "Is China at the Forefront of Drone Technology?" CSIS Drone report, 2019, https://chinapower.csis.org/china-drones-unmanned-technology/.

544 Ivan Willis Rasmussen, "Everyone Loves Drones, Especially China," November 9, 2014, Working paper, http://web.isanet.org/Web/Conferences/ISSS%20Austin%202014/Archive/b429b86f-27b8-4341-9372-a28ca52ee6df.pdf.

545 Shahryar Pasandideh, "The Zhuhai Airshow Confirms China's Emergence as a Defense Industrial Power," *World Politics Review*, December 7, 2019, https://www.worldpoliticsreview.com/articles/26935/the-zhuhai-airshow-confirms-china-s-emergence-as-a-defense-industrial-power.

546 P. Chow, *The One China Dilemma*, 2008, p. 225.

547 "Who Has What: Countries That Have Conducted Drone Strikes," New America, Accessed June 30, 2020, https://www.newamerica.org/international-security/reports/world-drones/who-has-what-countries-that-have-conducted-drone-strikes/.

548 Rick Joe, "China's Growing High-End Military Drone Force," *The Diplomat*, November 27, 2019, https://thediplomat.com/2019/11/chinas-growing-high-end-military-drone-force/.

549 Kyle Mizokami, "All the New Tech from China's Big Air Show," *Popular Mechanics,* November 6, 2018, https://www.popularmechanics.com/military/aviation/a24680684/all-the-new-tech-from-chinas-big-airshow/.

550 "Air Show China 2018: CH-7 Stealth Drone Makes First Public Appearance," Army Recognition, November 8, 2018, https://www.armyrecognition.com/airshow_china_2018_zhuhai_news_show_daily_coverage/air_show_china_2018_ch-7_stealth_drone_makes_first_public_appearance.html.

551 Global Security website Cai Hong Drones, https://www.globalsecurity.org/military/world/china/ch.htm.

552 Ibid.

553 Joseph Trevithick and Tyler Rogoway, "China's Biggest Airshow Offers More Evidence of Beijing's Stealth Drone Focus," The Drive, November

2, 2018, https://www.thedrive.com/the-war-zone/24645/chinas-biggest-airshow-offers-more-evidence-of-beijings-stealth-drone-focus.

554 "Air Show China 2018: CH-7 Stealth Drone Makes First Public Appearance," Army Recognition, November 8, 2018, https://www.armyrecognition.com/airshow_china_2018_zhuhai_news_show_daily_coverage/air_show_china_2018_ch-7_stealth_drone_makes_first_public_appearance.html.

555 CSIS, China Power Project, SIPRI data.

556 "China to Unveil GJ-2 Drone at Air Show," XinhuaNet, November 2, 2018, http://www.xinhuanet.com/english/2018-11/02/c_137577268.htm.

557 *The Drone Handbook*, Center for the Study of the Drone. p. xiii.

558 Rasmussen, p. 3.

559 Seth J. Frantzman, "The U.S. Risks Losing the Drone-War Arms Race," *National Review*, May 4, 2020, https://www.nationalreview.com/2020/05/drone-war-arms-race-united-states-risks-losing/.

560 "UAV Export Controls and Regulatory Challenges," Working Group Report, Stimson, 2015, https://www.stimson.org/wp-content/files/file-attachments/ECRC%20Working%20Group%20Report.pdf.

561 Andrea Shalal, Emily Stephenson, "U.S. Establishes Policy for Exports of Armed Drones," Reuters, February 17, 2015, https://www.reuters.com/article/us-usa-drones-exports/u-s-establishes-policy-for-exports-of-armed-drones-idUSKBN0LL21720150218.

562 Jeff Abramson, "New Policies Promote Arms, Drones Exports," Arms Control Association, May 2018, Accessed May, 1, 2020, https://www.arms-control.org/act/2018-05/news/new-policies-promote-arms-drone-exports; See also Arron Mehta, "Trump Admin Roles Out New Rules for Weapon, Drone Sales Abroad," Defense News, April 19, 2018, Accessed May 1, 2020, https://www.defensenews.com/news/pentagon-congress/2018/04/19/trump-admin-rolls-out-new-rules-for-weapon-drone-sales-abroad/.

563 Natasha Turak, "Pentagon is Scrambling as China 'Sells the Hell Out of' Armed Drones to US Allies," CNBC, Feb. 21, 2019, Accessed May 1, 2020, https://www.cnbc.com/2019/02/21/pentagon-is-scrambling-as-china-sells-the-hell-out-of-armed-drones-to-americas-allies.html.

564 WikiLeaks, "[OS] US/CHINA/MIL – Global Race on to Match U.S. Drone Capabilities," *The Global Intelligence Files,* July 5, 2011, https://wikileaks.org/gifiles/docs/30/3005214_-os-us-china-mil-global-race-on-to-match-u-s-drone.html.

565 WikiLeaks, "CHINA/HONG KONG – Chinese Military's Unmanned Aerial Vehicle Crashes – Hong Kong Paper," *The Global Intelligence Files,* August 26, 2011, https://wikileaks.org/gifiles/docs/69/693866_china-hong-kong-chinese-military-s-unmanned-aerial-vehicle.html.

566 WikiLeaks, "Situation Report: More on Bombers to Australia; Chinese Drones to Jordan; and European Forces to Libya," May 15, 2015, https://wikileaks.org/berats-box/emailid/41807.

567 "Is China at the Forefront of Drone Technology?" CSIS, China Power, 2019, https://chinapower.csis.org/china-drones-unmanned-technology/; The Covid-19 pandemic called into question China's ability to host an air show in 2020. The website for the 2020 China International Airshow can be seen here, Accessed July 12, 2020, http://www.airshow.com.cn/Category_1216/Index.aspx.

568 Edward Wong, "Hacking U.S. Secrets, China Pushes for Drones," *The New York Times*, September 20, 2013, https://www.nytimes.com/2013/09/21/world/asia/hacking-us-secrets-china-pushes-for-drones.html#:~:text=BEIJING%20%E2%80%94%20For%20almost%20two%20years,at%20least%2020%20in%20all.

569 Rob O' Gorman and Chris Abbott, *Remote Control War*, Open Briefing, September 20, 2013, https://www.files.ethz.ch/isn/170021/Remote-Control-War.pdf.

570 "The Role of Autonomy in DoD Systems," Department of Defense: Defense Science Board, Office of the Under Secretary of Defense for Acquisition, Technology and Logistics, July 2012, https://fas.org/irp/agency/dod/dsb/autonomy.pdf.

571 Greg Waldron, "PICTURE: China's Global Hawk Counterpart Breaks Cover," FlightGlobal, June 30, 2011, https://www.flightglobal.com/picture-chinas-global-hawk-counterpart-breaks-cover/100992.article.

572 "Soar Dragon UAVs Deployed to Yishuntun Airbase," Bellingcat, March 23, 2018, https://www.bellingcat.com/news/rest-of-world/2018/03/23/soar-dragon-uavs-deploy-yishuntun-airbase/.

573 See @Rupprechtdeino, June 23, 2019, https://twitter.com/RupprechtDeino/status/1142820724945686528.

574 David Axe, "China's Enormous Spy Drone Has Its Eyes Set On The U.S. Navy," National Interest, September 8, 2019, https://nationalinterest.org/blog/buzz/chinas-enormous-spy-drone-has-its-eyes-set-us-navy-78546.

575 Tweet @RupperechtDeino May 29, 2018, https://twitter.com/RupprechtDeino/status/1001460311948517378.

576 Tyler Rogoway, "Highly Impressive Lineup of Chinese Air Combat Drone Types Caught by Satellite," The Drive, December 8, 2019, https://www.thedrive.com/the-war-zone/31378/highly-impressive-lineup-of-chinese-air-combat-drone-types-caught-by-satellite; See also Joseph Trevithick and Tyler Rogoway, "China's Biggest Airshow Offers More Evidence of Beijing's Stealth Drone Focus," The Drive, November 2, 2018, https://www.thedrive.com/the-war-zone/24645/chinas-biggest-airshow-offers-more-evidence-of-beijings-stealth-drone-focus.

577 See @nktpnd, October 1, 2019: https://twitter.com/nktpnd/status/1179096634707320833.

578 Andreas Rupprecht, "Images Suggest WZ-8 UAV in Service With China's Eastern Theatre Command," Janes, October 4, 2019, https://www.janes.

com/defence-news/news-detail/images-suggest-wz-8-uav-in-service-with-chinas-eastern-theatre-command.

579   Jon Harper, "More Drones Needed to Fight Two-Front War," *National Defense*, March 10, 2020, https://www.nationaldefensemagazine.org/articles/2020/3/10/more-drones-needed-to-fight-two-front-war.

580   Zhenhua Lu, "China Sells Arms to More Countries and iss World's Biggest Exporter of Armed Drones, Says Swedish Think Tank SIPRI," *Southern China Morning Post*, March 12, 2019, https://www.scmp.com/news/china/military/article/2189604/china-sells-weapons-more-countries-and-biggest-exporter-armed.

581   Jakob Reimann, "China is Flooding the Middle East With Cheap Drones," Foreign Policy in Focus, February 18, 2019, https://fpif.org/china-is-flooding-the-middle-east-with-cheap-drones/.

582   Sharon Weinberger, "China Has Already Won the Drone Wars," Foreign Policy, May 20, 2018, Accessed May 1, 2020, https://foreignpolicy.com/2018/05/10/china-trump-middle-east-drone-wars/; Michael Peck, "A Really Big Deal: China is a Drone Superpower," *National Interest*, March 16, 2019, https://nationalinterest.org/blog/buzz/really-big-deal-china-drone-superpower-47692.

583   Greg Waldon, "China Finds its UAV Export Sweet Spot," FlightGlobal, June 14, 2019, https://www.flightglobal.com/military-uavs/china-finds-its-uav-export-sweet-spot/132557.article; "China Takes Lead In Military Drone Market," *Asia Times*, December 31, 2019, Accessed May 1, 2020, https://asiatimes.com/2019/12/china-targets-world-uav-market/; David Axe, "One Nation Is Selling Off It's Chinese Combat Drones," *National Interest*, June 5, 2019, Accessed May 1, 2020, https://nationalinterest.org/blog/buzz/one-nation-selling-its-chinese-combat-drones-61092.

584   Center for the Study of the Drone, 2019, page ix.

585   Center for the Study of the Drone, 2019, page xv.

586 Catherine Philp, "China's Drones Help It Become Second Biggest Arms Exporter," *The Times,* June 9, 2020, https://www.thetimes.co.uk/article/china-s-drones-help-it-become-second-biggest-arms-exporter-c9h9h0cn8.

587 Patrick Tucker, "New Drones, Weapons Get Spotlight In China's Military Parade," Defense One, October 1, 2019, Accessed July 8, 2020, https://www.defenseone.com/technology/2019/10/new-drones-weapons-get-spotlight-chinas-military-parade/160291/.

588 Report of UNOMIG on April 20, 2020 incident: https://www.securitycouncilreport.org/atf/cf/%7B65BFCF9B-6D27-4E9C-8CD3-CF6E4FF96FF9%7D/Georgia%20UNOMIG%20Report%20on%20Drone.pdf.

589 "Georgian Rebels Say Shot Down Georgian Spy Drone-Ifax,", Reuters, May 8, 2008, https://www.reuters.com/article/idUSL08767080?edition-redirect=in.

590 Nicholas Clayton, "How Russia and Georgia's 'Little War' Started a Drone Arms Race," PRI, October 23, 2012, https://www.pri.org/stories/2012-10-23/how-russia-and-georgias-little-war-started-drone-arms-race.

591 Ryan Gallagher, "Russia Tries to Remove Images of New Drone from the Internet," *Wired,* February 20, 2013, https://slate.com/technology/2013/02/russia-tries-to-remove-images-of-altius-drone-from-the-internet.html.

592 "The Czar of Battle: Russian artillery in Ukraine," Janes, 2014, https://www.janes.com/images/assets/111/80111/The_Czar_of_battle_Russian_artillery_use_in_Ukraine_portends_advances.pdf.

593 Dan Peleschuk, "Ukraine is Fighting a Drone War, Too," PRI, https://www.pri.org/stories/ukraine-fighting-drone-war-too.

594 Robert Farley, "Meet the 5 Weapons of War Ukraine Should Fear," *National Interest,* November 26, 2018, https://nationalinterest.org/blog/buzz/meet-5-russian-weapons-war-ukraine-should-fear-37112.

595   Joseph Hammond, "Ukraine Drones Show Sanctions Don't Clip Russia's Wings," The Defense Post, October 4, 2019, https://www.thedefensepost.com/2019/10/04/ukraine-russia-drones-sanctions/.

596   "Russia's New Drone-Based Electronic Warfare System," UAS Vision, no publication date, Accessed July 8, 2020, https://www.uasvision.com/2017/04/04/russias-new-drone-based-electronic-warfare-system/.

597   Dylan Malyasov, "Ukrainian Forces Shoot Down Russian Drone in Donetsk Region," Defence Blog, April 6, 2020, Accessed July 8, 2020, https://defence-blog.com/news/ukrainian-forces-shoot-down-russian-drone-in-donetsk-region.html.

598   Alex Hollings, "Here's Why Elon Musk is Wrong About Fighter Jets (But Right About Drones)," Sandboxx, March 6, 2020, Accessed May 1, 2020, https://www.sandboxx.us/blog/heres-why-elon-musk-is-wrong-about-fighter-jets-but-right-about-drones/; See Elon Musk Tweet, Feb. 28, 2020, Accessed May 1, 2020, https://twitter.com/elonmusk/status/1233478599170195457.

599   Interview with Stephen Jones, USAF, June 28, 2020.

600   Tom Hobbins, "Transforming Joint Air Power," *JAPCC Journal* Edition 3, 2006, p. 6, http://www.japcc.org/wp-content/uploads/japcc_journal_Edition_3.pdf.

601   Jeffrey J. Smith, *Tomorrow's Air Force: Tracing the Past, Shaping the Future*, Indiana University press, p. 221.

602   Dubester, interview, February 2020.

603   Dubester, interview, February 2020.

604   Rossella Tercatin, "Israeli Scientists Study Secrets of Human Brain to Bring AI to Next Level," *The Jerusalem Post*, April 23, 2020, Accessed May 1, 2020, https://www.jpost.com/health-science/israeli-scientists-study-secrets-of-human-brain-to-bring-ai-to-next-level-625693.

605   "The Role of Autonomy in DoD Systems," Department of Defense: Defense Science Board, Office of the Under Secretary of Defense for Acquisition,

Technology and Logistics, July 2012, https://fas.org/irp/agency/dod/dsb/autonomy.pdf.

606   Ibid, p. 71.

607   Valerie Insinna, "Boeing Rolls Out Australia's First 'Loyal Wingman' Combat Drone," Defense News, May 4, 2020, https://www.defensenews.com/air/2020/05/04/boeing-rolls-out-australias-first-loyal-wingman-combat-drone/?fbclid=IwAR0KlCrhH2m9PfwJbpLktcFrZ8gcljgwnAX-44_5uuSRQvonxIcDtaB7WlkI.

608   John Keller, "Boeing To Convert 18 Retired F-16 Jet Fighters Into Unmanned Target Drones for Advanced Pilot Training," Military & Aerospace Electronics, March 23, 2017, https://www.militaryaerospace.com/unmanned/article/16725836/boeing-to-convert-18-retired-f16-jet-fighters-into-unmanned-target-drones-for-advanced-pilot-training; See also Colin Dunjohn, "Boeing Converts F-16 Fighter Jet Into an Unmanned Drone," New Atlas, Sept 27, 2013, https://newatlas.com/boeing-f16-jet-unmanned-drone/29203/.

609   Mark Cancian, US Military Forces in FY 2019, Center for Strategic and International Studies, Rowman and Littlefield, p. 51.

610   Ibid, p. 40.

611   Interview with an anonymous former Air Force drone pilot source, February 28, Washington DC.

612   Unmanned Ambitions: Security Implications of Growing Proliferation of Emerging Military Drone Markets, Pax for Peace, July 2018.

613   Interview with Gal Papier of Rafael about FireFly: Seth J. Frantzman, "Israel Acquires FireFly Loitering Munition for Close Combat," C4ISRNet, May 5, 2020, https://www.c4isrnet.com/unmanned/2020/05/05/israel-acquires-firefly-loitering-munition-for-close-combat/.

614   Seth J. Frantzman, "Greece And Israel Deal Spotlight Leasing Model for Military UAVs," Defense News, May 8, 2020, https://www.defensenews.com/global/europe/2020/05/08/greece-and-israel-deal-spot-

light-leasing-model-for-military-uavs/#:~:text=JERUSALEM%20
%E2%80%94%20Greece's%20Hellenic%20Ministry%20of,-
pricey%20acquisitions%20amid%20budgetary%20constraints.&tex-
t=Greece%20will%20have%20an%20option,term%20ends%20in%20
three%20years.

[615] Petraeus to author, March 14, 2020.

[616] European Forum on Armed Drones, May 19, 2020, Tweet, Accessed May 23, 2020: https://twitter.com/EFADrones/status/1262765402846724096.

[617] Seth Cropsey to author, March 19, 2020.

[618] Peter Singer to author March 23, 2020.

[619] Raphael S. Cohen, Nathan Chandler, *et. al.*, *The Future of Warfare in 2030: Project Overview and Conclusions,* RAND Corporation, May 2020, Accessed may 15, 2020, https://www.rand.org/pubs/research_reports/RR2849z1.html.

[620] Ibid, p. 21.

[621] See Franz-Stephan Gady, @HoanSolo, Tweet, May 12, 2020, Accessed May 15, 2020, https://twitter.com/HoansSolo/status/1260300283785158665.

[622] See @LTCKilgore Tweet, May 9, 2019 video, Accessed July 12, 2020: https://twitter.com/LTCKilgoreJr/status/1126463724540153857.

[623] See @theRealBH6 Tweet, April 16, 2020, Accessed May 15, 2020: https://twitter.com/theRealBH6/status/1250561981154603008.

[624] See @TheRealBH6 Tweet, Accessed May 15, 2020, https://twitter.com/theRealBH6/status/1258556133037363200.

[625] Lockheed Martin Press Release, "Dominate the Electromagnetic Spectrum: Lockheed Martin Cyber/Electronic Warfare System Moves Into Next Phase of Development," Lockheed Martin, April 29, 2020, https://news.lockheedmartin.com/dominate-electromagnetic-spectrum-lockheed-martin-cyber-electronic-warfare-systems-moves-into-next-phase-development.

[626] Brad Bowman interview, March 2020.

627   David B. Larter, "A Classified Pentagon Maritime Drone Program is About to Get Its Moment in the Sun," Defense News, March 14, 2019, https://www.defensenews.com/naval/2019/03/14/a-classified-pentagon-maritime-drone-program-is-about-to-get-its-moment-in-the-sun/.

628   Christian Brose, *The Kill Chain: Defending America in the Future*, May 2020.

629   Ibid, p. xxix.

630   Ibid, p. 121.

631   Ibid, p. 98.

632   Barbara Starr and Ryan Browne, "US Increases Military Pressure on China as Tensions Rise Over Pandemic," CNN Politics, May 15, 2020, https://edition.cnn.com/2020/05/14/politics/us-china-military-pressure/index.html.\

633   Rick Francona to author, May 20, 2020.

634   Greg Allen, "Understanding AI Technology," JAIC, April 2020, https://www.ai.mil/docs/Understanding%20AI%20Technology.pdf.

635   Lockheed Martin, Inside Skunk Works Podcast, "Dull, Dirty, Dangerous," Produced by Claire Whitfield and Theresa Hoey, July 2019, Accessed May 17, 2020, https://podcasts.apple.com/us/podcast/dull-dirty-dangerous/id1350627500?i=1000445596240.

636   Caleb Larson, "The X-44 MANTA Was a Futuristic Version of Lockheed's F-22 Fighter," *National Interest*, June 9, 2020, Accessed June 15, 2020, https://nationalinterest.org/blog/buzz/x-44-manta-was-futuristic-version-lockheed%E2%80%99s-f-22-fighter-161911.

637   Lockheed Martin, Inside Skunk Works Podcast, "Dull, Dirty, Dangerous," Produced by Claire Whitfield and Theresa Hoey, July 2019, Accessed May 17, 2020, https://podcasts.apple.com/us/podcast/dull-dirty-dangerous/id1350627500?i=1000445596240.

638   Interview with Brad Bowman, March 2020.

639   Ibid.

640 Ibid; Also see Bradley Bowman, "Securing Technological Superiority Requires a Joint US-Israel effort," Defense News, May 22, 2020, https://www.defensenews.com/opinion/commentary/2020/05/22/securing-technological-superiority-requires-a-joint-us-israel-effort/.

641 Interview with Behnam Ben Taleblu, March 1, 2020.

642 Peter L. Hickman, "The Future of Warfare Will Continue to be Human," War on the Rocks, May 12, 2020, Accessed May 17, 2020, https://warontherocks.com/2020/05/the-future-of-warfare-will-continue-to-be-human/.

643 Elbridge Colby, "Testimony before Senate Armed Services Committee," January 29, 2019.

644 Andrew Chuter, "British Defense Ministry Reveals Why a Drone Program Now Costs $427M Extra," Defense News, January 24, 2020, Accessed July 7, 2020, https://www.defensenews.com/unmanned/2020/01/24/british-defence-ministry-reveals-why-a-drone-program-now-costs-245m-extra/.

645 "New Training Pathway Paves Way for Protector," Royal Air Force News, July 1, 2020, Accessed July 7, 2020, https://www.raf.mod.uk/news/articles/new-training-pathway-paves-way-for-protector/.

646 George and Meredith Friedman, The Future of War, St. Martins: 1998, p. 150.